First World War
and Army of Occupation
War Diary
France, Belgium and Germany

4 DIVISION
12 Infantry Brigade
Lancashire Fusiliers
2nd Battalion
23 August 1914 - 28 February 1919

WO95/1507

The Naval & Military Press Ltd
www.nmarchive.com
Published in association with The National Archives

Published by

The Naval & Military Press Ltd

Unit 10 Ridgewood Industrial Park,
Uckfield, East Sussex,
TN22 5QE England
Tel: +44 (0) 1825 749494

www.naval-military-press.com
www.nmarchive.com

This diary has been reprinted in facsimile from the original. Any imperfections are inevitably reproduced and the quality may fall short of modern type and cartographic standards.

© Crown Copyright
Images reproduced by permission of The National Archives, London, England, 2015.

Contents

Document type	Place/Title	Date From	Date To
Heading	4th Division War Diaries 2nd Lancashire Fies, August To December 1914 Feb 1919		
Heading	12th Brigade 4th Division 2nd Battalion Lancashire Fusiliers August & September 1914 Attached, Reports On Crossing Of R. Marne & R. Aisne.		
War Diary		23/08/1914	28/08/1914
Miscellaneous	Lancashire Fus 2/20th-24th-26th August, 1914		
Diagram etc	From XX Annual Showing Positions of 2/20 Aug 26 1914		
Diagram etc	From XX Annual Showing		
Diagram etc	From XX Annual Showing Positions of 2/20th Aug 26 1914		
Diagram etc	From XX Annual Showing Positions of 2/20th Aug 26th 1914		
Map	From XX Annual Showing Positions of 2/20 Aug 26th 1914		
War Diary		09/09/1914	17/09/1914
Miscellaneous	Crossing of R. Marne 9.9.14		
Miscellaneous	Crossing of the MARNE		
Miscellaneous	The Battle of Ligny		
Miscellaneous	Crossing of R Owsne 13.9.14		
Miscellaneous	The Crossing of the Aisne		
Heading	12th Brigade 4th Division 2nd Battalion Lancashire Fusiliers October 1914 Attached. Report on Operations 13th-22nd.		
Heading	For entries 1st & 2nd October 1914 see diary for September 1914		
War Diary		29/08/1914	16/10/1914
War Diary	Le Touquet	22/10/1914	31/10/1914
Heading	Operations 13-22 October 1914		
Miscellaneous			
Heading	12th Brigade 4th Division 2nd Battalion Lancashire Fusiliers November 1914		
War Diary		01/11/1914	30/11/1914
Miscellaneous	Strength Return.		
Heading	12th Brigade 4th Division 2nd Battalion Lancashire Fusiliers December 1914		
War Diary		01/12/1914	31/12/1914
Heading	4th Division War Diaries 12th Infantry Bde 2nd Lancs Kes To 108th Bde 4-11-15 January To October 1915		
Heading	4th Div 12th Inf. Bde War Diary 2nd Battn. Lancashire Fusiliers January 1915.		
War Diary		01/01/1915	31/01/1915
Heading	4th Div 12th Inf. Bde. War Diary 2nd Battn. Lancashire Fusiliers February 1915.		
War Diary		01/02/1915	28/02/1915
Heading	4th Div 12th Inf Bde War Diary 2nd Battn. Lancashire Fusiliers March 1915.		
War Diary		01/03/1915	31/03/1915

Heading	4th Div. 12th Inf. Bde. War Diary 2nd Battn. Lancashire Fusiliers April 1915		
War Diary		01/04/1915	30/04/1915
Heading	4th Div. 12th Inf. Bde. War Diary 2nd Battn. Lancashire Fusiliers May 1915		
War Diary		01/05/1915	31/05/1915
Heading	4th Div. 12th Inf. Bde. War Diary 2nd Battn. Lancashire Fusiliers June 1915		
War Diary		01/06/1915	30/06/1915
Heading	4th Div. 12th Inf. Bde. War Diary 2nd. Battn. Lancashire Fusiliers July 1915		
War Diary		01/07/1915	31/07/1915
Heading	4th Div. 12th Inf. Bde. War Diary 2nd Battn. Lancashire Fusiliers August 1915		
War Diary		01/08/1915	31/08/1915
Heading	4th Div. 12th Inf. Bde. War Diary 2nd Battn. Lancashire Fusiliers September 1915		
War Diary		01/09/1915	30/09/1915
Heading	4th Div. 12th Inf. Bde. War Diary 2nd Battn. Lancashire Fusiliers October 1915		
War Diary		01/10/1915	31/10/1915
Heading	36th Division 108th Infy Bde 4 Div 12 Bde 2nd Bn Lancs Fus. Nov 1915		
Heading	4th Division XXXVI Transferred to 108 Bde Nov 5-Dec 10 Vol XIV		
War Diary	Field	01/11/1915	30/11/1915
Heading	4 Div 12 Bde 2nd Bn Lancashire Fusiliers Dec 1915-Jan 1916		
Heading	4th Div 2/Lanc. Fusrs. Dec Vol XV 121/7930		
War Diary	Active Service	01/12/1915	31/12/1915
Heading	2/Lancs. Fusrs. Jan Vol XVI 36 Div		
War Diary	Field	01/01/1916	31/01/1916
Heading	4th Division War Diaries 12th Infantry Bde 2nd Lancs Fus With Private Diary of St Hewpins February To July 1916		
War Diary	Field	01/07/1916	31/07/1916
Miscellaneous	Casualties on 1st July 1916 Officers		
Heading	12th Brigade 4th Division 2nd Battalion The Lancashire Fusiliers February 1916		
War Diary	Field	01/02/1916	29/02/1916
Heading	12th Brigade 4th Division 2nd Battalion The Lancashire Fusiliers March 1916		
War Diary		01/03/1916	31/03/1916
Heading	2nd Battalion The Lancashire Fusiliers April 1916		
War Diary	Field	01/04/1916	30/04/1916
Heading	12th Brigade 4th Division 2nd Battalion The Lancashire Fusiliers May 1916		
War Diary	Field	01/05/1916	31/05/1916
Heading	12th Brigade 4th Division 2nd Battalion The Lancashire Fusiliers. June 1916		
War Diary	Field	01/06/1916	30/06/1916
Operation(al) Order(s)	Operation Order No 1		
Miscellaneous	Distribution of Officer		
Miscellaneous	Parade State		

Miscellaneous	Operation Orders By Lieut Colonel G.H.B. Freeth C.M.G. D.S.O. Commanding 2nd Bn Lancashire Fusiliers.	30/06/1916	30/06/1916
Heading	War Diary of 2nd Bn. Lancashire Fusiliers for July 1916		
War Diary	Diary of Lieut. V.F.S. Hawkins, 2/Lanc. Fusiliers.	01/07/1916	01/07/1916
Miscellaneous	Copy of Raid Orders.	06/07/1918	06/07/1918
Operation(al) Order(s)	Lancashire Fusiliers Order No. 17	03/07/1918	03/07/1918
Operation(al) Order(s)	12th Infantry Brigade Operation Order No.139	04/07/1918	04/07/1918
Miscellaneous	Table "A"		
Miscellaneous	Table "B"		
Miscellaneous	Enemy Withdrawal From Pacaut Wood. August 5th-15th 1918		
Miscellaneous	Operation Order Lan Fus.		
Miscellaneous	Raid By Lancs. Fus. On Night 15/16th November.		
Diagram etc	Table of Barrage		
Miscellaneous	Legend.		
Miscellaneous	4th Div. No. G.A.3/19	08/10/1918	08/10/1918
Miscellaneous	12th Inf. Brigade. No.B.M.1/57/4		
Miscellaneous	Report By Capt. A Howarth. M.C. Commanding "D" Coy 2nd Lancashire Fusiliers. On enterprise 3/6th October 1918		
Miscellaneous	12th Infantry Brigade	05/10/1918	05/10/1918
Miscellaneous	Raid Orders By Lieut Colonel G.H.B. Freeth b.m.G.D.S.O. Commanding 2nd Bn Lancashire Fusiliers.		
Heading	4th Division War Diaries 12th Infantry Bde 2nd Lancs Fus, August To December 1916		
Heading	12th Brigade 4th Division. 2nd Battalion The Lancashire Fusiliers August 1916		
War Diary	Field Camp. O. A. 30 D. 2.9.	01/08/1916	03/08/1916
War Diary	Bde Reserve Fusiliers	04/11/1917	08/11/1917
War Diary	Trenches	04/11/1917	08/11/1917
War Diary	Bde Reserve	09/11/1917	11/11/1917
War Diary	Trenches	12/11/1917	17/11/1917
War Diary	Bde Reserve	18/11/1917	22/11/1917
War Diary	Trenches	23/11/1917	28/11/1917
War Diary	Div Reserve	29/11/1917	30/11/1917
Heading	12th Brigade. 4th Division 2nd Battalion The Lancashire Fusiliers September 1916		
War Diary		01/09/1916	30/09/1916
Heading	12th Brigade. 4th Division 2nd Battalion The Lancashire Fusiliers October 1916		
War Diary	Albert Combined Sheet. 1 40.000 51/D SE 5/C S/C 62D N.E. 62 C N.W.	01/10/1916	10/10/1916
War Diary	Map Ref CE	11/10/1916	31/10/1916
Miscellaneous	Appendix (1) Report of the Operations on Oct 12th		
Miscellaneous	Appendix (ii) A Important Messages received From 12th Brigade		
Miscellaneous	Appendix (II) B Important Messages received from Companies.		
Miscellaneous	To 2nd Lancashire Fusiliers		
Miscellaneous	Appendix (iii) Important Messages Dispatched		
Miscellaneous	Report On Operations Carried Out By 2nd Bn Lancashire Fusiliers On October 23rd 1916		
Miscellaneous	Appendix V A Important Messages Received From Companies and Battalions To 2 Lan. Fus.		

Miscellaneous	Appendix V B Important Messages Received From Brigade.		
Miscellaneous	Appendix VI Important Messages Dispatched To Capt Salt		
Heading	12th Brigade 4th Division The Lancashire Fusiliers November 1916		
War Diary	Field	01/11/1917	30/11/1917
Heading	12th Brigade. 4th Division 2nd Battalion The Lancashire Fusiliers December 1916		
Heading	War Diary of 2nd Bn. Lancashire Fusiliers From 1st December 1916 To 31st December 1916 Volume		
War Diary	Maieneville	01/01/1917	02/01/1917
War Diary	Oisemont	03/01/1917	03/01/1917
War Diary	L.2.G	04/01/1917	04/01/1917
War Diary	H.26 3.3.0.	05/01/1917	06/01/1917
War Diary	Trenches Close Support	07/01/1917	11/01/1917
War Diary	Front Trenches Left Sub Sector	12/01/1917	15/01/1917
War Diary	Fregicourt Bde Reserve	16/01/1917	19/01/1917
War Diary	Front Trench Left Sub Sector	20/01/1917	23/01/1917
War Diary	Camp 107	24/01/1917	27/01/1917
War Diary	Camp 124	28/01/1917	31/01/1917
Heading	4th Division 12th Infantry Bde. 2nd Lancs. Fus. January To December 1917		
Miscellaneous	2nd Bn Lancashire Fusiliers Regt. From 1st January 1917 To 31st Jany 1917		
War Diary	Camp 124 J.35.b.9.0 Le Plateau F.20	01/01/1917	11/01/1917
War Diary	Camp 124	12/01/1917	22/01/1917
War Diary	Camp 112 L 2G	23/01/1917	23/01/1917
War Diary	Suzanne	24/01/1917	31/01/1917
Heading	War Diary of 2nd Bn Lancashire Fusiliers From 1st February 1917 To 28th February 1917 Volume No.2		
War Diary	Suzanne Bouchauesnes	01/01/1917	04/01/1917
War Diary	Left Front Sector	05/01/1917	09/01/1917
War Diary	Junction Wood	10/01/1917	12/01/1917
War Diary	Left Sub Sector	13/01/1917	16/01/1917
War Diary	Camp 17	17/01/1917	19/01/1917
War Diary	Camp 112	20/01/1917	20/01/1917
War Diary	Corbie	21/01/1917	28/01/1917
Heading	War Diary of 2 Bn Lancashire Fusiliers From 1st March 1917 To 31st March 1917 Volume 3		
War Diary	Corbie	01/03/1917	03/03/1917
War Diary	Villers Bocage	04/03/1917	04/03/1917
War Diary	Beauval	05/03/1917	05/03/1917
War Diary	Wavans	06/03/1917	06/03/1917
War Diary	Vaulx	07/03/1917	21/03/1917
War Diary	Ostreville	22/03/1917	31/03/1917
Miscellaneous	Lieut Colonel Bf Griffin D.S.O. Commanding 2nd Lancashire Fusiliers In The Field Ref March 51 B N.W. 1/2000		
Miscellaneous	Appendix B Time Table Of Creeping & Protective Barrages.		
Miscellaneous	Appendix A Time Table.		
Miscellaneous	General Idea		
Miscellaneous	Ref Para I. Add. Party J Battn Carriers A B C D		
Miscellaneous	Addition to Operation Orders issued 29-3-17		

Heading	War Diary of 2nd Bn Lancashire Fusiliers From 1st April 1917 To 30th April 1917 Volume No 4		
War Diary	Ostreville	01/04/1917	07/04/1917
War Diary	Y Hutments	08/04/1917	13/04/1917
War Diary	Ct.11.b.	14/04/1917	19/04/1917
War Diary	Montenescourt Manin	20/04/1917	22/04/1917
War Diary	Etree Wamin	25/04/1917	26/04/1917
War Diary	Beaufort	27/04/1917	27/04/1917
War Diary	Lauresset	28/04/1917	30/04/1917
War Diary	G. 17	29/04/1917	30/04/1917
Heading	War Diary of 2nd Bn Lancashire Fusiliers Regt From 1st May 1917 To 31st May 1917 Volume 5		
War Diary		01/05/1917	12/05/1917
War Diary	Penin	13/05/1917	31/05/1917
Operation(al) Order(s)	Operation Orders by Major H.W. Glennr Commanding 2nd Lancashire Fusiliers		
Heading	War Diary of 2nd Bn. Lancashire Fusiliers Regt From 1st June 1917 To 30th June 1917 Volume		
War Diary	Penin	01/06/1917	09/06/1917
War Diary	Arras	10/06/1917	10/06/1917
War Diary	Fife Camp	11/06/1917	14/06/1917
War Diary	Trenches E of Chemical Wks N. of Fampoux Plouvain Rly.	15/06/1917	17/06/1917
War Diary	In Trenches	18/06/1917	19/06/1917
War Diary	Dingwall Camp	20/06/1917	27/06/1917
War Diary	Trenches S of Teuchy 11th German System H 28 a Control	28/06/1917	30/07/1917
Heading	War Diary of 2nd Bn Lancashire Fusiliers From 1st July 1917 To 31st July 1917 Volume 7		
War Diary	Himalaya Trench	01/07/1917	01/07/1917
War Diary	Left Subsector Front Trenches	02/07/1917	05/07/1917
War Diary	Himalaya Trench	06/07/1917	08/07/1917
War Diary	Front Fusiliers Left Sub Sector	09/07/1917	13/07/1917
War Diary	Barossa Camp G 13	14/07/1917	28/07/1917
War Diary	Balmoral Camp G.13	29/07/1917	31/07/1917
Heading	War Diary of 2nd Bn Lancashire Fusiliers From 1st Aug 1917 To 31st Aug 1917 Volume 8		
War Diary	Barossa Camp G.18.a 4.6	01/08/1917	01/08/1917
War Diary	Himalaya Trench H.28.02	02/07/1917	06/07/1917
War Diary	Front Line Left Sub Sector I. 31 5.6 to I. 25	07/08/1917	14/08/1917
War Diary	Barossa Camp G.18.a 4.6.	15/08/1917	30/08/1917
War Diary	Camp H.25.C.25.3		
Heading	War Diary of 2 Lancashire Fusiliers From September 1st 1917 to September 30th 1917 Volume No 9		
War Diary	H.25.c.5.3	01/09/1917	03/09/1917
War Diary	Trenches	04/09/1917	07/09/1917
War Diary	No.4 Camp Hendecourt	08/09/1917	20/09/1917
War Diary	Sutton Camp	21/09/1917	26/09/1917
War Diary	To Wolfe Camp	27/09/1917	27/09/1917
War Diary	Canal Bank C.13.c	28/09/1917	30/09/1917
Heading	War Diary of 2nd Lancashire Fusiliers From 1st October 1917 To 31st October 1917 Volume 10		
War Diary	Dursionil Resinal (Canal Bank)	01/10/1917	01/10/1917
War Diary	Roussel Camp	02/10/1917	05/10/1917
War Diary	Wolf Camp	06/10/1917	07/10/1917
War Diary	Front Line	08/10/1917	10/10/1917

War Diary	Redan Camp	11/10/1917	12/10/1917
War Diary	Penton Camp	13/10/1917	14/10/1917
War Diary	Purbrook Camp	15/10/1917	16/10/1917
War Diary	Road Camp	17/10/1917	19/10/1917
War Diary	Habarcq	20/10/1917	24/10/1917
War Diary	Arras	25/10/1917	25/10/1917
War Diary	Bois Des Boeufs Bois des Boeufs	26/10/1917	29/10/1917
War Diary	Front Line	29/10/1917	31/10/1917
Operation(al) Order(s)	Operation Orders By Lancashire Fusiliers		
Miscellaneous	Copy No 11 War Diary		
Heading	War Diary of 2nd Bn. Lancashire Fusiliers Regt. From 1st November 1917 To 30th November 1917 Volume II		
War Diary	Lojeul Sector (Goemappe)	01/11/1917	01/11/1917
War Diary	Schramm Barracks	02/11/1917	08/11/1917
War Diary	Monchy Defences	09/11/1917	12/11/1917
War Diary	Left Sub Sector	13/11/1917	15/11/1917
War Diary	Brown Line	16/11/1917	21/11/1917
War Diary	Left Sub Sector	22/11/1917	24/11/1917
War Diary	Schramm Barracks	25/11/1917	30/11/1917
Heading	War Diary of 2nd. Bn. Lancashire Fusiliers Regt. From 1st. December 1917 To. 31st. December 1917 Volume 12.		
War Diary	Arras	01/12/1917	01/12/1917
War Diary	N8T 5.7	02/12/1917	18/12/1917
War Diary	Arras Roe Frederick De George	19/12/1917	24/12/1917
War Diary	Arras	24/12/1917	26/12/1917
War Diary	N5a 0-8	27/12/1917	31/12/1917
Heading	4th Division 12th Infantry Bde 2nd Lancs Fus, January To December 1918		
Heading	War Diary of 2nd Battalion Lancashire Fusiliers Regiment From. 1st January 1918 To 31st. January 1918 Volume 2		
War Diary	Right Sub. Sector	01/01/1917	03/01/1917
War Diary	Bde. Reserve N.3.b.	04/01/1917	06/01/1917
War Diary	Right Sub Sector	08/01/1917	11/01/1917
War Diary	Arras	12/01/1917	15/01/1917
War Diary	Wilderness Camp H.31.a	16/01/1917	19/01/1917
War Diary	Fosse Farm N.II.G. 95.40.	19/01/1917	22/01/1917
War Diary	Right Sub-Sector 0.5.a. & O.8c.	23/01/1917	26/01/1917
War Diary	Brown Line N.4	27/01/1917	31/01/1917
Heading	War Diary of 2nd. Bn. The Lancashire Fusiliers Regt. From. 1st February 1918 To. 28th February 1918 Volume 2		
War Diary	Line	01/02/1918	05/02/1918
War Diary	Arras	06/02/1918	06/02/1918
War Diary	Bernville	07/02/1918	28/02/1918
Heading	War Diary 12th Inf. Bde. 4th Div. 2nd Battn. The Lancashire Fusiliers. March 1918		
Heading	War Diary of 2nd Bn. The Lancashire Fusiliers Regt. From:- 1st March 1918 To 31st March 1918 Volume 3		
War Diary	Field Bernaville	01/03/1918	11/03/1918
War Diary	Arras	11/03/1918	19/03/1918
War Diary	Line	19/03/1918	28/03/1918
War Diary	Lemon Tr. Bde Support	28/03/1918	28/03/1918
War Diary	Line Lemon Tr.	29/03/1918	31/03/1918
Miscellaneous	Appendix 1.		

Heading	12th Brigade 4th Division 2nd Battalion Lancashire Fusiliers April 1918		
Heading	War Diary of 2nd Bn Lancashire Fusiliers. From April 1st 1918 To April 30th 1918 Volume 4		
War Diary	Line Fampoux Sector Arras	01/04/1918	07/04/1918
War Diary	Simencourt	08/04/1918	12/04/1918
War Diary	Busnes L'Ecleme Map Sheet	13/04/1918	13/04/1918
War Diary	36 A 1/40000 14	14/04/1918	14/04/1918
War Diary	36A SE 1/20000	15/04/1918	15/04/1918
War Diary	Line	16/04/1918	16/04/1918
War Diary	Riez Du Vinage	17/04/1918	24/04/1918
War Diary	Eblinghem	25/04/1918	30/04/1918
Operation(al) Order(s)	Operation Orders No. 2 by Lieut Colonel J.W. Watkins, D.S.O., M.C. Commanding-Lancashire Fusiliers.	22/04/1918	22/04/1918
Heading	War Diary of 2nd Lancashire Fusiliers From May 1st 1918 To May 31st 1918 Volume 5		
War Diary	Pacaut Wood La Pannerie Map Sheet 36a Se	01/05/1918	01/05/1918
War Diary	1/20000	02/05/1918	02/05/1918
War Diary	Les Harisoirs	03/05/1918	06/05/1918
War Diary	L'Ecleme	07/05/1918	11/05/1918
War Diary	Riez Du Vinage	01/05/1918	19/05/1918
War Diary	L'Ecleme	20/05/1918	22/05/1918
War Diary	Pacaut Wd La Pannerie	23/05/1918	23/05/1918
War Diary	Le Cauroy	24/05/1918	25/05/1918
War Diary	Pacaut Wd La Pannerie	26/05/1918	26/05/1918
War Diary	Le Cauroy	27/05/1918	31/05/1918
Heading	War Diary of 2nd Lancashire Fusiliers From June 1st 1918 To June 30th 1918 Volume		
War Diary	Sheet 36A 1/20000 Line	01/06/1918	01/06/1918
War Diary	Line Pacaut Wd to La Pannerie	01/06/1918	02/06/1918
War Diary	L'Ecleme	03/06/1918	08/06/1918
War Diary	Riez Du Vinage	08/06/1918	19/06/1918
War Diary	L'Ecleme	20/06/1918	24/06/1918
War Diary	Line Pacaut Wd La Pannerie	25/06/1918	30/06/1918
Heading	War Diary of 2nd Battalion The Lancashire Fusiliers From. 1st July, 1918 To. 31st July, 1918 Volume 7		
War Diary	Pacaut	01/07/1918	01/07/1918
War Diary	Sector	02/07/1918	02/07/1918
War Diary	Line	03/07/1918	08/07/1918
War Diary	L'Ecleme	08/07/1918	13/07/1918
War Diary	Line	14/07/1918	14/07/1918
War Diary	Vinage Sector	15/07/1918	22/07/1918
War Diary	Line	23/07/1918	29/07/1918
War Diary	L'Ecleme	30/07/1918	31/07/1918
Heading	War Diary of 2 Lancashire Fusiliers From August 1st 1918 To August 31st 1918 Volume 8		
War Diary	L'Ecleme	01/08/1918	01/08/1918
War Diary	Cantrainne	03/08/1918	03/08/1918
War Diary	Line	04/08/1918	15/08/1918
War Diary	L'Ecleme	16/08/1918	21/08/1918
War Diary	Map Sheet Lens	11/08/1918	11/08/1918
War Diary	Ligny Les Aires	22/08/1918	25/08/1918
War Diary	Croisettes	26/08/1918	26/08/1918
War Diary	Burles	27/08/1918	31/08/1918
Heading	War Diary of 2nd Lancashire Fusiliers From Sept 1st 1918 To Sept 30th 1918 Volume 9		

War Diary	Remy Sector Arras Mapolut 51 B.S.E 1/20.000	01/09/1918	05/09/1918
War Diary	Map Sheet 44 B1/40,000	05/09/1918	05/09/1918
War Diary	Magnicourt	06/09/1918	19/09/1918
War Diary	Map Sheet 51 3. 1/40000	20/09/1918	20/09/1918
War Diary	Battery Valley	20/09/1918	23/09/1918
War Diary	Map Sheet 51 B.N.W. 51 B.W.1/4000000	24/09/1918	24/09/1918
War Diary	Line	25/09/1918	28/09/1918
War Diary	Reserve	29/09/1918	30/09/1918
Heading	War Diary of 2 Lancashire Fusiliers From Oct 1st 1918 To Oct 31st 1918 Volume 10		
War Diary	Map Sheet 51 B.N.W. 120000 Line	01/10/1918	02/10/1918
War Diary	Sailly-En Ostrevant 15 Hamblain Sheet 51B 1/10000 51B. 1/20000	03/10/1918	03/10/1918
War Diary	Line	03/10/1918	06/10/1918
War Diary	Battery Valley	07/10/1918	07/10/1918
War Diary	Habarcq.	08/10/1918	11/10/1918
War Diary	Bourlon	12/10/1918	13/10/1918
War Diary	Cambrai	14/10/1918	18/10/1918
War Diary	Iwuy	18/10/1918	18/10/1918
War Diary	Area near Iwuy	19/10/1918	21/10/1918
War Diary	Villers En Cauchie Map 51A 1/40000	22/10/1918	24/10/1918
War Diary	Precentral Verchain	24/10/1918	24/10/1918
War Diary	Verchain	25/10/1918	25/10/1918
War Diary	Map 51ASE 1/20000	25/10/1918	25/10/1918
War Diary	Querenaing	25/10/1918	26/10/1918
War Diary	Artres & Querenaing	27/10/1918	28/10/1918
War Diary	Haspres	29/10/1918	31/10/1918
Heading	War Diary of 2 Bn. Lancashire Fusiliers Regt. From 1st. November. 1918 To 31st. November. 1918 Volume. II		
War Diary	Haspres	01/11/1918	02/11/1918
War Diary	Villers-En Cauchie	03/11/1918	06/11/1918
War Diary	Artres	06/10/1918	19/10/1918
War Diary	St Sauve	20/11/1918	30/11/1918
Heading	War Diary of 2nd Bn. Lancashire Fusiliers Regt. From 1st. Dec. 1918 To 31st Dec. 1918 Volume 12		
War Diary	St Saulve	01/12/1918	31/12/1918
Heading	2nd Lanc. Fus. Jan-Feb. 1919		
War Diary	St Saulve	01/12/1918	02/12/1918
War Diary	St Saulve to La Hestre	03/12/1918	03/12/1918
War Diary	Lahestre	04/01/1919	28/02/1919
Heading	4th Division War Diaries All Formation 1919		

4th Division
War Diaries
2nd Lancashire Fus.

August to December
1914

Feb - 1919

12th Brigade.
4th Division.

Disembarked Boulogne 23.8.14.

2nd BATTALION

LANCASHIRE FUSILIERS

AUGUST & SEPTEMBER 1914.

Attached:-
Reports on Crossing of R. MARNE & R. AISNE.

Aug 23rd Disembarked at Boulogne at 6am
       proceeded to rest camp
   24th Proceeded to BARTRY by rail &
       marched to LIGNY
   25th Marched to VIESLY were shelled
       for short time in evening, no casualties
25-26th Marched via CAUDRAI-LIGNY to
       high ground by WAMBAIX STA. arrived
       there about 4 am & proceeded to site
       & dig trenches. Heavy tools not available
       owing to heavy roads. Heavy shell & M.G
       fire opened at 6am. Pos held pos until
       about 9 am falling back to pos above
       HADCOURT. Brigade retired late in the afternoon
       to SELVIGNY thence to VENDHUILLE at night.
       Casualties

   27th Marched to ROISEL as A.G. to Division, entrenched
       at ROISEL, returning to HANCOURT.
   28th Night marched to VOYENNES

2/20th

Lancashire Fus.

2/20th - 24th-26th August, 1914.

Extract from Regtl. Journal 1914/15, vols XXIV and XXV in one.

    Maj.C.J.Griffen,   C.O. (Lt.Col.R.H.K.Butler,Dorset Regt. had been apptd. to the Cdt. in June 1914, but was retd. on Staff at Aldershot.)

    Capt. A.H.Spooner,   Adjt.
    Lt.W.K.Humfrey,   M.G.O.
    Lt.J.S.Fulton,   T'port Off.
    Capt.H.B.Roffey,   Actg. 2nd in cmmd.
    Capt.J.E.S.Woodman, "A" Coy.
    "   R.H.M.Moody,   "C" "
    "   A.C.Ward,D.S.O. "D" "
    "   J.A.Davenport.   "B" "

Total strength of Reserve, of 2/20th, on 1st Aug., 1914:-

    Sergts.   12,
    Corpls.   67,
    Drummers.   2,
    Privates.   1495.

Those who came up on 5th Aug. were:-

    Sergts.   10,) Since then men came in from Australia,
    Corpls.   62,) Canada,U.S.A. and S.America.
    Drummers.   2,) Only 36 then remained, many of whom were
    Privates.   1340.) permanently unfit.

To 2/Bn 20th, were sent:-

    Sergts.   4,
    Corpls.   41,
    Drummers.   2,
    Privates.   614.

Strength of 2/20th on disembkn at BOULOGNE in a.m. of 23/VII/14

                1,002.

1(Spec.Res.) 2/Lt. & 70 went direct from Dover to Havre. They joined 2/20th during the Retreat.

Extract from Journal of the
2/20th, 24th-26th Aug.1914.(contd).

Aug.23. 11pm. Started in train from Boulogne.

24, p.m. Detrained Bertry. Marched to Ligny & bivcd.there.

25th,early a.m. Marched to Quievy, N.N.E. of Caudry,and entrenched. Tropical rain twds evg,and sky illuminated
by burning Mons.
Few Ger. shell landed nr 2/20th's trenches. No one hit.

9.30pm. 12th I.B./H.F.M.Wilson_/marched in hvy rain to a posn
5 m N.N.W. of Ligny.
/The posn appears to have been only abt 3 m from Ligny./

The article states:- that the Ger. plan was to overwhelm the
L of the Allies and crush the British.
To assist in the effective retirement of the Second and First
Corps Sir J.French had ordered the Fourth Div. to take up a
posn with its R on Solesmes and left on Cambrai-Le Cateau rd.
S of La Chaprai /? La Chapelle //This statement must refer
to 25 Aug./

Aug. 26. 3.45a.m. 2/20th reached Longsart Fme. The ground was a
boggy stretch of moorland. It was still pitch dark,there
were no guides and the tool limbers had stuck fast 2 m back.
C.O. went in search of 1/4th; 2nd in cmd posted picquets.
When light came C.O.began to site the trenches. B.G.C. 12th
I.B. arrvd and pointed out where the trenches were to be dug-
some distance in rear of the original posn. Also he ordered
that some shd be dug for 1/4th who were entangled in the T'pt
some distance back.
Griffin & Woodman marked one line; Roffey & Ward settled the
second line.
Men v tired but set to work digging at once with their "grub-
bers".

Shortly after dawn a Fr.cav.patrol reported to C.O.that the
front ef was clear for miles.

5.45a.m. shallow trenches completed by A.C. & D. Only 2
pltns of A had trenches quite ready for occpn. "B" in res.
1 pltn of A behind a small bank.
T'pt of 2/20th reached Longsart Fme.& b'fast was prepared.
1 Sgt. & 10 men D,acted as covering party and went out abt
300 yds to L front of Bn line. From this pt no Br. or Fr.
troops were seen to the L. After a short interval fire
was opened on this post from their R front and from m.gs in
the corn-stooks. The Sgt. was severely W & was kicked into
a quarry by the Gers.

6a.m. 1/4th arrvd and sat down in ¼ col. to await the issue
of their tools. Part of A,2/20th, also moved down to draw
some tools,when a heavy fire - m.gs and S burst over 1/4th
wh suffered hvily. /See B.Genl.Higgins/,. After 1/4th had got
under cover,this fire turned on 2/20th. It was thought that
a Ger. maxim Btty turned onto the Bn at 1,000 yds range.
Ger. cav. led the attack;but after their guns had opened
dense masses of inf. issued from wood & farm buildings.
The 2/m.gs,2/20th,now came into action between the 2 coys.
1 gun jammed at once & was taken to Longsart for the armourer
to attend to it. The other did good execution. It was moved
several times to fire more effectively.

The L flank of the Bn gave cause for anxiety. It was spptd
by 1 coy of 56.
The L coy.

Extract from Journal of the
2/20th, 24th-26th Aug., 1914.

Aug. 26th.(contd).

The L coy of 2/20th was now withdrawn by the Coy.cmmdr.(Ward)
The 2nd in cmmd who had visited the L thought it shd be withdrawn further back; but Vandeleur(56)considered it shd remain as it was.
The main force of the attack had been thrown on the R flank,
but it suddenly developed with greater force agst the L and
the Gers. advcd agst Ward's coy wh suffered hvily.
In trying to get touch with Vandeleur the 2nd in cmmd was
seriously W & Vandeleur himself was also shot. Ward's coy
and the L pltn of A were now much harassed by m.gfire. It
was not long before all the offs. of D were K or W. The effect of the enfilade fire was severe & Gers. were seen working round the L flank. Retirement was clearly necessary.
A coy withdrew to the cover of a hedge Sidebottom's coy [Side-
bottom was in Moody's coy,C,. Apptly Moody had been W by this
time] followed. Many were K and W in this opern and the Gers
reached within 300 yds and a m.g. was particularly deadly. Sidebottom
collected a party to rush it, but fell dead before the attempt
was made.   Lt.Humfrey & Sgt.Roch carried off the m.g. of
the 2/20th. In the retirement the Gers. gained on 2/20th.
The unequal contest between a line of inf. and massed guns &
m.guns had lasted for 3 hrs.

At 9a.m. 2/20th rallied on a saddle-back ridge and opened fire
on the pursuers, who came on in dense col. with their rifles
held agst their hips.
Assisted by our art. the 2/20th, under Capt.Woodman, with
Capt.Spooner and Lt.Cross asstg him, held the ridge.
As the Ger. advance was checked the 2/20th withdrew a few
hundred yds and the 3 offs rounded up and gathered others together and attempted to est. touch with the Bde.Staff.
A hvy S fire now opened on the Bn and cover was taken behind
a fm building wh soon fell in ruins.

By 2p.m. it was thought that the Gers. had in action in this
section of the field from 90 to 150 guns. The whole sect. as
far back as Selvigny, was now thoroughly searched. The bulk of
the 12th I.B. was now ordered back to Selvigny, some troops
being left above Haucourt to cover the retirement of our guns.
One of these parties consisted of men collected by Capt.Daven-
port. By this time 2/20th and 108th were considerably inter-
mingled. Various parties of 2/20th assembled on the rd under
the C.O.(Maj.Griffin) and were ordered by the Staff of the
Fourth Div.to march until 10pm.when they b'lltd in some fm
buildings.
The cas..on 26th were - 2 offs K,
                         3 " W,
                        10 " W & M, 2 of these rejnd later.

            402 NCOs & men failed to answer the
roll that night; on Sept.9th 143 of these rejnd; wh leaves
259 NCOs & men as K.W.M. on 26th Aug.

" 27th. Noon. 2/20th reached Voyennes.

FROM XX ANNUAL

SHOWING POSITIONS OF 2/20" AUG 26" 14

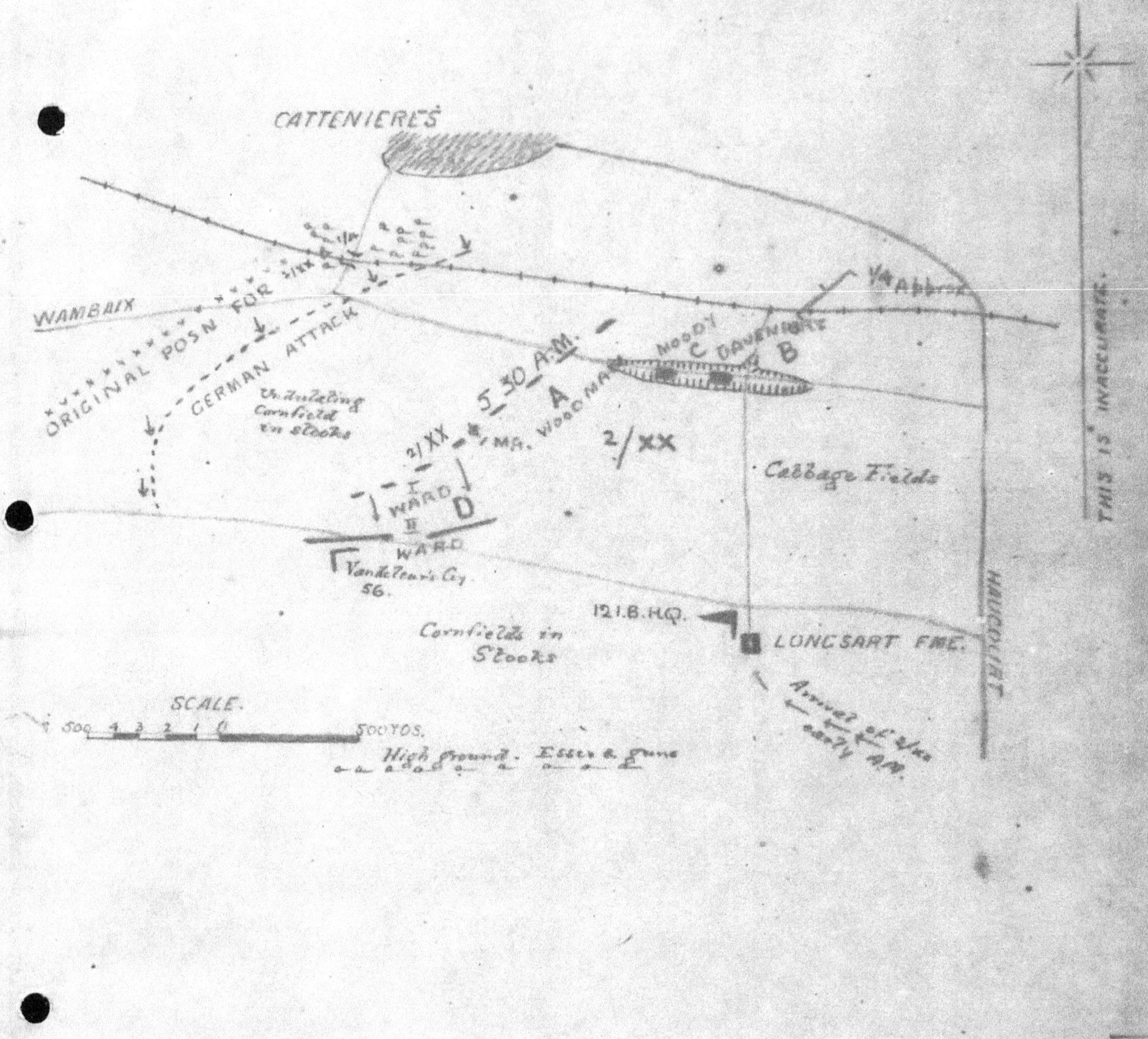
CATTENIERES
WAMBAIX
ORIGINAL POSN FOR 2/XX
GERMAN ATTACK
Undulating Cornfield in stooks
5.30 A.M.
A
C
B
2/XX
Cabbage Fields
THIS IS INACCURATE
WARD
D
56.
121.B.HQ.
LONGSART FME.
HAUCOURT
Cornfields in Stooks
SCALE.
500YDS.
High ground.

FROM XX ANNUAL

SHOWING POSITIONS OF 2/20th AUG 26th 1914

FROM XX ANNUAL

SHOWING POSITIONS OF 2/20th AUG. 26th 914

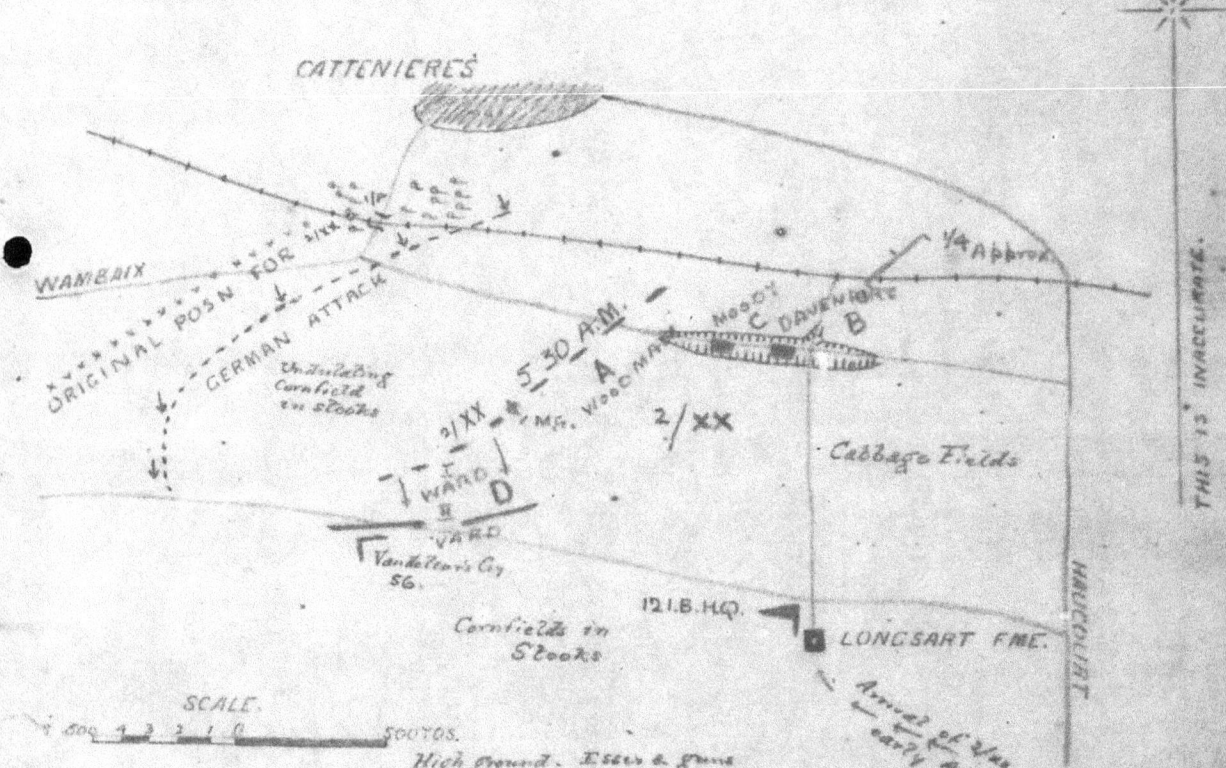

FROM XX ANNUAL

SHOWING POSITIONS OF 2/20th AUG 26th 14

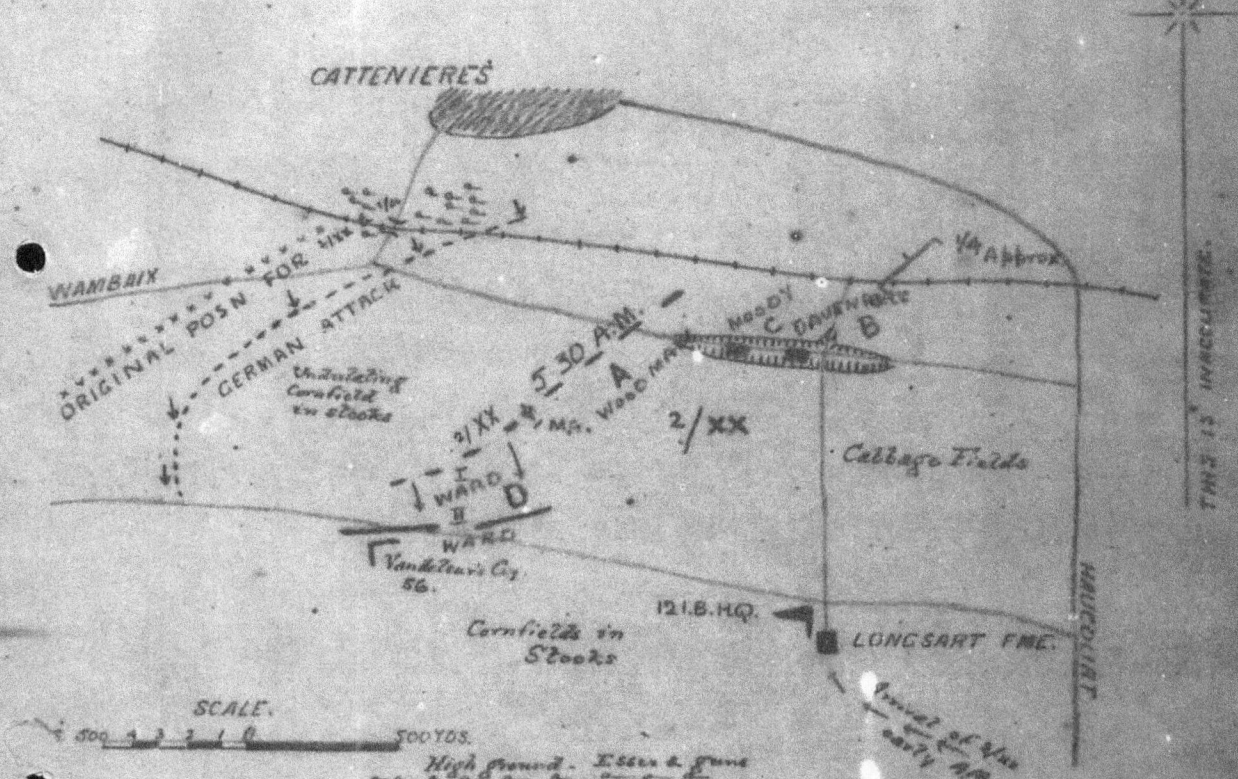

FROM XX ANNUAL

SHOWING POSITIONS OF 2/20th AUG 26th 14

Sept 10 — CHAMIGNY, remainder in position to cover the crossing of the remainder of Division over R MARNE. In the afternoon proceeded to VAUX when brigade was outpost to the Division. No incident.

Sept 11 — marched to CHOUY no incident

Sept 12 — marched to Septmont, avoided to full heavy guns up the hills got to bivouac about 11pm no action

Sept 13 — crossed the R Aisne under fire — had one killed one wounded. In the afternoon proceeded to St Marguerite & proceeded to attack Chivres, met with heavy fire frontal & flank; held on to far & pushed forward through wood, got not progress further but held on till dusk when relieved by the Manchester Regt.
Killed Lt Stirret & 6 men
46 men N. Major Griffin, Lt Fulton 2/Lt
2 Lt Rowlinson (since died)
11 9. M & Lt Page (injured)

Sept 14 — Battn continued nearer St Margarite the Bn men in reserve & employed in digging trenches

---

Sept 9th — Small village 1 mile S.E. of LA FERTE assisted high ground of TARTARE at 9 am in conjunction with 10 Brigade. Proceeded to cross the R. MARNE below Chamigny with Essex Regt. Occupied high ground N of Chamigny before dusk, killed 2 captured 6 German. Two men slightly wounded by own shrapnel.

Sept 8th — LA HAUTE MAISON proceeded via PIERRE LEVEE through JOUARE dug forward without incident to the R...

Sept 7th — VILLIERS marched via SAMEY to LA HAUTE MAISON was shelled by enemy but had no casualties. R.I.F. Lot 1 off. 2 men 1 S.W.

Sept 6 — BRIE no incident
Sept 5 — FERRIERS
Sept 3 — SERRES
Sept 2 — DAMMARTIN, stayed all 3rd also

Sept 15th: Battle continued two wounded died during night Ptes Binden & Reid.
"" Our moved inured have till by
the Essex Regt + they are
to mar[?]lable [?] Battn [?]
Major Balfour took [?] O. [?] men
[?] Pen.

Sept 16th: Heavy shelling of position continued all day seven men wounded with exception of Pte Murphy (abdomen) wounds were not dangerous. The men were not in their trenches at the time, but either carrying water or on fatigues. No one in dugs [?] trenches has been hit so far.

Sept 17th: Position the same as yesterday
O.C. Coys at present
A.   2 Lt Cross
B.   Capt Hodgson Risketts (S R)
C.   Lieut Blancour
D.   Capt Davies Tooth (S.R.)

6 men wounded

Crossing of
R. Marne
9-9-14

The Crossing of the MARNE.

The next important event in which the Battalion took part... ... was the crossing of the MARNE.

Steep banks lead down on the western side of this swiftly flowing, broad river, a flat open plain about 1000 yards across with a high ridge beyond it and the main road to PARIS at the back, made it look a formidable undertaking.

Luckily the Germans had become demoralised in their retreat and careful leading enabled the crossing to be effected with a total loss of 2 wounded Essex Regiment

A party with machine guns worked down unseen through the woods to about 200 yards from the lock gates and lay low: two parties went about 400 yards up and down stream respectively and at a given moment all three parties opened fire on the German force. The sudden burst of enfilade fire from both flanks had the desired effect and they fled precipitately.

The Battalion crossed the river man by man over the lock gates and extending on the opposite bank pushed forward through the village of
                    to the heights beyond
which they occupied without loss; a few Uhlans retiring were fired on, and one killed and three wounded and 6 prisoners taken

Unfortunately a section of our artillery opened fire on us at dusk wounding two men and killing one German prisoner

The Battle of Ligny.

The Battalion left Boulogne on August 23rd in the evening and after a long train journey with no halts long enough to be of use, detrained at BERTRY in the afternoon of the 24th. After teas had been made in an adjoining field we then marched to LIGNY where we bivouacked for the night, headquarters being most hospitably dined by the Maire of the Town. Early next morning 26th August the Brigade marched to VIESLY about 12 miles NE where we entrenched ourselves. Late in the afternoon heavy rain began to fall with tropical severity and the sky was illuminated with light from MONS which had been set on fire by the Germans. A few shells landed near our trenches but no one in the Brigade was injured.

At 9.30 pm the Brigade started back from VIESLY to march to a position about 5 miles slightly N.W. of LIGNY amidst rain and ever deepening mud.

About 3.45 am a thoroughly tired battalion had reached the high ground near LONGSTART FARM and between the village of HARCOURT and WAMBEAUX STATION. It was pitch dark. There were no guides and the tool limbers were stuck in the mud a couple of miles back. As soon as it was light enough to see, Major Griffin began to site our trenches and General Wilson came up and gave us directions where to put the trenches and also instructed us to begin some for the King's Own Regiment, who having been entangled in the masses of transport in LIGNY had not yet arrived.

This work was taken in hand with the entrenching tools carried on the men, and by 5.45 a.m. shallow shelter trenches had, in most cases been completed by A. C. and D. Coys,- B Coy being in reserve (though only two platoons of 'A' Company had trenches ready for occupation) in a sunken road, and one platoon 'A' Company behind a small bank.

At 6 a.m. the King's Own Regiment arrived and sat down in quarter column to await the issue of engineers tools which were then coming towards them under Captain Horch (L.F.). Part of A. Coy L.F. were on their way to these waggons also to draw tools, when an appalling burst of shrapnel and machine gun fire was opened on the King's Own. Colonel Dykes and many men were killed before the Regiment could get under cover on the reverse side of the hill; where they had gone this fire was turned onto our trenches. The Companies stuck gallantly to their posts, but the casualties were very heavy, the shallow rifle pits being of little protection from the artillery. For about three hours the unequal contest was carried on, our infantry receiving no support from our artillery which had not yet arrived. One by one the trenches were enveloped and enfiladed and the survivors forced to retire. Captain Ward and Lieut Boyle were killed, Captains Roffey and Moody, Lieuts Corbett-Winder, Rowley and Helps were wounded. Captain Davenport, Lieuts Humfrey Bass and Wilkinson were not seen again and grave doubts as to their safety are entertained Lieuts Fulton, Stewart and Smyth rejoined some days later.

The survivors fell back to the next ridge

and opening fire on the pursuing Germans with the artillery which had now begun to come into action drove them back.

An advance back to the old position was made by portions of the line, but the arrival of fresh German artillery drove them back.

About 2pm the German artillery began a thorough searching of our position and the plain, back to the village of SELVIGNY, guns variously computed from 90 to 150 in number being employed. Most of the brigade were ordered back to SELVIGNY a small party being left above HARCOURT to cover the retirement of our artillery. Further casualties were incurred here and during the final withdrawal to SELVIGNY, including Capt. Davenport wounded in the arm and subsequently taken prisoner in the temporary hospital at HARCOURT.

Total casualties during the action as far as can be ascertained are as follows:-

K. 2 Officers (Ward & Boyle)
W. 5 Officers. (Roffey, Moody, Sidebottom, Rowley, Kelpe).
M. 7 Officers. (Davenport, Cubett-Winder, Bass, Wilkinson, - (wounded & missing).
Humfrey - missing.
Fulton, Stuart & Smyth, who joined a few days after.

Men - K. - 1 Offl & 8 men.
Wd 48.
Wd (Shrateni medium) 38.
Missing.

Crossing of
R. Aisne

13.9.14

The Crossing of the AISNE

Early in the morning of the 13th Sept 1914 the Brigade left SEPTMONTS to clear the enemy from the adjacent heights and try and effect the crossing of the River AISNE.

The Brigade reached the village of VENIZEL on the banks of the river without opposition and then halted for information from the 10th Brigade who were A.G.

While halted the enemy began to search the village with their big guns, one shell landing in the midst of a Company of the Kings Own about 20 yards from ourselves the other side of the road, causing about 6 casualties. Other shells began to get unpleasantly close so the Battalion and the Essex Regiment were at once moved forward.

The Bridge had been partially destroyed and had to be crossed in single file, the Lancashire Fusiliers forming a succession of skirmishing lines on the left and right of the road to BUCY-LE-LONG, the Essex Regiment on our right.

The lines moved forward across the plain under a heavy cross shell fire from the direction of SOISSONS and FORT CONDÉ, and the heights above CHIVRES village. These shell burst too high or scattered too much and our casualties were only 1 killed, 2 wounded.

After halting at BUCY-LE-LONG and reforming the Battalion, we were ordered to form A.G. to the Brigade as far as ST. MARGUERITE where further orders would be issued.

Reaching there without incident, we were ordered to attack the enemy who had been located at CHIVRES and on the high ground N.W. of that village.

Major Griffin pushed forward under cover through ST. MARGUERITE towards MISSY and turning N.W. by a less direct route through a wood, advanced as far as possible towards CHIVRES village.

The ground was very swampy, making progress slow, and the thick undergrowth in the wood combined with the scanty information available with regard to the direction and extent of the enemy's position made it practically impossible to ascertain from which direction the bullets were coming when once firing began, and whether they were being fired by our own troops or the enemy.

On nearing CHIVRES the Companies came under heavy fire from entrenched positions S. of the village and also from the Western slopes of the CHIVRES HILL.

"A" Company under Captain Woodman pushed forwards towards the village and was joined by "D" Company. "B" Company under 2/Lieut. Evatt opened fire on the trenches on the hill and drove the enemy out of the advanced trenches or silenced their fire.

The Essex Regiment supported the attack as far as possible from the hill above ST MARGUERITE with rifle and M.G. fire but the position was far too strong for one Regiment to assault.

The Battalion held onto their ground until dark suffering heavy losses, and at night were relieved by the Manchester Regiment; it is consoling to think that 3 weeks later, no troops had got so far forward as the Regiment did that evening.

Our casualties were:—

Killed:— Lieut. C. E. Stuart, 2/Lieut. J. S. Paulson and 14 other ranks.
Wounded:— Major C. J. Griffin, Lieut. J. S. Hutton, 2/Lieut. J. W. Evatt and 44 other ranks.
Missing:— 83 other ranks

Many under the heading of missing got to within 100 yards of the enemy and whether killed or wounded, with the exception of 5 or 6 of the latter, who were brought in after dark, could not be recovered, and it can only be hoped that we shall meet the majority restored to health on entering BERLIN.

12th Brigade.
4th Division.

2nd BATTALION

LANCASHIRE FUSILIERS

OCTOBER 1 9 1 4

Attached:-
 Report on Operations 17th-22nd.

For entries 1st & 2nd October 1914 see diary for September 1914.

WAR DIARY
or
INTELLIGENCE SUMMARY.

Army Form C. 2118.

(Erase heading not required.)

Instructions regarding War Diaries and Intelligence Summaries are contained in F.S. Regs., Part II. and the Staff Manual respectively. Title pages will be prepared in manuscript.

Hour, Date, Place	Summary of Events and Information	Remarks and references to Appendices
29th August 1914.	The Battalion marched to SEMPIGNY.	
30th August 1914.	Marched from SEMPIGNY to GUISE-LA-MOTTE Halt to 5 p.m. The Rest? then took up Outpost position for the night & marched off at	
31st August 1914 4-30am	to VERBOGGE arriving at 7pm	
1st September 1914.	Marched from VERBOGGE to BARRON. Battalion sent to the support of the 2nd Dragoon Guards who were severely attacked on left flank, but did not come into action	
1st September 1914.	ST. MARGUERITE. in position to protect Sappers of little front. Enemy fell back.	
	Our CONDÉ Pinissary. Searchlights sweeping and fired.	
	A file from the river. Bomb and Howyshelling	do	
10/9/14 - 11/10/14		
2nd October 1914.	marched from ST. MARGUERITE over pontoon bridge to Piomico at MISSY-SUR-AISNE where we relieved R.W.Kent High Living	

Army Form C. 2118.

WAR DIARY
or
INTELLIGENCE SUMMARY.
(Erase heading not required.)

Instructions regarding War Diaries and Intelligence Summaries are contained in F.S. Regs., Part II. and the Staff Manual respectively. Title pages will be prepared in manuscript.

Hour, Date, Place	Summary of Events and Information	Remarks and references to Appendices
3rd October 1914	MISSY. Excellent fire on enemy at Chavonne & outpost	
4th October 1914	"	
5th October 1914	Hooper battery heavily engaged by enemy positions	
6th October 1914	" and also	
7th October 1914	Visited MISSY by front trenches. Marched at 6am for CIRY and SERMOISE and visited Queen's West infantry on position there	1/20
8th October 1914	Relieved at CIRY and SERMOISE by French troops, handed it	
9th October 1914	SEPTMONTS arriving at 3am. Left at 3pm and marched	
10th October 1914	CHACRISE. Battalion billeted.	
11th October 1914	CHACRISE. Route march and skirmishing	
12th October 1914	Left CHACRISE by Motor Lorries for LE MEUX. Equipment entrained at LE MEUX at 5am, arriving at HAZEBROUCK at 10 pm. BILLETED	
13th October 1914	Marched from METEREN to BAILLEUL. Billeted.	
14th October 1914	" BAILLEUL to LE LEUTHE.	
15th October 1914	" "	
16th October 1914	marched to PLOEGSTEERT. Night outposts	

Army Form C. 2118.

WAR DIARY
or
INTELLIGENCE SUMMARY.
(Erase heading not required.)

Hour, Date, Place	Summary of Events and Information	Remarks and references to Appendices
22nd October. LE TOUQUET	6 men wounded by snipers. Relieved at night by Rifle Brigade and marched to billets in LE BIZET. Relief without incident.	
23rd October	Remained in billets until 6.15 p.m. when Bn marched to ARMENTIERES and relieved the LEINSTER & N. STAFFORD Regts in trenches.	
24 October	In trenches south of ARMENTIERES. Enemy attacked WEZ MACQUART village on our right but were repulsed with loss. Bn had 2 wounded only.	
25 October	Quiet day (nothing of interest)	
26 October	Relieved Kings Own Regt in early morning arrived in billets at 4 a.m [remainder of day spent in cleaning up]	
27 October	Two Coys occupied reserve trenches in the morning & Battalion relieved Kings Own at night in the same trenches. H.Q. Farm had been burnt but good dug out was erected by R.E in reserve trench. Casualties. One man wounded during relief.	
28 Oct.	Enemy made a night attack at 2 a.m repulsed. Whole position heavily shelled during day. Made another attack early morning on E YORKS but got hung up in wire entanglements between first and second line of trenches, were counter attacked by E YORKS. and by B Coy LAN FUS. Enemy's losses estimated 200 killed at least Our losses 4 men killed, Capt Birkett 7 men wounded.	

Army Form C. 2118.

WAR DIARY
or
INTELLIGENCE SUMMARY.
(Erase heading not required.)

Instructions regarding War Diaries and Intelligence Summaries are contained in F.S. Regs., Part II. and the Staff Manual respectively. Title pages will be prepared in manuscript.

Hour, Date, Place	Summary of Events and Information	Remarks and references to Appendices
29th Oct.	Quiet day. Relieved by King's Own in trenches though relief made very late owing to heavy rifle fire.	
30th Oct.	Quiet day in billets.	
31st Oct.	At 11 pm ½ Bn under Capt. WOODMAN were sent to PLOEGSTEERT to the assistance of 11th Brigade. At 1 am H.Q. & remainder of Battalion were ordered up also.	

Operations

13–22d

October

1914

The Battalion detrained at HAZEBROUCK about 3 am on 13th October & proceeded to billets. About 11 am the Bn marched as part of the Brigade towards METEREN. The Brigade commenced an attack on the latter place, the Kings Own moving on the south side of the COURT CROIX road with the Lan Fus in support. "C" Coy under Capt. LUKER reinforced the left centre of the Kings Own Regt. B Coy were echeloned on right rear of "C" Coy to watch a gap between the 4th & 6th Divisions.

The firing line reached a bank by the road but owing to open ground & heavy firing were unable to advance.

At dark the Regt. were ordered to push round the east side of the village or storm it, Col Butler decided on the latter alternative and about 11 pm formed the battalion along the road to METEREN in single file on either side with bayonets fixed & orders not to fire but charge if fire were opened.

It was a pitch dark night & the approach to the village was unknown, or the exact positions of the enemy's trenches & posts.

3. The village was reached without incident, strong platoons were sent through the village to seize the further edge and block the roads. A search was then made through the houses and eight Germans discovered, three more being found next morning. A couple of dead Germans were picked up & buried by B Coy after daylight.

The French inhabitants were delighted to see us & gave the whole battalion hot coffee in the early morning.

Casualties Killed Lt Ecmeror
 9339 Pte Holt
 247 " Foole.

Wounded
 7 OR

On 17th Oct the Batt (?) was covering PLOEGSTEERT towards the south with an outpost line extending from NIEPPE exclusive to the PLOEGSTEERT-ARMENTIERES road. In the evening the Bn moved towards the French-Belgian frontier taking up an outpost line from a Cavalry Brigade stretching from the R. LYS at HOUPLINES through LE TOUQUET STA towards LE GHEER, the Innis Fus connecting on our left flank about 1 mile S.E of the last village.

On the morning of 18 Oct as soon as the Kings Own came up, Col Butler was put in command of the two Regts & ordered to attack LE TOUQUET in order to assist the 10th Brigade who were attacking on the S.E side of the R. LYS.

The Bn were allotted the village of LE TOUQUET as their objective, the K.O. Regt the trenches between the village & the river. The two Battalions advanced to the attack, one Coy (K.O.R) supported by another Coy on the south of the road, two Coys LF supported by one Coy to the N of the road. One Coy LF and two Coys K.O being held in reserve.

The village was strongly held, the houses being loopholed & trenches were dotted over the open ground between the village & river while a cross fire of artillery & rifle fire was maintained from

2

the opposite side of the river & loopholed houses of FRELINGHIEN.

The Battalions pushed forward slowly under cover of artillery fire & the fire of their own supports and by evening had got a strong hold of the village with the exception of the last few houses at the road junction. During the night Col Butler sent up some engineers and a strong barricade was built across the street & the firing line of both Batts strongly entrenched on both sides of the village.

On 19 Oct the day was devoted to improving the position the 10th Brigade not having been able to advance so quickly and to suit arrangements further N the left of the line was thrown forward towards PONT ROUGE On 20th additional artillery both Howitzer & field guns came up & materially assisted the 10th Brigade. Early in the morning 21st a strong attack was made by the enemy on the portion of the line held by the Innis. Fus. who gave way.

The left Coy of the Kings Own who had been sent to that flank the night before were thus enfiladed and had to retire a short distance, but they refused to be driven further

3

It was however imperative to reinforce the left accordingly Lieut Northover & 3 platoons L.F. were sent to their assistance and later Lieut Seckham & one platoon were withdrawn from the right and sent up to fill the gap between B Coy on our left & the Kings Own Coy.

The strong defence put up combined with a powerful artillery support finally broke the attack. The enemy began to retire & our machine guns had the time of their lives. The German casualties were extremely heavy, several hundred it is estimated were lying in front of our position.

During the night 21/22/ a counter attack on the Germans that still remained was made by some of the E. Lanc Regt & Somersets & again the enemy were driven back with heavy casualties.

The following letter was sent by the 4th Div to the 3rd Army. "The staunchness of the Kings Own & Lan. Fus. after their flank was turned was most commendable & I beg to bring to notice Lt Col Butler L.F who commanded these two Battalions with great success during these two days

12th Brigade.
4th Division.

2nd BATTALION

LANCASHIRE FUSILIERS

NOVEMBER 1914

1st November	Two companies pushed forward on MESSINES Road in local support of SOMERSET. L.INF. Remainder of Bn in Brigade reserve at PLOEGSTEERT.
2nd November	Col Butler takes over command of Section of Defence. One Company into fire trenches at ST.YVES to support SOMERSETS. Casualties Killed Capt SNEYD & 4 men. Wounded 19 other ranks.
3rd November	Battalion in trenches at ST YVES. Casualties mostly from shell fire. KILLED two men. WOUNDED 14 men.
4th November	As yesterday Killed one Wounded 6 men.
5th November	As yesterday 4 killed one wounded.
6th November	Relieved at night by SOMERSETS Casualties during day 5 wounded.

Army Form C. 2118.

WAR DIARY
or
INTELLIGENCE SUMMARY.
(Erase heading not required.)

Instructions regarding War Diaries and Intelligence Summaries are contained in F.S. Regs., Part II. and the Staff Manual respectively. Title pages will be prepared in manuscript.

Hour, Date, Place	Summary of Events and Information	Remarks and references to Appendices
7th November	Battalion west in dug outs in PLOEGSTEERT WOOD 3 men wounded.	
8 November	Battalion went into trenches at ST YVES recover trenches. Wood heavily shelled. Casualties 1 killed 15 wounded.	
9th November	Germans broke through trenches held by WORCESTERS, the men in the trenches having been killed by shell fire. Preparations made for night attack. Argyll Sutherlands to make attack. LAN FUS in support. Attack practically successful only, trenches when occupied were enfiladed & had to be abandoned again; other trenches were occupied to watch Germans & prevent any further progress into wood. Casualties 2 killed at hothoer & 15 other ranks wounded.	2/2
10th		
11	Battalion took over front trenches from the ARGYLLS 7 on by SEAFORTHS Wounded 3 men.	
12th	In trenches. Continuous shell fire 12 men wounded.	
13	Do do 1 man killed 6 wounded.	
14th	do Occasional shells & deadly sniping killed 3 men.	
15th	do do Casualties nil.	

WAR DIARY or INTELLIGENCE SUMMARY.

(Erase heading not required.)

Army Form C. 2118.

Hour, Date, Place	Summary of Events and Information	Remarks and references to Appendices
16th November	In trenches in PLOEGSTEERT WOOD. Two men wounded.	
17th November	do do One man wounded.	
18 & 19th November	do do 1 wounded each day.	
20 November	Relieved from trenches and marched to billets in LE BIZET.	
21 November	In billets during day. Relieved KINGS OWN Regt at LE TOUQUET	2/20
22 November	Two men killed by snipers during day. [Lt SECKHAM bitten by dog in deserted farm & sent to PASTEUR's Institute Paris]	
23rd November	Day passed without incident. Digging as usual.	
24th November	Good work done at communication trenches. Capt Brisley and 80 men arrived to join Battalion.	
25th November	Battalion relieved by Kings Own in trenches and marched to billets at NIEPPE.	
26th November	Battalion in the Baths. Hot wash very refreshing & much appreciated.	
27 & 28th November	In fresh billets. Two Corpl recruits march in morning two in the evening.	
29th November	Church Parade in the morning. Relieved Kings Own at LE TOUQUET	Capt & Adjt
30th November	A quiet day. Progress in trench repairs & communication trenches reported by all Companies	[signature] Col on [?]

STRENGTH RETURN.

Detail.	Officers Number.	Other ranks Number.	Remarks.
Strength of Unit on 30th Nov. 1914.	14	804	
Details, by arms attached to unit as in War establishment) A.S.C.	—	4	
) R.A.M.C.	1	5	
) etc.	—	1	Am Sgt
Total	18	814	

Signature _____
Unit Lanc. Fus.

Date 2/12/1914.

URGENT.

This return to be completed and forwarded through the usual channel to reach Div. H.Q.'s by 12 M.D. on 3rd Dec. 1914.

(Sd) G. Smyth Osborne

2/12/14.

Lt. Col.
A.A. & Q.M.G. 4th Div.

12th Brigade.
4th Division.

2nd BATTALION

LANCASHIRE FUSILIERS

DECEMBER 1914

Army Form C. 2118.

WAR DIARY
or
INTELLIGENCE SUMMARY.
(Erase heading not required.)

Instructions regarding War Diaries and Intelligence Summaries are contained in F. S. Regs., Part II. and the Staff Manual respectively. Title pages will be prepared in manuscript.

Hour, Date, Place	Summary of Events and Information	Remarks and references to Appendices
1 December 1914.	In trenches at LE TOUQUET. Enemy machine guns considerably interfered with our working parties but no casualties. Communication trenches widened & improved	
2 December	In trenches good progress made on trenches. No shelling.	
3 December	Enemy continued. Three or four light shrapnel shells burst near Bn. H.Q.	7/20 f.
4 December	Relieved from trenches. Billets in LE BIZET	
5 December	Billets. Two companies out route marching	
6 December	Billets. Other two companies route march.	
7 December	Billets until evening. Back to trenches. No incident	
8 December	Trenches. Snipers fairly active. Draining trenches occupies all available time	
9 December	Had to abandon left supporting trench owing to flood	
10 December	Quiet day but water is rising in the trenches which are in places waist & in places chest deep.	
11 December	Our artillery shelled enemy's houses in LE TOUQUET & demolished them. Sniping has ceased. Relieved in evening to Billets at LE BIZET	

WAR DIARY
or
INTELLIGENCE SUMMARY.
(Erase heading not required.)

Army Form C. 2118.

Hour, Date, Place	Summary of Events and Information	Remarks and references to Appendices
12, 13 & 14th December	In billets two Coys went march daily. 2 Lt Hawkins + 108 other ranks joined Bn. 13th inst.	
15th December.	Relieved the Kings Own in the trenches. Our guns shell FRELINGHEIN at night.	
16th December.	Quiet day in trenches which are still very wet. One killed one wounded	
17 December	Work in trenches continued. One man killed one wounded by enemy	
18 December	Quiet day no casualties. Work or drainage continued	
19th December	Headquarters from heavily shelled in response to our artillery maintained heavy fire during day in support of 11th Brigade no casualties. One killed two wounded in trenches by snipers	2/2.6"
20th December	Intermittent shelling by Germans no damage. Relieved by the Kings Own without incident	
21, 22 December	In billets without incident men get hot baths	
23 December	Inspected by the Brigadier General Haig 25 mm fan Bn.	
24 December	Return to the trenches in relief of the Kings Own	
25-26 December	The firing Xmas day, practically none 2 2/4" but one man killed.	
27th December	Quiet day no casualties.	

WAR DIARY
or
INTELLIGENCE SUMMARY.
(Erase heading not required.)

Army Form C. 2118.

Hour, Date, Place	Summary of Events and Information	Remarks and references to Appendices
28th – 31st December	In billets. Het bath for the Battalion. Route marches by Companies. Working parties of 200 men found each night to build new high command trenches to replace those now full of water. Two men wounded by one bullet night 30/31 while working	

4th Division

War Diary
12th Infantry Bde
2nd Lancs Fus To 108th Bde 4-11-15

January to October, 1915

4th Div.
12th Inf.Bde.

WAR DIARY

2ND BATTN. LANCASHIRE FUSILIERS

JANUARY

1915.

Army Form C. 2118

WAR DIARY
or
INTELLIGENCE SUMMARY of Lancashire Fusiliers
January 1915

(Erase heading not required.)

Hour, Date, Place	Summary of Events and Information	Remarks and references to Appendices
1st January 1915	New Years day. Germans opened a heavy rifle & machine gun fire at midnight as a feu de joie to celebrate the New Year, did no harm. Relieved the Rifle Corps in the trenches in the evening.	7/20
2nd, 3rd, 4th & 5th January	In trenches very quiet practically no snipers.	
6th, 7, 8, 9 January	In billets. Germans threw about 50 shells round the billets but no one was hit.	
10, 11, 12, 13 January	In trenches again. Floods very high, had to abandon some trenches & put our men in houses. Had to dig more trenches as possible refuge in case of shelling. Our snipers claim 11 Germans on 12 inst. Average of sick remains satisfactorily low.	
14, 15, 16, 17 January.	In billets. Day trenches in case billets are shelled by big guns otherwise in case of shrapnel & small shell men are safer in the houses. Men forbidden to remain in the streets. Inoculation again entered is being strenuously pushed forward.	
18, 19, 20, 21 January	In trenches very wet weather making it difficult to obtain much of the trenches. Quiet generally but occasional bursts of machine gun fire generally about 7 pm & 3 am	

Army Form C. 2118.

WAR DIARY
or
INTELLIGENCE SUMMARY.
(Erase heading not required.)

Instructions regarding War Diaries and Intelligence Summaries are contained in F.S. Regs., Part II. and the Staff Manual respectively. Title pages will be prepared in manuscript.

Hour, Date, Place	Summary of Events and Information	Remarks and references to Appendices
January 22, 23, 24, 25	In billets. The battalion were unable to go to Brigade Baths owing to the pipes being flooded over. Grenadiers from Coys practised in throwing from bombs from trenches & in the open.	
January 26, 27, 28, 29	In trenches. The Kaiser's birthday passed off very quietly on our front. AMELIA shelled a German horse and trenches but no men were seen to leave.	
January 30, 31st	In billets. Relief in spite of bright moon was carried out without casualties. Battalion had baths at NIEPPE return fresh shirts & underclothing were issued to them. No shelling.	

Capt. & Adjt
Albany Jan
Lt Col

4th Div.
12th Inf. Bde.

WAR DIARY

2ND BATTN. LANCASHIRE FUSILIERS

FEBRUARY

1915.

Army Form C. 2118.

WAR DIARY
or
INTELLIGENCE SUMMARY.
(Erase heading not required.)

2nd Bn Lancashire Fusiliers

Instructions regarding War Diaries and Intelligence Summaries are contained in F.S. Regs., Part II. and the Staff Manual respectively. Title pages will be prepared in manuscript.

Hour, Date, Place	Summary of Events and Information	Remarks and references to Appendices
1910		
1st, 2nd February	In Billets. Hot baths for men. Working parties at night.	
3rd, 4th February	Relieved King's Own in trenches. Three men wounded. 2/Lt Bowen arrived.	
5th, 6th February	In trenches. One man wounded. 2Lts Powell & Doaty & 2 men joined Bgt.	
7, 8, 9, 10th February	In Billets. Hot baths for men. Working parties at nights	
11th	In trenches. One man wounded	
12th	One killed two wounded. Put one section in g.5.7.10. house beyond SNIPERS HOUSE and are working at communication tracks	
13th	Two killed two wounded.	
14th	One killed two wounded. 2/Lt Clayen proceeded to join Highland L.Inf.	29th
15, 16, 17, 18th	In Billets. One man wounded whilst working with King's Own. Incendiary shells fired into LE BIZET, one fire started but quickly put out by "A" Coy.	
19th	In trenches. South Lancs trenbucks and one company to the trenches with battalion. One killed two wounded. Also on S danos killed.	
20th	Last night many rifle grenades were fired at railway barricade only one however did damage killing one and wounding one. Reinforcements arrived 2/Lt Harrison and 60 men	

Army Form C. 2118.

WAR DIARY
or
INTELLIGENCE SUMMARY.
(Erase heading not required.)

Instructions regarding War Diaries and Intelligence Summaries are contained in F. S. Regs., Part II. and the Staff Manual respectively. Title pages will be prepared in manuscript.

Hour, Date, Place	Summary of Events and Information	Remarks and references to Appendices
21st & 22nd February	In trenches. One man wounded. Houses in LE TOUQUET from snipers have completed. A barricade is being erected behind two walls on right front of these houses as cover in case wall is blown down. Frequent visits from staff to see houses.	
23rd, 24, 25, 26 February	In billets. [Hot baths at PONT DE NIEPPE.] Reinforcements arrive 2 Lts Martin & Roberts with 40 men. The battalion are now twenty one over strength.	
27th February	In trenches. One company S. Lancs Territorials attached to battalion for instruction. Two men wounded.	
28th February	In trenches. One man of S. Lancs killed and two Km. Gns wounded. Some light shells fell near the new trenches behind on H.Q.	

A.H.Hoblasm Capt & Adjt.
Hampshire Fusiliers

4th Div.
12th Inf.Bde.

WAR DIARY

2ND BATTN. LANCASHIRE FUSILIERS

MARCH

1915.

WAR DIARY or INTELLIGENCE SUMMARY.

Army Form C. 2118.

Hour, Date, Place	Summary of Events and Information	Remarks and references to Appendices
March 1st	In Kinchio. Enemy very active with rifle grenades. 1 killed 5 wounded.	
March 2nd	Have actively with rifle grenade. 1 killed 7 wounded. Our supply of rifle grenades has run out & cannot be replaced yet. Relieved by the Kings Own in the evening.	
March 3rd, 4th, 5th	In Billets. 2nd Lt Macdonald & 26 men joined Battalion. 1 killed 1 wounded for working parties.	2/2°
March 6, 7, 8, 9	In Kinchio. Rather a quiet tour until evening of when 5 men were wounded four of them by rifle grenade.	
March 10, 11, 12, 13	In Billets. ["C" Coy inspected by Brigadier. Capt Aiken injures his knee owing to his horse coming down.]	
March 14, 15th	Four men wounded. Capt Aiken to hospital with injured knee.	
March 16th	Three men wounded. Reinforcements 122 men joined Battalion.	
March 17th	Six men wounded mostly rifle grenade. Battalion 70 over strength.	
March 18, 19, 20, 21	In Billets. 2nd Lt Granger joins Battalion [but went to hospital two days later. Brigadier inspects "D Coy."]	
March 22, 23, 24, 25	A very quiet tour in trenches. Three men wounded. Lt Cowly ? Battalion which is now (on paper) overstrength in officers and men	

Army Form C. 2118.

WAR DIARY
or
INTELLIGENCE SUMMARY.
(Erase heading not required.)

Instructions regarding War Diaries and Intelligence Summaries are contained in F. S. Regs., Part II. and the Staff Manual respectively. Title pages will be prepared in manuscript.

Hour, Date, Place	Summary of Events and Information	Remarks and references to Appendices
March 26, 27, 28, 29.	In Billets. 2 Lt Wells joins the Battalion. Corps have not bathe in NIEPPE, and Scott trains the bomb throwers of the 5th Leicesters (Territorials)	
	In trenches 1 killed 6 wounded. Lieut wounded by rifle grenade which have become frequent gun principally on the LE TOUQUET	
March 30, 31.	During the month 165 yards have been made in the drainage of trenches and in the construction of new ones. Good communication trenches now exist up to most of the front trenches. B Coy and Capt BLENCOWE have made & traversed some excellent trenches. Work still continues	2/20 [signature] Capt & Adj.

(9 29 6) W 2794 100,000 8/14 H W V Forms/C. 2118/11.

4th Div.
12th Inf. Bde.

WAR DIARY

2ND BATTN. LANCASHIRE FUSILIERS

A P R I L

1 9 1 5

Army Form C. 2118.

WAR DIARY
or
INTELLIGENCE SUMMARY. 2nd Bn Lancashire Fusiliers

(Erase heading not required.)

Hour, Date, Place	Summary of Events and Information	Remarks and references to Appendices
1915		
1st April	Bismarck contour quiet day on trenches	
2 and 3rd April	Still in trenches. 2/Lt Wells and 4 men wounded very slightly. "B"	
	Wells ought to return to duty in a week.	
4th 5th 6th 7th		
8th April	2nd Lts Greaves and Hartley joined the battalion.	
	A German sniper's nest was observed last night by one of our	
	gallers. It was decided to blow it up. Day spent in laying the	
	gunpowder and tamping mine. A trench mortar put into	
	position in Snipers House.	
9th April	Artillery & trench mortars opened fire on German houses at 8am	
	and all trenches opened musketry fire from 8 – 8.30am on	
	trenches in front & houses. At 8.30am mine was blown up	
	Very successful. Our stores going up to be position at 1pm	
	saw 29 Germans carried across river on stretchers, presumably	
	the majority of the wounded were carried across before that hour.	
	Our infantry fire appeared very accurate, our men being able	
	to entirely enfilade themselves. In the afternoon we were heavily	
	shelled with little damage. A 5.9 shell through Guard room full of men	
	slightly wounded four. Total casualties thirty-four for the day	

Army Form C. 2118.

WAR DIARY
or
INTELLIGENCE SUMMARY.

1/4th Bn. Lancashire Fusiliers

(Erase heading not required.)

Instructions regarding War Diaries and Intelligence Summaries are contained in F.S. Regs., Part II. and the Staff Manual respectively. Title pages will be prepared in manuscript.

Hour, Date, Place	Summary of Events and Information	Remarks and references to Appendices
1915		
10th April	were 1 killed 17 wounded. Some of the latter by falling bricks etc from our own shells which fell 300+ back, three men will return in a day or so	
11th April	About 300 shells settle Willies own next our during day but no damage was done. Two men wounded. LE TOUQUET village shelled by Germans 5.9 Batterie. About 60 shells were fired. Two sheds in NORTH BLOCK set on fire & burnt down. Two or three walls knocked down in SNIPERS HOUSES. No casualties. Three men wounded in legs by rifle grenade late in the evening	
12th 13th 14th do do	In Billets. Capt. Salt joined 13th inst	
15th	Moved back from old Billets to the BLUE FACTORY where the Battalion is to rest and get in marching & fighting trim	
16th to 27th	Route marches, free gymnastics, running, football in the daily routine. Transport inspected by Divcav. Horses and vehicles in a very satisfactory condition	
28th	Received orders to move at mid-day. Battalion partly proceed to BOULEUR	

Army Form C. 2118.

WAR DIARY
or
INTELLIGENCE SUMMARY.

(Erase heading not required.)

1st/4th Lancashire Fusiliers

Army Form C. 2118.

Instructions regarding War Diaries and Intelligence Summaries are contained in F. S. Regs., Part II. and the Staff Manual respectively. Title pages will be prepared in manuscript.

Hour, Date, Place	Summary of Events and Information	Remarks and references to Appendices
1915 April 29th	In billets S.E. of BAILLEUL	
April 30th	Left billets at 7.45 am and marched work. Very hot and dusty march toward VLAMERINGHE about 2 pm bivouacked in fields, proposed to move again about 5 pm	

(9 29 6) W 2794 100,000 8/14 HWV Forms/C. 2118/11.

4th Div.
12th Inf. Bde.

WAR DIARY

2ND BATTN. LANCASHIRE FUSILIERS

M A Y

1 9 1 5

Army Form C. 2118

WAR DIARY
or
INTELLIGENCE SUMMARY.
(Erase heading not required.)

Instructions regarding War Diaries and Intelligence Summaries are contained in F.S. Regs., Part II. and the Staff Manual respectively. Title pages will be prepared in manuscript.

Hour, Date, Place	Summary of Events and Information	Remarks and references to Appendices
May 1st	No treated near village of "WIELTJE". Heavily shelled during the day. Casualties 3 men killed and 28 wounded.	
2nd	During the night about 11 p.m. enemy attacked our position by means of gun fire. This was immediately followed by a heavy infantry attack on our right flank. Casualties 1 man killed. [Captain Adams D.S.O. Bnl. Suffolk Regt.] [attached, wounded. Captain Warburton V.C. & Spencer Regt. Lieut H.P. McCormick D.C.L.I. Lieut Powell D.W.L. Hound Enzel B.R. Blum S.R. Beck C.E. Capt. F. R. Lund Capt. Sew R.W. Watts & H. Curtis R.C. Stewart R.E. Little R.W. Arthur J.B. Evans J. David W. Wray. G. also ?????? admitted to hospital since 17.4.15 the names of officers of Eastern Reinforcement sent on 19.4.15 were ?????? joining Battalion and killed or missing regret to report Major Griffiths O.C. attached from ?????? of Lancashire. Major Griffiths O.C. attached from 4 LANCASHIRE (Wounded) ????? was on escort of a 2/Yorkshire	

Army Form C. 2118

WAR DIARY
or
INTELLIGENCE SUMMARY.
(Erase heading not required.)

Instructions regarding War Diaries and Intelligence Summaries are contained in F. S. Regs., Part II. and the Staff Manual respectively. Title pages will be prepared in manuscript.

Hour, Date, Place	Summary of Events and Information	Remarks and references to Appendices
May 11	Battalion went into Bivouac about 4 miles N. of POPERINGHE	
May 9th to 13th	Battalion in Bivouac. Reinforcement 187 men joined.	
May 14th	Moved onto Reserve trenches dug in left of VLAMERTINGHE	
May 15th	Relieved Royal Scots in trenches W. of SHELL TRAP FARM	
May 16, 17th	In trenches. Reinforcement joined 201 men	
" 18 & 19th	Continuously shelled. Many killed by Cavalry Killed 18 men wounded	
" 20th	Relieved in trenches by Hampshire Regt. and Wiltshires	
" 21 & 22nd	In support in support line 4 Bomb Throwers	
" 21 & 22nd	In support trenches. Reinforcement Lieut Crawford Lieut A. Brew to M.S. Lieut Heald Lieut J. 226 men were attached. Continued shelling ah(?) and ahh(?)	
" 23rd		
" 24	At 2.30 A.M. the Germans attacked our front trenches were attacked by asphyxiating gas and after a shell from "2" compartment the support line from Regt. Capt. Birnham and 8 other only reaching this. It enabled B.C. & D. Coy to hold up by rifle and machine gun fire shot up North behind enemy	

Army Form C. 2118.

WAR DIARY
or
INTELLIGENCE SUMMARY.
(Erase heading not required.)

Hour, Date, Place	Summary of Events and Information	Remarks and references to Appendices

May 25th — 1 should [Lieut Charles E.?] and 12 other ranks killed. Captain Oller-Browne, [Lieut?] Hall to south Eye [wood?] [4 other ranks?] wounded.

26th — Heavy shell[ing?] during the day. 2 men wounded.

27th — Battalion withdrawn to Divisional reserve line in dug-outs.

Casual [events?] in early morning. Reinforcement joined 187 men.

28th — 1st Divisional Reserve line.

29th — Battalion relieved Essex Regt in trenches N. of [Inver?] Farm.

L. trenches. Heavily shelled in evening and also in coming casualties.

9 men wounded.

30th — Heavily shelled in evening. 1 man killed and 10 wounded.

Artillery continued during the night. Battalion relieved in the trenches by 2nd Lancs Fusiliers. One officer 1 man

31st — knocked at night by [Lieut?] [illegible] [illegible] [illegible] near PLOEGSTEERTE killed, 10 wounded. Bn. Proceeded to [new?] [illegible] [illegible]

C. J. [Griffin?] Major
Commanding [illegible] [illegible]

4th Div.
12th Inf. Bde.

WAR DIARY

    2ND BATTN. LANCASHIRE FUSILIERS

        J U N E

            1 9 1 5

Army Form C. 2118

WAR DIARY
or
INTELLIGENCE SUMMARY.
(Erase heading not required.)

Instructions regarding War Diaries and Intelligence Summaries are contained in F.S. Regs., Part II. and the Staff Manual respectively. Title pages will be prepared in manuscript.

Hour, Date, Place	Summary of Events and Information	Remarks and references to Appendices
1915		
June 1st to 5th	Battalion at rest in bivouac at Dernancourt Headquarters Chateau. VLAMERTINGHE	
June 6th	Relieved French (Zouaves) in trenches. 2 Lieut A.S. Fletcher junr.	
" 7th	On front line trenches. Enemy artillery active all day.	
" 8th	Heavily shelled in trenches in morning. 6 men wounded by shell fire	
" 9th	Quiet day. 1 man wounded by snipers.	
" 10th	Shelled at intervals during the day, 2 men killed 2 wounded.	
" 11th	Continuous shelling during early morning. 2 men wounded.	
" 12th	Reinforcement Lieut H.G. Birchall and 30 other ranks joined. 4 Their wounded by enemy snipers. Lieut Billing Rts.C.C. Loucks, R.C. Marsh (S. Lan. Regt) and 4 L.E. Marne (S. Lanc. Regt) joined.	
" 13th	One man killed, 2 wounded by enemy snipers.	
" 14th	Some shelling took place about midday but no damage done. One man was killed and 2 wounded by enemy snipers.	
" 15th	2 men killed and 2 wounded by enemy snipers. Battalion relieved in trenches by Warwicks Regt. and withdrawn	

(9 29 6) W 2794 100,000 8/14 H W V Forms/C. 2118/11.

WAR DIARY or INTELLIGENCE SUMMARY.

(Erase heading not required.)

Army Form C. 2118

Instructions regarding War Diaries and Intelligence Summaries are contained in F.S. Regs., Part II. and the Staff Manual respectively. Title pages will be prepared in manuscript.

Hour, Date, Place	Summary of Events and Information	Remarks and references to Appendices
June 15	Withdrawn to reserve trenches at Chateau Trois Tours "Brielen". One man was killed whilst relief was being carried out. Lieut. E.H. Kelly (Border Reg) joined Batln. During this period in the trenches, much good work was done in strengthening and generally improving the trenches.	
June 16-18	Battalion in trenches at BRIELEN. Major Mc.Pherson (R.W. Kent) joined and Lieut. E.H.D. Day rejoined from Hospital. Battalion relieved Essex Regt in front line trenches.	
" 19th	2 men wounded.	
" 20th	Quiet day. Work at improvement of trenches carried out. 2 men killed and one wounded	
" 21st		
" 22nd	Slight shelling by enemy's "trench" artillery. 30 damage done.	
" 23rd	In trenches. Battalion relieved by Essex Regt and withdrawn to 2nd line trenches at "La Belle Alliance" Farm, No Company to trenches "Irish Farm". Captain A.H. Spooner, D.S.O. rejoined Battalion.	

Army Form C. 2118.

WAR DIARY
or
INTELLIGENCE SUMMARY.
(Erase heading not required.)

Instructions regarding War Diaries and Intelligence Summaries are contained in F.S. Regs., Part II. and the Staff Manual respectively. Title pages will be prepared in manuscript.

Hour, Date, Place	Summary of Events and Information	Remarks and references to Appendices
June 21st 27th	Bn. in front line trenches. Quiet day spent in cleaning and strengthening trenches. Relieved Essex Regt. in front line trenches. 2 men wounded.	
28	In firing line. Working parties sent out at night, and general work on trenches carried on. 3 men wounded by snipers.	
29.	Enemy's Artillery active and shelling us continued throughout the day. 4 men were killed and 3 wounded by Enemy snipers. One man wounded by stell fire.	
30th	Enemy mortars were busy, but caused no casualties.	

W. Gorm Capt + Adjt
2 Essex Regt

4th Div.
12th Inf. Bde.

WAR DIARY

2ND. BATTN. LANCASHIRE FUSILIERS

J U L Y

1 9 1 5

Army Form C. 2118.

WAR DIARY
or
INTELLIGENCE SUMMARY.

(Erase heading not required.) **2nd Bn The Lancashire Fusiliers.**

Instructions regarding War Diaries and Intelligence Summaries are contained in F.S. Regs., Part II. and the Staff Manual respectively. Title pages will be prepared in manuscript.

Hour, Date, Place	Summary of Events and Information	Remarks and references to Appendices
July 1st	Battalion in trenches N. of Ypres. Enemy Artillery active during the morning. Reserve and support trenches heavily shelled. Some slight damage done to parapets and 3 men wounded, the chaplain relieved in trenches in evening and billets were bivouacked and marched to rest camp about 3 mile N.E. of POPERINGHE	
2nd	Battalion in bivouac. Reinforcements 50 men joined	
3rd H	-do- Company inspections and reorganisation.	
5th	Battalion marched to Elverdinghe and where they bivouacked for the night	
6	Lieuts C.C. Butler and 16 S.M Cohen admitted to Hospital. In evening Battalion marched to PILKEM where they relieved Rifle Brigade in trenches captured in early morning. Trenches improved and parapets repaired the whole continued until day break on 7th inst.	

(9 29 6) W 2794 100,000 8/14 H W V Forms/C. 2118/11.

Army Form C. 2118

WAR DIARY
or
INTELLIGENCE SUMMARY.
(Erase heading not required.) 2nd Bn The Lancashire Fusiliers.

Hour, Date, Place	Summary of Events and Information	Remarks and references to Appendices
July 7.14	Owing to the very severe fighting in which the Battalion was involved on which 2 Coys and the Regimental Head Quarters bore the brunt so severe mention is to be made. The casualties on these 2 days were as follows:- Officers Killed. Captain J Smith, Lieut A R Humfrey (Queen's R Chillington Regt) W A Clements, G R Dickinson (N Staffs Regt.) Lieut [?] (L North Regt) Ra Russell (Somerset L.I.)	
	F E Kelly (Worcster Regt), Wyndham, Major C P Griffin DSO. Captain A O Shane DSO. Lieut in [?] A Mitchison. Lieut J Christie, C B Johnson F W Gourlay, B Worthington (N Staffs R.) Kilmer W G [?] (Cheshire Regt) Other Ranks:- Killed 79, Wounded	
	204, Missing 19.	
	On 7th inst Lieut J [?] (N Staffs Rgt) and 30 mn Reinforcements joined. Regimental transport On arrival of 9th Batt. men were relieved in the trenches by 9th/Lancs Rft and marched into bivouac near POPERINGHE.	
10h	Marched to Bullets at Brew Renforencher 30 men joined	

Army Form C. 2118.

WAR DIARY
or
INTELLIGENCE SUMMARY.

(Erase heading not required.) 2nd Bn The Lancashire Fusiliers.

Hour, Date, Place	Summary of Events and Information	Remarks and references to Appendices
July 11-12th	Battalion at rest in Sillob. Company inspection and general reorganisation etc.	
13th	Brigade inspected by 2nd Army Commander	
14-18th	In rest Sillob. Lt Col G.S. Butler joined Brigade inspected by Commander in Chief	
19th	In rest Sillob.	
20th	Marched to "Doirnancourt" and entrained at 11.37pm where we arrived 12.30 am & 22nd	
21/22	At DOULLENS where we arrived 12.30am & 22nd	
22nd	Detrained and marched to bivouac at POTHIEULE	
23rd	Marched to billets at "FORCEVILLE" Battalion fatigue carrying Ammunition to trenches	
24th	Front line & Laviers South from East Ends Redt." Battalion (and 12 b Brigade) inspected by 2nd Army Commander (Lieut Genl Munro.)	
25th-26th	In billets at FORCEVILLE. Inspections - Route marches etc	

WAR DIARY or INTELLIGENCE SUMMARY.

(Erase heading not required.) 2nd Bn The Lancashire Fusiliers.

Army Form C. 2118.

Hour, Date, Place	Summary of Events and Information	Remarks and references to Appendices
July 27th	carried out.	
" 28th	Battalion marched to Lillile or MAILLY MAILLET. One Company (B) and M.Gunners to Fyegade Reserve in Auchonvillers	
" 29th	Capt W.O'Neill R.A.M.C. posted to be attached to Bath and Coln J Roberts late R.A.M.C. attached. Capt W.D.P. Mansell, Lieut R.S. McIver, 2o Lieut C Arnold, J Brennell, O.H. McMullan, M.P. Sanders, C.A. Reid and 13 Other Ranks joined.	
" 30th	—do— Maillet	
" 31st	2ᵈ Lieut Boyd Roughton and 95 other ranks joined the Battalion	What Kind and Holidays L. Cause, Lui

4th Div.
12th Inf. Bde.

WAR DIARY

2ND BATTN. LANCASHIRE FUSILIERS

A U G U S T

1 9 1 5.

Army Form C. 2118.

WAR DIARY
or
INTELLIGENCE SUMMARY.

(Erase heading not required.) **2nd Bn The Lancashire Fusiliers.**

Instructions regarding War Diaries and Intelligence Summaries are contained in F.S. Regs., Part II. and the Staff Manual respectively. Title pages will be prepared in manuscript.

Hour, Date, Place	Summary of Events and Information	Remarks and references to Appendices
August 1st	Battalion in billets at MAILLY. Muster day celebration.	
2nd	Working parties were found for Reserve trenches.	
3rd	Relieved King's Own in trenches N. of AUCHONVILLERS. "A" "C" "D" Companies in firing line. "B" Company in Reserve. Quiet day. Work of repairing trenches and parapets carried on.	
4th–9th	In trenches. General work in trenches, improvement of parapets were undertaken &c.	
10th	Battalion relieved by King's Own and marched to Divisional Reserve billets at FORCEVILLE.	
11th–17th	In Reserve billets at FORCEVILLE. Company inspections, reorganisation, instruction and route marching carried out.	
18th	Relieved King's Own Regt in trenches at RICHONVILLERS.	
19th–23rd	In trenches. Occasional shells from enemy's artillery arrived at our front line trenches. Work in trenches and improvement of parapets, dug outs etc.	

Army Form C. 2118.

WAR DIARY
or
INTELLIGENCE SUMMARY.

(Erase heading not required.) 2nd Bn The Lancashire Fusiliers.

Instructions regarding War Diaries and Intelligence
Summaries are contained in F.S. Regs., Part II.
and the Staff Manual respectively. Title pages
will be prepared in manuscript.

Hour, Date, Place	Summary of Events and Information	Remarks and references to Appendices
August 24th	"C" Company's trench shelled by enemy. One man killed and eleven wounded.	
25th–31st	In trenches. Point A.2 Trenches front 29th and admitted to No 9. 10% General work in trenches.	
31st	One man wounded by rifle and hand grenade. During the month much work in improvement of trenches was carried out, drainage of communication trenches etc receiving attention. One Company at St Baths East Lancs Reg and attached for instruction in trench duties from 29th inst.	Albert Rind and Aylock No Cause for

4th Div.
12th Inf.Bde.

WAR DIARY

2ND BATTN. LANCASHIRE FUSILIERS

S E P T E M B E R

1 9 1 5

WAR DIARY or INTELLIGENCE SUMMARY.

(Erase heading not required.)

Army Form C. 2118.

Instructions regarding War Diaries and Intelligence Summaries are contained in F. S. Regs., Part II. and the Staff Manual respectively. Title pages will be prepared in manuscript.

Hour, Date, Place	Summary of Events and Information	Remarks and references to Appendices
September 1st	In trenches N. of Auchonvillers, quiet day. Work of improving trenches generally carried out.	
2nd	In trenches. Quiet day. Relieved in trenches at night by 1st Royal Irish Fusiliers and marched to Rest Billets at "Acheux".	
3rd	At Billets at Acheux, general reorganisation and refitment of Companies. Lieut. J.O. Rotcliffe assumed to strength.	
4th to 8th	At Billets at "Acheux". Working parties daily sent for support and Reserve Line trenches.	
9th	Marched to "Auchonvillers" where we relieved R.D.F. in trenches.	
10th to 14th	In trenches. Enemy's artillery active and our slight shelling at front trenches by enemy artillery. Little damage was done to trenches. One Pte. Watson, [?] man was killed and 4 wounded by a rifle grenade which exploded in the trench. Quiet day on 15th. Nothing of note occurred.	
15th		

Army Form C. 2118.

WAR DIARY
or
INTELLIGENCE SUMMARY.
(Erase heading not required.)

Instructions regarding War Diaries and Intelligence Summaries are contained in F. S. Regs., Part II. and the Staff Manual respectively. Title pages will be prepared in manuscript.

Hour, Date, Place	Summary of Events and Information	Remarks and references to Appendices
Sept 16th	Relieved by 2 L Div in trenches and marched to billets at Troiville.	
17th to 21st	In Divisional Reserve billets in Troiville. Working parties for 2nd & 3rd line trenches employed daily and general work of preparation of Defences, etc.	
22nd	Marched to Anchonvillers and relieved R.D. Div in trenches.	
23rd	Intermittent bombardment of our Artillery of enemy's trenches during the day. 2 men wounded Col. Surveying grounds Betw[ee]n 22 men joined Battn.	
24th	Bombardment of our Artillery continued at intervals during the day. One man killed by enemy's sniper.	
25th	Further bombardment of enemy's trenches. During this 3 day bombardment much gun activity was observed and a great deal of damage appeared to be inflicted on enemy's defences. 3 Taubes were	

Army Form C. 2118.

WAR DIARY
or
INTELLIGENCE SUMMARY.
(Erase heading not required.)

Instructions regarding War Diaries and Intelligence Summaries are contained in F.S. Regs., Part II. and the Staff Manual respectively. Title pages will be prepared in manuscript.

Hour, Date, Place	Summary of Events and Information	Remarks and references to Appendices
Sep 25th (Cont)	wounded by enemys hand grenade	
26th	Enemys grenadiers more than usually active One man killed & one wounded	
27th	Quiet day	
28th	A few shells from enemys artillery dropped in Auchonvillers and in front of village (one man killed) One wounded by grenade.	
29th	Quiet day. Our artillery shelled enemys trenches in intervals. Relieved in evening by 1st Royal Scots Fusiliers and marched to billets at MAILLY-MAILLET	
30th	Billets at Mailly. Working parties on trenches and second line, also instructions from 10th Brigade	

J.C. Mort. Lieut
Adjutant, 2nd Lancashire Fusiliers

4th Div.
12th.Inf.Bde.

WAR DIARY

2ND BATTN. LANCASHIRE FUSILIERS

OCTOBER

1915.

4 RWF: Jan: Dec

Army Form C. 2118

WAR DIARY or **INTELLIGENCE SUMMARY.**
(Erase heading not required.)

WAR OFFICE RECEIVED -3 NOV 1915

Hour, Date, Place	Summary of Events and Information	Remarks and references to Appendices
Oct. 1st to 5th	Battalion in billets at Mailly Maillet forming the reserve battalion to the 10th Infantry Brigade. Three companies were employed daily for work in support trenches to the front line and defences generally.	
6th	Major Spooner rejoined the Battalion on the 3rd. The Battalion relieved the Royal Irish Fusiliers in the trenches (North of Auchonvillers) Relief was carried out easily and without any casualties. Capt: Q.M. Scott R.A.M.C. relieved Lieut: Copland R.A.M.C. as M.O. to the Battalion.	
7th	Enemy snipers very active. One man was slightly wounded.	
8th	Enemy working parties were observed to be busier than usual, especially just North of Beaumont Hamel than the garrison of Pt Genin.	
9th	Quiet day. Pt Genin slightly wounded while on patrol at night.	

WAR DIARY or INTELLIGENCE SUMMARY.

(Erase heading not required.)

Army Form C. 2118.

Hour, Date, Place	Summary of Events and Information	Remarks and references to Appendices
9th	One Corporal missing believed wounded on patrol prisoner (also whilst on patrol)	
10th	Very quiet day	
11th	Very quiet day	
	One company of 2nd Royal Irish Rifles attached to the Battalion for instruction in trench duties. 2nd Lieut. Dunne admitted to Hospital.	
12th	Sniping fairly heavy, otherwise a quiet day. Lieut Crowley admitted to Hospital.	
13th	Relieved in the trenches by the Royal Irish Fusiliers and march to billets at Authieux.	
14th	Companies at disposal of their Officers for reorganisation	
15th	Working party of 250 men called for to dig 2nd and 3rd line in front of the Carlos line	
16th	Battalion Route march in the afternoon. Inspected by Brigadier General & Gen. Anley. - 12th Infantry Brigade on an attack across Country.	

WAR DIARY
or
INTELLIGENCE SUMMARY.
(Erase heading not required.)

Army Form C. 2118.

Hour, Date, Place	Summary of Events and Information	Remarks and references to Appendices
17th to 20th	Battalion in Divisional Reserve billets at Authuis. Working parties found daily on Corps line defences; training & general reorganisation carried on.	
20th	The Battalion relieved the Royal Irish Fusiliers in the trenches South of Auchonvillers; the relief was completed early and without casualties.	
21st	Quiet day. One company 11 Royal Irish Fusiliers 108th Brigade attached for instruction in trench duties.	
22nd	Enemy exploded a mine opposite the Redan at 5.15AM directly after the explosion killed one man and wounded four. Redan, two mortars fired during the morning, was shelled with about 50-60 light shells, however no damage done. Remainder of day quiet.	
23rd	Enemy exploded large mine on right of Redan	

WAR DIARY or INTELLIGENCE SUMMARY.

Army Form C. 2118.

(*Erase heading not required.*)

Hour, Date, Place	Summary of Events and Information	Remarks and references to Appendices
Oct 23rd	Occupying our parapet for about 25 yards. There were no serious casualties. Enemy shelled Redan all evening to in the evening with much rostan. Killing one and wounding five men.	
Oct 24th	Very quiet day.	
Oct 25th	Very quiet day.	
26th	Our artillery and hostile artillery very active. No damage done by hostile artillery fire.	
27th	Quiet day	
28th	Quiet day	
30th	At 12.45 a.m. we blew in a German mine just in front of the Redan by means of a camouflet. Believed to be fairly successful. In the evening the Royal Dublin Fusiliers relieved the Battalion in the trenches. Battalion in billets in small Forceville	O.C. Harte Ft and Adj. 2nd Rre cachine fur lien

36TH DIVISION
108TH INFY BDE

4 DIV
12 Bde

2ND BN LANCS FUS.
NOV 1915.

36TH DIVISION
108TH INFY BDE

1/4 Division

XXXVI Transferred Nov. 5th
2/ Lanc: Fus. 6.15 Bde
Nov 5- Dec 10"

36
12/
7636

Nov 1915 only

Vol XIII

2nd Lancashire Fusiliers

Army Form C. 2118.

WAR DIARY
or
INTELLIGENCE SUMMARY.
(Erase heading not required.)

Instructions regarding War Diaries and Intelligence Summaries are contained in F.S. Regs., Part II. and the Staff Manual respectively. Title pages will be prepared in manuscript.

Place	Date	Hour	Summary of Events and Information	Remarks and references to Appendices
Field.	1/11/15 & 4/11/15.	5 & 6 11/15	Battalion in billets at Freville.	
	7th & 21st 22nd 2-3rd		Battalion marched to Renescure in stages. Nov. 5th marched to and spent the night at Rubempré. Nov. 6 marched to Freiville. Temporarily attached to 108th Infantry Bde.; 36th Division. Battalion in billets at Freiville (Company & Battalion training) Battalion inspected by Major General Nugent in field Exercise Major General Nugent inspected Battalion hand Renews at Ефекаму?	
	24-26. 27th		Company training in neighbourhood of Battalion moved to S. Riquier. A.& C coys billeted in a village called S'hoqwille (South of S. Riquier). B&D at Velville (N.E. q S. Riquier).	
	28th-30th		Company Training.	
	20th		Change from 7th into 13th Corps.	

J.P. Matin. Lieut & Adjt.
2nd Bn Lancashire Fusiliers.

4 DIV
12 BDE

2nd Bn Lancashire Fusiliers
Dec 1915 - Jan 1916

4th Bn

2/Lancs. Fusrs.

Dec

Vol XV

121
793

H.V.
4 sheets

Army Form C. 2118.

WAR DIARY
or
INTELLIGENCE SUMMARY.
(Erase heading not required.)

Instructions regarding War Diaries and Intelligence Summaries are contained in F.S. Regs., Part II. and the Staff Manual respectively. Title pages will be prepared in manuscript.

Place	Date	Hour	Summary of Events and Information	Remarks and references to Appendices
Active Service	1st to 9th		Battalion in Billets in outskirts of St Riquier. A & C Coys in Bthosville B & D in heuville	
	10th.		Outdoor training disturbed by the bad weather. Battalion moved to Billets in Buigny on exchange of billets with 11th R.I.R.	
			Battalion rejoined 12th Bn.	
	11th		Brigade Route march.	
	11th 12 13th		Settling in and improvement of billets.	
	14th		Brigade Route March.	
	15th - 16th		Company training	
	17"		Battalion Day Practice final stages of attack as a Battalion.	
	18 - 21st		Company training.	
	22nd		Brigade Route march.	
	23rd		General Nugent G.O.C. 36th Division inspected billets In the afternoon G.O.C. 12th Infantry Bde. inspected a Company in marching order.	

Army Form C. 2118.

WAR DIARY
or
INTELLIGENCE SUMMARY.
(Erase heading not required.)

Instructions regarding War Diaries and Intelligence Summaries are contained in F.S. Regs., Part II. and the Staff Manual respectively. Title pages will be prepared in manuscript.

Place	Date	Hour	Summary of Events and Information	Remarks and references to Appendices
Acline Sector	24th		O.D.C. 12th Bn inspected 1 Platoon "B" Coy in a practice trench attack at Bossus.	
	25th		Christmas day. No work.	
	26th		Sunday.	
	27th		Battalion Route March.	
	28th		Lt Col H. Breeth DSO. took over temporary command of 12th Inf Bde during the absence on leave of Brigadier General F Gore Anley.	
	29th		Brigade Route March.	
	30th			
	31st		Company training.	

JW Watt Lt Colly
2nd Monmouthshire Fusiliers

2/ franco. francs

$\frac{\text{dam}}{\text{vol. XVI}}$

36 ηPiv

WAR DIARY
or
INTELLIGENCE SUMMARY.

(Erase heading not required.)

Army Form C. 2118.

Instructions regarding War Diaries and Intelligence Summaries are contained in F. S. Regs., Part II. and the Staff Manual respectively. Title pages will be prepared in manuscript.

Place	Date	Hour	Summary of Events and Information	Remarks and references to Appendices
Sailly	1/11/16 to 3/11/16		Company training in billets at Bussy Pabbe	
	4/11/16		Commenced move to Sailly du Bois. Battalion billeted at Bonneville	
	5/11/16		Marched from Bonneville to Rousseauxcourt, where the Battalion billeted for the night. Came under the command of the G.O.C. 48th Division	
	6/11/16		Marched from Rousseauxcourt to Sailly au Bois. Halting to Ra Haie Farm. Arrived in billets about midday and settled in.	
	7/11/16		Settled in billets	
	8/11/16		Village was shelled, with about 60 to 100 shells. Very little damage. Casualties. One man wounded.	
	9/11/16 to 18/11/16		Battalion worked on dug-outs and Hurdel lines of trenches.	
	19/11/16		Major General Blomfield visited the Battalion. Work finished at midday. The General addressed (1) the two Coys in Sailly (2) the two in Ra Haie. Usual work carried on.	
	20th to 31/11/16			

Q Want P4 AG
3rd Rd Ru au lie Grup Coy

1st Division
War Diaries
12th Infantry Bde.
2nd Lancs Fus,
With Private Diary of Lt Hawkins

February to July
1916

WAR DIARY
or
INTELLIGENCE SUMMARY.
(Erase heading not required.)

Army Form C. 2118.

2 Lanc Fus

Place	Date	Hour	Summary of Events and Information	Remarks and references to Appendices
Field	July 1st		Ref: map 57D.S.E 1/20,000	
		12.15 AM	The Battalion passed the starting point East of BERTRANCOURT for the Assembly trenches	
		2.50 AM	Battalion was settled in Assembly trenches at Q.I.A	
		7.30 AM	The 11th Bde: attacked the German front line System (See Operation Order by Lt. Col. G.H.B. Freeth C.M.G. D.S.O dated 26/6/16)	
		8 AM	Battalion moved out of Assembly trench in Artillery formation. The band drove everyone day dawn and ascended further down.	
		8.30 AM	Battalion advanced, checking (flank moved at 50" a minute) nothing retarded the advance until shortly after 9 AM when the head of the Battalion passed over the line of Ballards trench. Directly the small parties crossed the above line they became subject to heavy Artillery, machine Gun and Rifle fire. A particularly heavy barrage had to be passed through on our front line and on all "No Mans Land" However the advance was still carried on, naturally faster than the 50" a minute	

21.V
10 sheets

WAR DIARY or INTELLIGENCE SUMMARY

Army Form C. 2118.

Place	Date	Hour	Summary of Events and Information	Remarks and references to Appendices
Field	July 1st	9.15 AM	About 9.15AM the Head of the Battalion crossed over our front line trench, the casualties in Officers and O.R. were by then fairly numerous. About 9.15AM the front companies had reached the German Third line of the Serre Ridge, Front Line. As it was impossible to advance further owing to the entire lack of support on either flank, an attempt was made to consolidate the position. The advance then began to filtrate. The first two companies and parts of the 3rd were collected in the German lines. The remainder collected in our old front line and led the forward line as well as possible with bombs. Owing to the Germans not being entirely driven out of their front line the ground occupied by our troops closed in round the area of the Quadrilateral. This area was successfully held by bombers, rifle and Lewis gun fire until the orders were given to evacuate the position. Machine gun, rifle and bayonet with hand grenades & Stokes mortar were used. About 11AM the following morning	

WAR DIARY
or
INTELLIGENCE SUMMARY.

(Erase heading not required.)

Army Form C. 2118.

Place	Date	Hour	Summary of Events and Information	Remarks and references to Appendices
	July 2nd		The wounded were carried out successfully and with few casualties. During the early hours of July 2nd the Bn. collected in ELLIS SQUARE trenches, and the 10% Reinforcement rejoined us. Salvage work commenced and collection and burial of the dead.	
	July 3rd	7 AM	The Battalion moved back into Brigade Reserve in the Assembly trenches at Q.1.A. Companies reorganised and at deficiencies made up. Owing to large movement of troops in rear of German lines being observed during the day, it was expected that the Germans might make a counter attack.	
		11.30 p.m	Consequently at 11.30 pm the Battalion moved up to defensive position. A, B and D Coys under Major B. Duncan to FORT HORSTED in SUCRERIE Q wood, but very wet night. Stood to until 7 AM on morning of 4th	
	4th			

Army Form C. 2118.

WAR DIARY
or
INTELLIGENCE SUMMARY.
(Erase heading not required.)

Instructions regarding War Diaries and Intelligence Summaries are contained in F. S. Regs., Part II. and the Staff Manual respectively. Title pages will be prepared in manuscript.

Place	Date	Hour	Summary of Events and Information	Remarks and references to Appendices
	July 4th	4pm	Rained hard all day. Battalion left B.1.a. to relieve Royal Irish Fusiliers in the trenches on other side of the Turmec Road.	
	5th		Casualties Nil. Artillery of both sides very active.	
	6th		Owing to one of our gas cylinders leaking Capt Ravenscroft & 8 R Rly and 2 O.R. were admitted to hospital suffering from the effects. Artillery active	
	7th		Our Artillery bombarded German lines to create a diversion so as to help an attack on our left. Enemy replied with a heavy barage on our front and reserve lines. Known casualties — recoving wounds from which he died on the 9th. 2 O.R. killed 7 O.R. wounded	
	8th 9th		Short bombardment of enemies trenches. Little retaliation. Smoke bomb discharge in Turmec Road. Heavy barrage on our front line and reserve lines.	

2353 Wt. W2514/1454 700,000 5/15 D. D. & L. A.D.S.S./Forms/C. 2118.

Army Form C. 2118.

WAR DIARY
or
INTELLIGENCE SUMMARY.
(Erase heading not required.)

Place	Date	Hour	Summary of Events and Information	Remarks and references to Appendices
	July 9th 1915		3 O.R. Wounded. (See Order for Raid by 2nd Col. G.H.R. Brett, O.C. 2/50 attached). The Raid was commenced as laid down in Order. A verbal order was given to the Officer in Charge that if by any sign the Germans made discovered the Raiding Party then the party was to endeavour to return to our own trenches. When it first arrived at the German lines he for was divided on the Brafs 150 x' Wayland who was in charge on finding that he was discovered lined the parapet and was successful in the way that the Raid was crawled back and in what should the Germans were lathe found him and in what should the Germans were 1 O.R. wounded. The remainder of them just about ... Usual artillery activity relieved in the evening by the Hampshire Regiment. Casualties nil	

WAR DIARY or INTELLIGENCE SUMMARY

Army Form C. 2118.

Place	Date	Hour	Summary of Events and Information	Remarks and references to Appendices
	July 4-10 inclusive		Throughout this period in the trenches the weather was very bad. All trenches were from ankle to knee deep and in places waist deep. The accumulation was due chiefly to the seepage it was very difficult to dry the clothes or socks of the men.	
	11th		On relief the Battalion went in to Corps Div'l Rest at BERTRANCOURT in Camp H.	
	12th	2 pm	The C.O. inspected Battalion.	
		6.30 pm	Lt General Hunter Weston inspected and spoke to the Battalion.	
	13th to 16th inclusive		Reorganisation and Company training.	
	17th		Moved to camp in Sq. P.17.b. (1000 x ROD city)	
			A wing to AVELUY-HEDAUVILLE. Battalion in Brigade Reserve.	
	18th to 20th		In camp. Working Party of 2 officers and 120 men found nightly to dig a new line in front of the present front line. 1 O.R. killed 2 O.R. wounded	
	21st		1 O.R. missing. Relieved by 7th Norfolks, marched to VARENNES.	

Army Form C. 2118.

WAR DIARY
or
INTELLIGENCE SUMMARY.

(Erase heading not required.)

Instructions regarding War Diaries and Intelligence Summaries are contained in F. S. Regs., Part II. and the Staff Manual respectively. Title pages will be prepared in manuscript.

Place	Date	Hour	Summary of Events and Information	Remarks and references to Appendices
	July 21st		Army found at U ROCHELLES	
	22nd	7 pm	Battalion moved to HUTTIQUE	
	23rd	7 am	Owing to an unforseen accident Bn entrained at 7 pm instead of 5.30. Entraining Stn Petite DOULLENS.	
		12.30 pm (about)	Detrained at CASSEL. Marched to HERTZEELE arriving there about 6.0 pm	
	24th 25th 26th		R. billets. Company training.	
			On 26th Lt. Col. Puch O/C Battalion to take over command of 167th Brigade. Major R. Curnow assumed command	
	27th	1.15 pm	Battalion moved to M camp west of POPERINGHE	
	28th	9 pm	Battalion moved to E. O. camp about 3 miles East of Poperinghe	
	29th 30th 31st		In camp Company training	

W.J.W. Blenkarne Major
Commdg 2 Lan Fus.

Casualties on 1st July 1916

Officers

Killed	Wounded	Missing
Captain H.W. Sayres	Captain J. Collis-Browne	Lieut. A.V. Davies
" M.P. Gamon	Lieut. G.G. Bowen	
Lieut R.S. MacIver	" A.D. MacDonald	
Lieut C.D. Roberton	Lieut H. Ravenscroft	
" H.C. Kenion	" C.L. Rougier	
" B. Farrow	" H.T. Williams	
	" J. Anderson	
	" C. Gregory	
	Captain G.M. Scott (RAMC) (Attached)	

Other Ranks

Killed	24
Wounded	273
Died from Wounds	7
Missing	48

Total. Officers. = 16

Total. O. Ranks. = 352

A   12th Brigade.

4th Division.

C

2nd BATTALION

THE LANCASHIRE FUSILIERS

FEBRUARY 1 9 1 6

WAR DIARY
or
INTELLIGENCE SUMMARY.
(Erase heading not required.)

Army Form C. 2118.

Place	Date	Hour	Summary of Events and Information	Remarks and references to Appendices
Field	February			
	1st to 3rd		Battalion in billets in Sailly. Battalion used for work on line of defences and erection of dug-outs from Fuquevillers to Hebuterne	
	4th		12th Bde relieved the IVth Division. Battalion moved from Sailly to Bertrancourt.	
	5, 6th		In huts in Bertrancourt.	
	7th		Left Bertrancourt and proceeded to Colincamps, where Battalion was in billets for night of 6/7th	
	8th		On night of 8/9th Battalion relieved the Kings Own in the trenches, West of Serre. Casualties Nil	
	9th		Enemy Artillery Active. Improvement of trenches commenced. Owing to the rain the trenches were in a dilapidated and filthy condition. Casualties Killed 1 O.R. Wounded 8 O.R. Accidentally 2 Sergeants.	
	10.		Enemy Artillery Active. Roughly 50% of their shells were duds. Casualties Killed 1 O.R. Wounded 1 O.R.	
	11th		Intermittent shelling of trenches by enemy guns, trench-mortars and rifle grenades. Casualties Nil	
	12th		Quiet day. Relieved at night by 1st King's Own Regt. Marched to billets in Colincamps. Casualties Nil	

WAR DIARY
or
INTELLIGENCE SUMMARY.

Place	Date	Hour	Summary of Events and Information	Remarks and references to Appendices
Field	February 13, 14, 15		In Billets in Chocques. Working parties found for front and reserve line	
	16		Relieved 1 K.O. Regiment in the trenches (West of Sevre) in the evening. Casualties: Nil.	
	17		Enemy shelled front line trenches with 5.9 Howitzers. Trench mortars and Cowenters. Company on left of front line heavily shelled (Casualties 6 men Buried, 2 wounded and a few suffering from shock) Casualties Killed 5 Missing believed killed 1. Wounded 4. Suffering from shock 3. Weather very bad	
	18		Bad weather still continues. General activity of Artillery on both sides.	
	19		About 6 p.m. in the evening about 100 Germans were seen in front of their trenches either their own. Our Artillery immediately opened on them. The Germans gave them began and plastered our trenches (front line, reserve line and communication trench) will all manner all kinds of shells and trench mortars. The Bombardment continued for about an hour and then lifted	

WAR DIARY
or
INTELLIGENCE SUMMARY.
(Erase heading not required.)

Place	Date	Hour	Summary of Events and Information	Remarks and references to Appendices
	Feb. 19th		A few Germans succeeded in getting into our trenches at different places but were soon ejected, leaving a few dead. The following is a copy of a wire received from the Corps Commander — "Message begins — The Corps Commander congratulates all concerned on last night's fighting. The manner in which the attack was anticipated by the higher Commander, the steps they took to meet it and this instantaneous and successful support given by the Royal Artillery was all that could be desired. The counterattack was delivered promptly and was well led. Both those in the trenches and those in the counterattack fought as Officers and men of the Lancashire Fusiliers always have fought and always will fight" from Seventh Corps endo. Casualties. Officers Wounded, 2. Captain Collins-Browne and Lieut Carter. Missing believed killed. 1. 2 Lieut Carter. O.R. Killed 11. Wounded 30. Missing B.K. 12. Missing 5.	

Army Form C. 2118.

WAR DIARY
or
INTELLIGENCE SUMMARY.
(Erase heading not required.)

Instructions regarding War Diaries and Intelligence Summaries are contained in F. S. Regs., Part II. and the Staff Manual respectively. Title pages will be prepared in manuscript.

Place	Date	Hour	Summary of Events and Information	Remarks and references to Appendices
Field	Feb. 20		Very quiet all day. Casualties Nil	
	21st			
	22nd		Battalion in billets in Blircampo.	
	23rd			
	24th		Relieved King's Own in trenches, West of Serre. Casualties Nil	
	25th		Snowed hard all day. Quiet. Casualties 1 O.R. Killed 1 O.R. Wounded (sniped)	
	26th		Snowing and freezing. Artillery active on both sides. Casualties 1 O.R. Killed 1 O.R. Wounded (sniped)	
	27th		Snowed in the morning but began to thaw towards the evening. General activity on both sides. Casualties 1 O.R. Killed 2 O.R. wounded.	
	28th		Thaw still continues. Trenches in very bad condition. Relieved by 1st K.O. Rgt in trenches. Casualties Nil.	
	29th		In billets in Blircampo.	

Ellent R. Miles
2nd Lancashire Fusiliers

12th BRIGADE

4th DIVISION.

--+++++--

2nd BATTALION

THE LANCASHIRE FUSILIERS

MARCH 1916

Army Form C. 2118.

WAR DIARY
or
INTELLIGENCE SUMMARY.
(Erase heading not required.)

17.V.
3 Meet

Place	Date	Hour	Summary of Events and Information	Remarks and references to Appendices
	MARCH			
	1972		Battalion in billets in Blaincourt.	
	3rd 4th		Battalion marched to Neuvillette. On 3rd marched to Hindecourt where it billeted the night and on the 4th marched to Neuvillette.	
	5.6.th		Battalion in billets.	
	7.8.th		For the first day battalion settled in and improved billets. For remaining time Company training was carried out. On the 13th & 14th the M.O. inoculated two companies	
	9.10.th			
	11th to 14th			
	15		Brigade route-marched.	
	16th		In billets.	
	17 & 18		Moved to BAILLEULMONT by Stages. 17th marched to Halloy & but night in huts. 18th marched to BAILLEULMONT.	
	19th		Relieved 13th Royal Fusiliers in trenches opposite Ransart. Very quiet, no casualties.	
	20.21.22.nd		"C" Coy trenches slightly shelled. One casualty. 1 O.R. Killed 1 O.R. Wounded	
	23rd		Very quiet day	
	24th		Relieved in trenches by King's Own Regiment, and marched to billets in BAILLEULMONT	
	25th			

Army Form C. 2118.

WAR DIARY
or
INTELLIGENCE SUMMARY.
(Erase heading not required.)

2

Place	Date	Hour	Summary of Events and Information	Remarks and references to Appendices
	MARCH			
	26th 27th 28th 29th 30th		In billets in BAILLEULMONT. All possible men were out working nearly everyday or night on front line, communication trenches and support lines	
	31st		Relieved 6/8 King's Own Regiment in trenches opposite "RANSART", by night	

Gilbert Pick.
2nd Lieut.
tue.

12th Brigade.

4th Division.

2nd BATTALION

THE LANCASHIRE FUSILIERS

APRIL 1916

WAR DIARY or INTELLIGENCE SUMMARY

Army Form C. 2118.

Place	Date	Hour	Summary of Events and Information	Remarks and references to Appendices
Field	APRIL 1st-5th		Battalion in trenches opposite RANSART.	
	6th		Quiet day. On night of the 6th relieved in trenches by 1st K.O. Regiment. Battalion returned to billets in BAILLEULMONT.	
	7th-11th		In billets in BAILLEULMONT. Working parties found by companies in front and reserve line.	
	12th		Battalion relieved 1st King's Own Regiment in trenches opposite RANSART.	
	13th-17th		A renewal in excess of activity in enemies artillery and sniping. On the 16th enemy shelled "B" Agro in GASTINEAU Fme. with High Explosive obtaining three (3) direct hits, without causing any casualties.	
	18th		Relieved in trenches by 1st K.O. Regt. Battalion returned to same billets.	
	19-23		In billets. Usual working parties.	
	24		Relieved King's Own in trenches. Enemies Artillery & snipers even more active.	
	25, 26		Except for above quiet days. Shelled "B" Coy's Company, 1 O.R. wounded.	
	27, 28		Quiet days.	
	26, 29		Enemy again shelled "B" Company, 5.4, 4.2 shells fired altogether. All failed	
	30		to explode except four (4).	

18 V
3 total

WAR DIARY or INTELLIGENCE SUMMARY

Army Form C. 2118.

Place	Date	Hour	Summary of Events and Information	Remarks and references to Appendices
Field	April 20th		Battalion relieved in trenches by 13th Royal Fusiliers. Very late relief. 10 R. wounded in leg on the RANSART-BERLES Road. In billets in BAILLEULMONT.	

A.L. Clark, Lt Adj
2nd Lancashire Fusiliers

12th Brigade.

4th Division.

2nd BATTALION

THE LANCASHIRE FUSILIERS

M A Y 1 9 1 6

WAR DIARY
or
INTELLIGENCE SUMMARY.
(Erase heading not required.)

Army Form C. 2118.

2 Knner Fus

Place	Date	Hour	Summary of Events and Information	Remarks and references to Appendices
Field.	May 1st, 2nd 3rd		Battalion in Bllts in Bailleulmont. At 5.15 pm Battalion marched from BAILLEULMONT to LE SOUICH arriving there at 2. A.M. 4/5/16.	
	4th–6th 7th 8th		Billeted in LE SOUICH. Company training & reorganisation. Battalion marched by night to BEAUSSART. Settled in and improved billets	
	9th–12		Day and night working parties found by the Battalion. A cay: dug Battalion Assembly Position round the SUCRERIE by night. B coy: dug trenches for and then buried Corps Cables by day. C coy: Lengthened and improved communication trenches between AUCHONVILLERS and SUCRERIE. D coy: helped 'B' coy and also worked for Artillery, digging new gun emplacements, Observation Stations etc.	
	12th		On night of 12th 2nd Lt F. Granger was wounded in the heel by shrapnel while working with A coy round Sucrerie.	
	13–22		Same work as from 9th to 12th.	

19.V
2 sheets

Army Form C. 2118.

WAR DIARY
or
INTELLIGENCE SUMMARY.
(Erase heading not required.)

Place	Date	Hour	Summary of Events and Information	Remarks and references to Appendices
Field	23rd		Battalion marched to Bernaville by night, leaving BEAUSSART at 6.45pm and arriving at BERNAVILLE at 9.15am, after halting from 2am to 6am near VERGRAND FME, West of BEAUQUESNE.	
	24th 25th		In Billets BERNAVILLE. Battalion marched to LE FESTEL and HANCHY. Hqrs A & C coys in LE FESTEL, B & D coys in HANCHY. Demonstration with Contact Aeroplane in afternoon.	
	26th		Company training.	
	27th 28th		Sucrerie and Assembly trenches marked out in Brigade Training Area. Battalion trains. Practice leaving Assembly trenches in Artillery formation, and preliminary stages of attack.	
	29th		Divisional exercise. Dismounted practice leaving Assembly trenches & advance to attack objective.	
	30th 31st		Company and Platoon training in the morning. Battalion practice preliminary and final stages of attack in the afternoon.	

E. Greene Lt. Colonel.
Commdg 2nd Bn; .... Fus.

12th Brigade.

4th Division.

2nd BATTALION

THE LANCASHIRE FUSILIERS.

JUNE 1916

WAR DIARY or INTELLIGENCE SUMMARY

2 Lancs Fus
Vol 21

20.V
12 sheets

Place	Date	Hour	Summary of Events and Information	Remarks and references to Appendices
Field	June 1-8th	-	Battalion in Billets at Pesle and Hardly. Divisional, Brigade, and Battalion training in Attack.	
	9th		Battalion moved to BERNAVILLE	
	10th		Hqrs A & B coys moved to BEAUVAL. C & D coys to Thumblet & Berneuil Respectively.	
	11th & 12th		Hqrs A, B & D coys marched to BOIS-DU-WARMINTON. A, B & D coys moved to BERTRANCOURT. Three officers and 100 O.R. moved to MAILLY.	
	13th & 14th		Hqrs and details of A B & D moved to BERTRANCOURT. Hqrs A B & D moved to BEAUSSART.	
	15th & 16th		Working Parties found day and night for Artillery and Signals. "C" coy found from Detachment.	
	17th to 23		Working Parties as above. (15th) 10 O.R. wounded.	
	24		Detachment found from hardly. Working Parties as above. Battalion moved to Camp West of BERTRANCOURT.	
	25.		Preliminary Bombardment of Enemy Trenches Commenced	

WAR DIARY
or
INTELLIGENCE SUMMARY.

(Erase heading not required.)

Army Form C. 2118

Place	Date	Hour	Summary of Events and Information	Remarks and references to Appendices
	June 26th		Brigade Exercise in Attack from 6 AM till 9.30 AM. Company training.	
	27th	11 AM	O.C. II Div. Major General Poultin addressed Battalion in coming Assault.	
		6.30 PM	G.O.C. 11th Inf. Bde. Brigadier General Combe informed Battalion in fighting order. Operation order (attached) issued. Battalion prepared for Assembly, which should have taken place on night of 28th/29th, but was postponed for 48 hours. Two O.R. wounded while on working party about 3 A.M. Company trainings.	
	28th			
	29th 30th	11.30 PM	Battalion Prepares for Assault. Battalion moved off to Assembly Area 11.30 P.M. See Operation Orders attached.	

G. [signature]
Lt. Col.
Comdg. 2nd Rang[..]

Diary
Secret.

No 6/103

Operation Order No 1
Ref. Maps Sheet 57d N.E. & S.E. (Trench maps 1/10,000
HEBUTERNE and BEAUMONT)

1. The VIII Corps will take part in an assault on the 29th inst.
   The 4th Dvn. attacks in the centre, the 31st Dvn. on the left, and the 29th Dvn. on the right. The 48th Dvn. is in Corps Reserve.

2. The object of the attack is to seize and hold the enemy trenches on the FRONCOURT–PUISIEUX Ridge from pt R.8.B.5.7 to L.11.c.5.6 and to form a defensive flank from the latter point to K.23.d.8.2, and thence to our present front line.
   The scheme of the attack of the 31st Dvn has been explained to all concerned.

3. The final objective is on a line in the enemy trenches running from pt R.2.B.3.0 (incl.) to Pt L.26.c.7.6 (incl.)

4. The attack of the 3 Divisions will be simultaneous.

5. The objectives of the 4th Dvn. are:—
   First Objective. German trenches on the line Q.5.a.9.1 (incl.) to Q.5.B.1.7. K.35.a.1.5. K.35.d.6.7 (all incl.). K.35.d.6.5 (incl.)
   Second Objective: German trenches on the line K.6.c.9.3 – K.6.c.7.6 – K.6.a.7.3 – K.4.a.6.7 – K.11.c.3.5 – K.11.a.8.2.
   Third Objective. German trenches on PUISIEUX – SERRE Ridge along the line R.2.c.0.5 – R.2.a.6.4 – R.1.a.6.6 – L.26.c.7.6

6. The attack will consist of the following phases:-

1st Phase - 5 days bombardment of the enemy's trenches.

2nd Phase - Intensive bombardment of the enemy's trenches with artillery and mortars.

3rd Phase - 11th Infy Bde assault and capture 1st and 2nd objectives and consolidate.

4th Phase - Artillery bombard final objective.

5th Phase - 10th and 11th Inf. Bdes attack and seize the Final Objective, and consolidate it. The 10th Bde will be on the right, and the 11th Bde on the left. The Dividing line between the 10th and 11th Bdes is the line K.34.c.0.5 - K.35.c.5.5 - K.36.c.0.5. Track and communication trench running eastward to pt L.31.c.6.5 - L.32.d.2.6 (all incl. to 10th Bde.) The Bat'n of the 10th Infy Bde, on the right, the Lancashire Fus" will be the 1st R. Irish Fusiliers. The Dividing Line between the 11th Bde, and the 31st Div'n is the line K.35.a.8.2. 7½ - K.36.a.6.3 (incl to 11th Bde) - S. corner of PENDANT Copse - L.26.c.3.5. During the advance, the left Battalion will overlap the 31st Div'n Area in a. North ex pt. 79 and 93.

7. The Bde will assemble for the attack in prepared Assembly Places as follows:-

Bde H.R. — ROMAN Rd, pt K.34.a.2.1.
Signal Section
1 Sect Dunpass M.G.Cº } — STIRLING Trench. S. O. SERRE Rd.

1st KINGS OWN
6 guns Battn M.G. Cº } — LYCEUM.

2nd ESSEX
4 guns, Bde M.G. Cº } — ELLES SQUARE

Duke of WELLINGTONS — SUCRERIE.
LANCASHIRE FUS" — Q.1.a.
11 N. Bde M.G. Cº — FORT HUYSTEAD
11 T.M. Batty — WOLF TRENCH (in action.)
Bde Carriers and
Bde Reserve Stores } — VALLADE Trench

3.

8. The Attack by the 12th Bde will be carried out as follows:—

(a) Objective. Enemy's trenches from L.32.d.2.6 – L.26.c.7.6.

(b) Disposition of Troops during the attack.

Firing Line and Supports.   Objective

Left Battn. KING'S OWN
with 2 guns, Bde M.G. Co.   } — L.32.b.0.6 – L.26.c.7.6
and Sect., 11th T.M. Batt.   (both inclusive.)

Right Battn. ESSEX   } — L.32.d.2.6 – L.32.b.0.6
with 2 guns Bde M.G. Co.   (both inclusive.)

Reserve.
Left. Duke of WELLINGTONS
Right. LANCASHIRE Fus.
6 guns Bde M.G. Co.
Sect. Res: from Fd. Co. R.E.
Sect. 11th T.M. Batty.

Special Mission. — 4 guns Bde M.G. Co.

For Time Table of Moves and Assaults see App. A.

9. Instructions for Attack of 12th Bde.

(i) The Dividing Line between Battns. is K.34.a.9.2½ (marked by White Diamond) – N. Western flank of the Quadrilateral. K.35.a.6.3. pt 50 yds S. of PENDANT COPSE – L.34.b.0.6.

(ii) Should the attacking battns. use up all their supports, and still require help the O.C. LANCASHIRE Fus. will place not more than one company at the disposal of each Battn.
"A Co." will then support the ESSEX, and "B Co." the KING'S OWN. If my Cmdy Hands B Co. will send up such reinforcements as may be demanded, notifying Batn. Hd. Co. that he has done so.

(iii) On capturing the position, the leading half Battns. of the attacking Battalions will push forward and cage the enemy's outpost line, and at 4.30 hours, will send out strong patrols with Lewis

4

Guns as are in the line L.32.d.5.7 – L.26.c.9.6, to cover the position while it is being consolidated. These strong patrols will dig in on this above line, which will be the line of observation.

The consolidation of the position will include the making of 5 Strong Points, as under:-

Point A, L.26.c.3.3 (pt 33), to be made by KING'S OWN.
" B, L.26.c.9.0. (pt 90)   . . . . "   "
" C, L.32.b.1.2. (pt 12)   . . . . . ESSEX.
" D, L.32.a.1.9½   . . . . . LAN. FUS.
" E, L.31.a.3.1.   . . . . . "   "

These strong pts will be constructed as per App. C, (copies of which have been supplied to all companies), to hold a platoon each, & or guns & Stokes mortar. The strong pts will be joined up eventually, by a continuous fire trench, and a Support Trench, 150 yds in rear will be made.

Wire entanglements will be put up all along the front.

(i) The Reserve Battns. will advance from Assembly Area in Artillery formation, moving in echelon, the LAN. Fus. leading, and following the ESSEX at 400 yds distance, the DUKE of WELLINGTON'S keeping at a distance of 400 yds from the leading line of the LAN FUS.

On the final objective being captured, the Battn. in Reserve will at once send forward all R.E. material to the Strong pts, A, B, and C, and working parties and material to Strong points D and E.

The DUKE of WELLINGTON'S will dig in and consolidate on the line L.31.a.9.4 – L.31.a.9½.2.

If the leading Battns have not enough men to hold the captured lines and consolidate them, the L. LAN. FUS. will send up further parties to help in the making of the Strong pts A, B, and C, notifying D. of W. R. if he does so. All spare men in Reserve will be used to make cover in Reserve in a line, joining PENDANT trench and Strong Pt E, passing through pt L.31. B.S.5.

10. Bdes HQrs will move to the MUNICH Trench on the line dividing battns during the advance.

11. Two new communication trenches will be constructed by parties from the Reserve battns. One running from L.32.a.55 to L.31.b.8.3 and one from PUISIEUX Alley at pt L.32.c.2.4. to the PUISIEUX Road at L.31.d.5.6. The latter will be constructed by D. of W., work being commenced at the west end of the trench.

12. Instructions regarding Signalling communications within the battn. have been circulated to companies.

3.

The Bde Forward Report Centre will be established at Thows at pt. K.36.a.6.3. and later, near L.31.a.3.3.
The S.O.S. Signal is 5 red rockets in quick succession. 12 red rockets will be carried during the advance.

13. The Line of Evacuation is via 6th Avenue. Collecting Posts will be established at the following points:-
 (a) Near HYDE PARK Corner.
 (b) Off ROMAN Rd. at K.34.c.3½.8½
 (c) In cellars at the SUCRERIE Cross Rds.
 (d) At pt. G.2.a.3.3.
 (e) At pt 45, after the Final Objective has been captured.

14. Prisoners of war will be sent to the 11th Bde at pt 63.

15. <u>Instructions applying to the Battalion only.</u>

(a) The Batn will assemble in the Assembly Area as follows, on the night of Jun 28th.
'A' and 'B' Coys in front and second trenches, ('A' on the rig[h]t.), each company on a front of 150 yds.
'C' and 'D' Coys, in the rear trenches, ('C' on the right.) to the left of Battn Hd. Qtrs.
Batn Hd. Qtrs and Signallers on the rig[h]t, in rear trench.

(b) The advance from the Assembly Area will be in Artillery Formation, on a front of 350 yds. 'B' Co will direct, the directing section marching on a bearing.
Each column will be preceded by 2 wound scouts who will clear ways to such entanglements etc, nor leaving each passage as they pass.

(c) On crossing the Sunken Rd., the advance will be continued on a bearing of ___, leaving the S' AVENUE and BORDEN Avenue to the west, as far as the junction of BORDEN AVENUE and VALLADE

(d) The advance will be continued on the same alignment until the front line of sections is on the line K.34.38.4./K.34.d.8.1½. In this position, the SERRE Bde Rd will be the dividing line between companies, 'B' and 'D' companies being on the left, 'A' and 'C' on the right.
The rear line of sections of the rear companies will be on a N. & S. line passing through the junction of the ROMAN and SERRE Roads.
The Batn should arrive at this position (Line A) at Z.+ hours.

6

(e) From "Line A" the advance will be continued at Z.15 hours, with the left moving along the Western bank of the Quadrilateral, across the final objective of the N Bde, and thence via pt 63, on a line moving 50 yds S. of PENDANT COPSE.

Unless orders to reinforce the front line are received the Batn will not proceed further than the line L.31.b.c.c. - L.31.d.c.5 (Line C). The Batn will not cross the PUISIEUX Road, except with the object of supporting, or carrying materials to the front line.

"Line C" should be reached at 3.30 hours.

14. On reaching Line "C", if the Batn is still intact, the following dispositions will be made without waiting further orders:—

"A" Co. will commence the communication trench referred to in para 11.

"B" Co. will report to the O.C. KING'S OWN, for work on the support line.

"C" Co. will despatch parties as follows:—

(i). To Strong pt C where material will be dumped, the party to proceed to pt. E, to work there.

(ii). To Pt E, the construction of which will be commenced immediately.

(iii). To report to O.C. ESSEX, with material for front line, and for work there if required. If not required to proceed to Pt E, to work on reserve line.

"D" Co. will despatch parties as follows:—

(i). To Pt A, to dump material there, and then proceed to pt D.

(ii). To Pt B, to dump material there, and to report to O.C. KING'S OWN for work if required. If not required, to proceed to pt D, for work on line connecting pts D and E.

(iii). To Pt E, the construction of which will be commenced immediately.

Each of the parties detailed by "C" and "D" Companies will consist of 1 N.C.O. and 6 other ranks, and will be detailed previously.

7.

If any part, or the whole, of 'A' Co. has been called upon to support the ESSEX, they will not be withdrawn, or took on other communication therewith, without the approval of the O.C. ESSEX. If retained with the ESSEX, that fact will be reported to Bttn. Hd. Qrs.

Similarly, if any part or the whole of 'B' Co. has been called upon to reinforce the KING'S OWN, the O.C. KING'S OWN will decide as to their further employment, Bttn. Hd. Qrs. being informed.

14. At this stage Bttn. Hd. Qrs. will be at the eastern end of TEN TREE ALLEY.

15. The only maps to be referred to in orders and messages, and to be carried on the attack are the 1/10,000 Sheet 57d N.E. and S.E., and 1/10,000 Trench map 57d N.E. and S.E. (HEBUTERNE and BEAUMONT).

No maps showing our trenches will be taken.

17. Any maps or papers taken from the enemy will be sent at once to Bttn. Hd. Qrs.

18. Officers & N.C.Os. & other O.R.'s will carry note books, but no other papers will be taken.

19. Situation reports will be sent in by Co's. not less than every half hour & until the position is taken & not less frequently. Estimated casualties will be reported every hour, but at apart every adverse occurrence of the gain time.

27/6/16.

J. Churton Biddulph
2 Lancashire Fusiliers

Distribution of Officers

Officers who will accompany Battalion in Assault.	Officers in Reserve.	Officers with Bde Carrying Party	Officers with Div Carrying Party	Officers otherwise employed	Remarks
Lt Col Stott. E.H.B. Commanding. C.M.G. D.S.O.	Major Blencowe A.E.G 2nd in Command	Captain Ramsay Jones & Capt Ravenscroft G. Woodward F.R.G.		Major Rowe W.	Quarter Master
Capt. Collin-Parsons. T.W	Capt. Garthwin. R.H.			Capt. Salt. W.P.	Embarkation Officer
Capt. Maxwell. M.D.P	" Keirn. A.L			Capt. Robertson. M	Div. Intelligence Officer
Capt. Sayers. H.W. K	" Powell. R.T.			" Harris	IIᵈ Army School
Capt. Seckham P.R.E.	" Haber. C.E.			" Hawkin	12ᵗʰ Inf. Bde
Capt. Gaunt. M.P. Lewis Gun Officer	" Shorley. G.R.			" Staff	Transport Officer
" Brown. G.G. W	" Kirkland L.			" Greaves	IV Div: School
" Martin. G.C. Adjutant.	" Watson. L.G.S.			" Wabon	&c—
" MacDonald A.D.W. M.G.O					
" Ravenscroft. H. W					
" Robertson. C.R. Reconnaissance Officer					
" Davis. A.V.M					
" Finley. J.					
" Frazer. C.R. W					
Lt Oliver. H.T. W					
Lt Farran. B.J. W					
" Anderson.					
" Poe. R.S. V					
" Hauger. C.P.					
" Watkins. T.W.					
" Kenton. H.C.K					
" Hall. W.T.					
" Gregory. C. W					
Capt. Scott. C.M. Medical Officer					

Lt Col
Commanding

Parade State.

2nd Lancashire Fusiliers

Assaulting Groups.

	Officers	O. Ranks
Headquarters.	6	71
A.	5	115
B.	5	111
C.	4	158
D.	4	156
Total	24	611

Total 24 Off. 611 O.R.

	Officers	A	B	C	D
Headquarters.	-	-	-	-	3
Q.M. Store.	1	-	5	2	1
Transport.	1	15	18	13	12
10% Reinforcements	8	20	20	14	17
Bn. Carriers	2	34	34	30	28
Div: Carriers	1	16	29	-	-
Trench Mortar Carriers	-	16	-	-	-
Cooks.	-	2	1	1	-
Total	13	103	97	60	61

Total. 321.

G. Greek Lt. Colonel.
Commdg. 2d Lancs Fus.

Operation Orders
By
Lieut Colonel G. H. B. Freeth. C.M.G. D.S.O.
Commanding 2nd Bn Lancashire Fusiliers.

Active Service.   30th June. 1916.

MOVE. Battalion will move to the Assembly Area tonight 30th June & 1st July.

ORDER OF MARCH. Coys will move off in the following order, and on arrival will march straight into the trenches allotted to them.—
"A" "C" "B" "D" Coys. Headquarters.
Companies will move at 4 minutes interval.
"A" Compy will march off at 11-30 pm.

LEWIS GUNNERS Lewis Guns, and Lewis Gun Magazines in their carriers to be ready to be packed on limbers at 5-15 pm. this evening.
Lewis Gun Teams under Lt Macdonald will accompany limber and will stay with the guns etc until the Battalion come up in the night.

ORDERS FOR CARRYING PARTIES. DIVIS'L CARRIERS will parade at 6-30 pm. at the Camp, and will be marched off by Capt. Ravenscroft to their rendezvous.
BRIGADE CARRIERS: Lt Lawson Lewis & the 13 other ranks will march off at 6-0 pm.
Lt Woodward & the 113 other ranks will march off at 6-30 P.M.

CARRIERS FOR T.M. BATTERY. Carriers to parade ready to march off at 4-0 pm. They will report to O.C. 12th T.M. Battery at BERTRANCOURT. who will give them instructions and a Guide.

DISCIPLINE. No Smoking or Lights will be allowed after leaving BERTRANCOURT, and the strictest silence will be observed during the march.

REPORTS Parade States to be rendered to O. Room by 6-0 pm. tonight, shewing strength for attack separate from the remainder.
Coys will report to Bn. Hd Qrs. as soon as they have settled down in the Assembly Trenches.

(Sd) G. C. Marten. Lt & Adjt
2 Bn Lancashire Fusiliers

12/4.

War Diary

of

2nd Bn. Lancashire Fusiliers.

for

July 1916.

Diary of Lieut. V.F.S. Hawkins, 2/Lanc. Fusiliers.

Battle of the Somme.

1st July 1916.

The Attack.

At 6:30 a.m. the artillery fire became rapid until 7 p.m. when it became intense. It was the most extraordinary sight. The Bosch line could not be seen for smoke and bursting shells. Bosch still hardly answered at all. The first mistake was made at 7:25 a.m. when the Beaumont Hamel line under the Hawthorne Ridge Redoubt went up. This gave the Germans 5 minutes to consolidate the crater which they made use of. Zero hour was at 7:30 a.m.

At 7:30 a.m. the first waves went over and then things began to happen. In spite of the six days bombardment German machine guns got going from every direction. Beaumont Hamel opposite the 29th Division was a veritable Fortress. The 29th Division never got near the Hun Front Line. The 93rd Brigade of the Division on our left never got more than half way over No Mans Land, although the left Brigade of that Division did get into Serre that day. The 11th Brigade got the first line fairly easy. Gen. Prowse left the Headquarters too soon and was killed rushing a machine gun. He was shot in the stomach and died at Maueux. Corps Headquarters that evening. The losses of the Brigade were awful. The Cos. of the Hampshires. The Rifle Brigade and the Sommerset Light Infantry were killed and most of the Officers were knocked out. They finally got held up somewhere in the 2nd line.

Meanwhile we were waiting in Brigade Headquarters for news. The Essex and King's Own were going over first with the Lan. Fus. and Dukes in support. The Kings Own and Essex were wonderful. The Kings Own got very nearly to Pendant Copse and the Essex to Munich trench. Martineau the Brigade Signalling Officer went off to raise a forward signal station which he did somewhere on 63 over and over again we got a message back from him saying the Essex were bombing in Munich trench and wanted more bombs. Of the Kings Own we never heard a word, beyond from the Adjutant who came in to Headquarters with a cracked head. This was the first action in which Steel Helmets were worn and they undoubtedly saved many lives.

Just before the Brigade went over the Division wired us to stop the Battalions and also stop the 10th Brigade Runners were immediately sent to the Kings Own and Essex Lan. Fus, Dukes.

They were too late however. The Kings Own and Essex were right on. The Lan. Fus. were mostly in the quadrilateral and one Coy. of the Dukes was in the Bosch line.

The result of all this was that the 93rd Brigade having failed on the left and the 29th Division on the right, the German came down from either flank and the Kings Own and Essex were practically missing. Major Bromilow✝ has not been heard of since. Col. Stirling the C.O. Essex was wounded twice at the beginning and got away Cadic the Adjutant of the Essex and the Adjutant of the Kings Own were both wounded.

Fighting went on all the afternoon. Some of the Seaforths of the 10th Brigade got over and joined up with the Lan. Fus in the quadrilateral. The C.D. of the Seaforths, Hodge, Bertie Ravenscroft, Hall, Watkins, Mansell, and Rougier in the Quad with him and stayed there till 2 a.m. July 2nd. bombing the whole time. C.S.M. Laverick and Sgt. Alben were in there too. These to found a stokes gun and although they had never seen one before worked it till they ran dry of ammunition.

B.Farrow was killed in No Mans Land on his way back having been with the others all the time.

The Roman Road on the afternoon of July 1st. was

✝ Body found August. 1917.

ghastly, wounded in every place conceivable coming up all the time. Macdonald with a bullet in his chest and a Bosch Helmet was the only one of the Officers I saw from the Regt. He was quite happy.

I heard nothing of Brain or Firth till well into the afternoon. They reported in writing that they were somewhere near the Quadrilateral and did we know where the others were they lost each other at the beginning of the show.

The attack finally ended as far as the Division was concerned at 2 a.m. July 2nd, when the last of our people came back from the Quadrilateral.

The sum total of the attack was a bad hammering and no ground captured, but from all accounts Bosch lost heavily too.

The following casualties and Officers in the 2nd Lan Fus.:- Sayers, Charlie Roberton, Farrow, Nipper Kennion, Gammon, and MacIver Killed.

Bertie Ravenscroft, Rougier, Williams, Gregory, Bowes Collis-Browne, Macdonald, Anderson, wounded, Daies Missing reported (prisoner) Firth, Brain, Hodge, Mansell, Watkins, Rougier and Hall came through.

Of these Sayers, Roberton, Bowes and Collis-Browne were hit before reaching our own front line.

The other Battalions except the Dukes had lost, worse than we had. The 110 Brigade practically did not exist.

While the 10th Brigade except for the Seaforths, had had been stopped by the Division and had not lost so badly.

The Bosch showed his fighting powers that day, and he put up a grand fight. It/however nearly all his Officers. The machine Guns in our vicinity were nearly all manned by Bosch Officers and all the prisoners told us the same. The prisoners No.15. All Wurtenburgers from the   Regt.

I first saw Brain about 5 p.m. the evening of the 12th. he seemed pretty broken up, but had not been hit. John Carr, the C.O's Orderly of course had'nt cared a hang for anything. Clegg Brains Orderly got wounded.

The Bosch had put up a very fine Barrage of 5.9 H.E. and Shrapnel. He put up every gun in a clump on to one small bit of the front, using his machine guns elsewhere. After 10 mins. or so he would shift all his guns to another small portion of the front and so on always having a machine gun Barrage where his guns were not firing. It was most effective. He also blew a couple of mines in No Mans Land under our first wave.

Official report of the attack with a map of operations is attached.

August 20th. 1916.

The Bluff terminates on one of the Biggest Mine craters on the front, its about 200 ft. long 80 ft. broad and 60 ft. deep.

Hill 60 was on the extreme left of our line. Bosch was right up at the top of it, we were at the bottom. After all the fighting we had expected rather a sizy hill. Hill 60 was scarcely more than a mound. Behind our lines there were Fir woods, not very deep or thick These were on the slope away from the Bosch and it was quite possible to get anywhere by day. The 10th Bde were on our left and the 12th Canadian Bde on our right. The character of this front line may be gauged from the fact that at one point a notice was stuck up which read "Do not fire at the trench opposite, it is ours". we were in this line from 24th to 31st.

October 10th 1916.

The dispositions in our neighbourhood at present are :-

In Front of Guendecourt 6th Div. From Guedecourt to Les Boeoffs 4th Div. who are in touch with French in front of Les Boeoffs.

Of the 4th Div. 10th & 12th Brigade are in the Line, with 11th Brigade in Trones Wood. Of the 12th Brigade the Bn. and the Duke of Wellingtons were in the line with the King's Own and Essex in the Flers Line.

It appears that we are in with Le Transloy as our final objective and here we stay until we've got it. We've got to get our jumping off line first, however, so there's two snaps ahead of the Battalion, anyway.

October 11th 1916.

Having spent an extraordinary uncomfortable night in a very small scoop which Johny Greave and I shared I crept out in the morning rather stiff. The first thing I discovered was that a soup tablet which I had had in my pocket had melted and made a filthy mess of my coat. Whilst scraping the remnants of the said soup tablet from off my person I got a message from H.Q. to say that Co. Comdrs had to meet the C.O. in the Line on the right of "D" Co. in order to reconoitre the trenches with an attack next day as the object of the reconnaisance I left Johny in Command and went up to Battalion H.Q. - 3 miles - for the conference, and found only Baks and Brain at H.Q. Blenks was coming up the Line instead of the C.O. so we started off together. After a somewhat venturesome journey we eventually arrived with more or less whole skins and found Daddy Mansell Uncle Salt and Robin waiting for us. Blenks told us the general idea and then as the other three had been in and knew the line, he and I went off along to "D" Co. The trench was simply a courtesy title for a very narrow ditch dug in a hurry like the trenches at Ypres in 1915. Nothing exciting happened until we turned back and went the other way. "C" Co. right we found was only seperated from the Hun by a barricade over which they periodically lobbed stray bombs at each other; and evidently there is a pocket of Hun between us and the Dukes in the same trench thus :-

```
              HUN
       ---------::::::::::---------------
  ::::::::::::                  ::::::::::::
  2nd Lan.Fus.                  Dukes.
```

Cheerful sort of disposition.

Having inspected everything there was of any interest we wended our way back again. On the way home we stopped to have a chat with Salt which same old gentleman produced a bottle of brandied Chems for our delectation. Having allowed us one cherry each the gods stepped in and caused the Hun to drop a whizz-bang on the parados above us. When we had risen from our humble position we discovered the bottle Chems to be full of earth.

As there seemed nothing more to stop up in the line for we left Salt moaning over the Chems and cursing the Hun at the same time, and having been held up by a strafe of 15 minutes eventually ggotbhekktboBBn. H.Q. The C.O. had not yet returned so I was bidden to remain to lunch, in case the C.O. had orders when he returned.

The C.O. appeared in the dug-out at about 3 p.m. having raced a 5.9 to the door and only just won. He had orders for a show to-morrow and having sent out for Daddy Salt and Robin gave us the following orders :-

The 4th Division in conjunction with the 6th Division on the left and the French on the right will attack on October 12th and capture the Brown line.

<u>Brown Line</u>   Map sheet 57.C.
                N.28.b.8 .1. N.29.c.3.3.
Bde. H.Q. will be at T.8.d.3.6.

<u>S. Boundary between 10th and 12th Bde</u> :-

N.34.D.0.0. N.34.D.6.6. thence along Les Boeuffs - Le Transloy Road.

N. Boundary. 12th Bde and 6th Division. N.34.A.1.9. - N.28.B.8.1.

Div. Front. N.28.B.9.0. - N.35.a.8.7. - T.6 .A.6-8. The 2nd Lan. Fus and 2 guns M.G.Co.will be on the left of the Bde.

Attack in 8 waves. 200 yards between 4th & 5th. 4 guns 12 M.G.Co. and 4 guns T.M.B. will be on special mission.

A & C Cos. have been digging saps out from the front line for assembly trenches which will be finished to-night 11/12th Oct. and with Spectrum trench will form Bn. assembly position.

A.Co. to assemble on right.
B.Co.
C.Co.
D.Co. " "   on left.
to be assembled by 5:15 a.m. Oct. 12th 1916.

Having had these orders I got back to the Co. in Cow trench as quickly as possible landing up there about 4 p.m.

I had my platoon Officers - Johnny Greaves-Fortescue - and Addison and my N.C.O's up and gave them orders.

At 5 p.m. I got a chit from Brain telling me to fetch the stores from D.Dump at 10:45 p.m. this evening These stores consisted of yellow flares for signalling to aeroplanes and wire cutters for the attack.

I had also to arrange to fetch rations to my C.H.Q. and issue them out to the other Cos. each of whom sent a party back for them.

Rations and stores were fixed up and the Co. ready to move by 12 midnight 11/12th.

Robin whi was at present in the support line, which was really the only communication trench arranged to be clear of this by 2:30 a.m. so as to enable me to get straight up to the line.

Accordingly I had given orders to the platoon Comdrs. to be ready to move off at 2:30 a.m. The men would wear fighting order Packs and Greatcoats being left in charge of Co. Q.M.S. Clifton in Cow trench.

Therefore everything being settled I turned in and slept till 1:30 a.m. Oct. 12th. 1916.

October 12th. 1916.

At 2:30 a.m. I started off to the assembly position with my Co. H.Q. which consisted of C.S.M. Laverick D.C.M. my runner Ginger Hodgkinson my servant Hargreaves and the Co. Signallers and Orderlies.

The platoon were to start off at 3:15 a.m. in the following order :- 5.6.7.8 .

I reached Robins H.Q. at 3 a.m. to find "A" Co. had not moved and were still sleeping the sleep of the just. This seemed to prophesy a bit of a muddle at dawn unless somebody hustled. So I chivied Robin up and his 3rd platoon were just getting away as Johny rolled up with No.5. They sat down and rested until "A" Co. were well clear and then went on up the line. Addison Commanding 7 platoon and Sgt. Bolton Commanding 8 platoon rolled up O.K. and were sent on up to the line but of Forterque and No.6. platoon there was'nt a sign. By 4:30 a.m. as Fortesque and 6 were still absent I left Ginger and another orderly to show them the way up and with Cottee went on up to see how the 3 platoons were getting on and after a little effort got them assembled with a certain amount of room and comfort and a space left for Fortesque. At 5:30 a.m. just as it was getting daylight. Fortesque with No.6. turned up. His guide had lost him compleyely and utterly and it had taken Fortesque some time to find his wat back. After a short time 6 platoon got settled in. By 6 a.m. we were assembled thus :-

10.

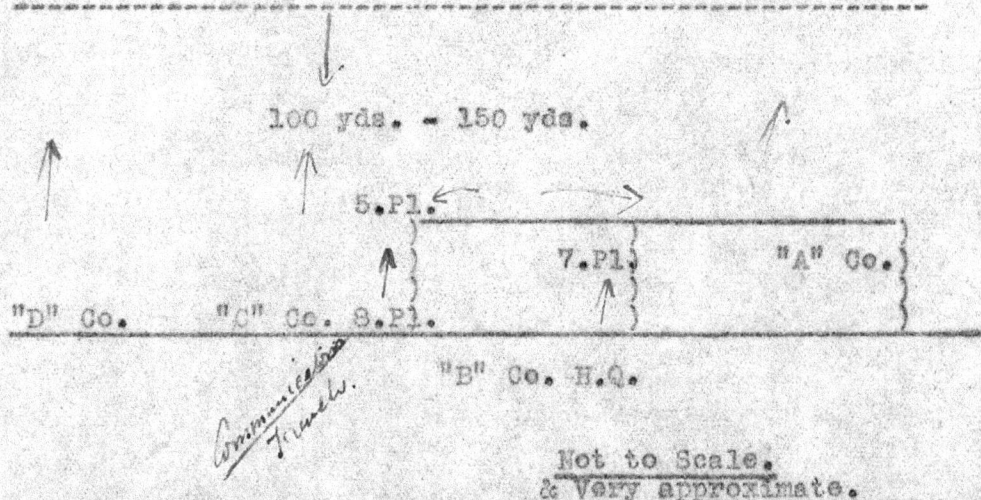

Not to Scale.
& Very approximate.

At about 6 a.m. the preliminary bombardment began and lasted all day until Zero Hour. It was very slow and very regular. A few shots fell short into "D" Co. but nothing very exciting happened at first. (The rest of this diary is written by Hour and minutes as the events of the day became somewhat crowded).

8 a.m. One C.O's, 6th Div. came along our trench he thought Zero hour was 2 p.m.

12 noon. Watkins came along from C.Co. for a last conflab Salt the Co. Comdr. is being sent back to Brigade with Blencowe as 10% reinforcements.

12:15 p.m. Several Huns running and crawling about in No Man's Land, carrying a Machine Gun. Had a few shots at them.

12:30 p.m. 12 Huns came into our line and surrendered. Some excitement. Things assume a rosy aspect and point to a fairly easy show.

1:0 p.m. Watches sent to Bn. H.Q. for synchonizing.

1:30 p.m. Watch sent back and following additional orders received from Brain. Zero hour 2.5.p.m. The Duke to attack the length of trench occupied by the Hun between A Co. and then At. 2.25 p.m. the rest of the Division to attack. Accordingly we sat down and waited for Zero hour.

2.P.m. Bombardment increased. Bayonets fixed.

2:3 p.m. Hunplan flew straight down own line about 300

feet up, must have seen trenches crowded with men. None of our planes in sight.

2:5 p.m. Fiendish Row. Zero hour. Heavy enemy barrage on 10th Brigade Machine Gun Barrage. Dukes attacking on our right but can't see much.

2:10 p.m. Shrapnel shell on top of us. Laverick hit on steel helmet and stunned several other casualties.

2:15 p.m. Awful noise impossible to make oneself heard Several men got excited and went over the top on their own. Keen as hell to go.

2:20 p.m. Shell landed on Co. H.Q. all Co. signallers and runners knocked out except Ginger Hargreaves badly knocked.

2:25 p.m. Johny Greaves and 5 platoon off followed by the rest of the Co. Johny shot through the lung 5 yards in front of our parapet. Enemy machine gun barrage pretty unhealthy our own barrage which should have waited for us has gone on with the Dukes and 25 mins. in front of us.

Ginger and I follow the Co. over. Run like hares and find ourselves well away in front of the Co.

2:50 p.m. 50% Co. already down. Whole Bde appears to be held up L/Cpl. Fenton one of my Lewis Gunners has got his gun going in a shell hole on my left. Awful din can hardly hear it yelled at Sgt. Manin to take the 1st wave on. He's lying just behind me. Ginger says he's dead. Sgt. Mann on my right of 7 platoon also dead. Most of the men appear to be dead. Shout at the rest and get up to take them on. Find myself sitting on the ground facing our own line with a bally great hole in my thigh, does'nt hurt much but bleeding like hell. Ginger also hit in the wrist. Awful din still. Most of the Co. now out. Ginger ties my leg up I put my tie round my leg as a torniquet Fortesque about 5 yds on my right still alive. He had had a bullet through his steal hat and another had broken the skin on his nose. Funny how one noticed these things.

Yell at him to come over to me. Show him my leg and tell him to carry on. He gets into a shell hole to listen while I tell what to do. Shot through the heart while I'm talking to him, Addison also wounded and crawling back to our lines. That all the Officers and most of the N.C.O's. cant see anything of Bolton and 8 Pl. Start crawling on back, back to our own lines. Bump. "Whats that Ginger" Dead man Sir, Dam;; Turns over and drag along on my stomach. Ginger helps me along. About 75 yds. to go. Leg still bleeding fast, and my trousers have been cut off me. Feel rather naked. Beastly uncomfortable also rather faint. Bloody row still. Make another effort and roll over our parapet on to Laverick who has recovered and is just coming up. Ginger dives off for stretcher bearers. Awful shindy still. Feeling rotten. Stretcher bearer arrives. Take my Field Dressing off. Hole in my thigh. I can put my fist into it. Full of mud to. They tie me up and cart me off to a small hole somewhere near in original assembly trench. Laverick goes off to collect the Co. Only about 12 men left out of a hundred.

2:40 p.m. Johny Greaves carried along and put in another small hole. Badly hit in lung. Can't get away till dark.

3. p.m. Got an awful pain. Laverick has collected the remnants of the Co. in the front line. Himself Sgt.Bolton and a dozen men. Attack an absolute failure.

5 p.m. Feeling rotten. Keeping loosing consciousness. Heard a Subaltern in the Dukes passes. Asks him how they did. He says he is the only Officer left. 9 Officers killed, 6 wounded. Ask him if he is going to Bn.H.Q. He is. Will he tell Brain how things are, and that Johny and I are here. He will. Must have fainted again.

6 p.m. Still in this beastly hole. Johny very quiet. 10% reserves come up.

11. p.m. Stretcher Bearers come up and Johny carried off

Another stretcher party come along and take me away. Beastly journey down. Essex and King's Own all coming up. Stretcher bearers have to get into the open. After a long time we get to the road. John Carr and L/Cpl Owen meet us with a stretcher. Take me over and send S.B's. back for someone else. John & Owen start off with me, to Bn. H.Q. Drop me off stretcher twice. John keeps patting my head and telling me I am O.K. Reach Bn. H.Q. Brain and Blence come out and give me a drink. Willis sends me a message to say, I'll soon be in town. Cheers me up a bit. Brain tells me our casualties.

Poor Old Daddy Mansell killed. Robin, Greaves, Kirkland, Addison and others wounded. Bolton missing. Watkins and Sammy Howarth, only 2 to get through. Whole show dud. The doctor decides to send me on at once. I am lying on a stretcher in a trench near Battalion H.Q. Damned shell bursts near, and covers me with mud. Don't seem to mind a bit. Seem apathetic since getting hit. Am sent off to a Dressing Station near Givenchy and thus sever connection with the Bn. again after ' months ' spell.

14.

October 7th 1917.

The attack was altered to take place on the 9th so the plan of Campaign now is 7/8th relieve the 10th & 11th Brigades.

9th Attack.

PRELIMINARIES TO THE ATTACK

The attack was to take place in accordance with the accompanying map.

The extreme left the French, on their Right the Guards Division. Of these two the French are to work round to the left and the Guards to the right of their main objective i.e. Houtholst Forest. On the right of the Guards are the 29th Division, the 4th Division and the 11th Division and the 2nd Army.

The 12th Brigade of the 4th Division is attacking with the 10th Brigade in support, the 11th in Reserve.

Dispositions of the 12th Brigade are :-

Left Front Battalion	2nd Lancashire Fusiliers.
Right Front Battalion	2nd Essex Regiment.
Support Battalion	2nd Dukes (West Ridings).
Reserve Battalion	1st King's own R.L. Regt.

Dispositions of the Battalion.

Left Front Company	"C" Company.
Right Front Company	"A" Company
Support Company	"B" Company
Reserve Company	"D" Company

In the 29th Division, 2 Brigades attack. The 86th Brigade being on the Right of the Division and the 1st Battalion Lancashire Fusiliers on the Right of the 86th Brigade. In other words the 1st and 2nd Bns. Lan. Fus. attack touching. This is the first time in history.

Of the 11th Division there is the 9th Battalion and of the 17th Division in Reserve there is the 10th Battn. so the Regiment is well represented.

Officers of the Battalion going into the attack.

Commanding Officer.	Major J.W.Watkins.
Adjutant.	Capt. G.G.Martin, M.C.
Signalling Officer.	2nd Lt. R.Gilmour.
Intelligence Officer.	Capt. S.Clarke,

"A" Coy.	"B" Coy.
2nd Lt. C.U.Lloyd	Capt. G.L.Elkington.
2nd Lt. A.Worrall	2nd Lt. C.H.Elliott.
2nd Lt. E.J.Howl.	2nd Lt. H.M.Dodson.
2nd Lt. C.Dunlavy.	2nd Lt. R.S.Thicknesse.

"C" Coy.	"D" Coy.
Capt. J.Judd.	Lt. A.D.Macdonald. M.C.
Capt. Lowe.(Essex Regt).	2nd Lt. W.H.Riley.
2nd Lt. E.S.Faragher	2nd.Lt.L.Shipman,
2nd Lt. Blewes	2nd Lt. E.G.Dalglish.

10% Reinforcements.

Lt. Col H.W.Glenn (W.Riding Regt).	Transport.
Capt. K.Guy.	Dragon Camp
Capt. V.F.S.Hawkins, M.C.	Transport.
2nd LT. G.N.Stange.	Herzeele.

Carrying Officer	2nd Lt. J.Grimshaw, V.C.
Quartermaster.	Major W.Bowes, D.S.O.
Transport Officer.	2nd Lt. A.R.Topping.

If on the 9th the 2nd Lan. Fus. and the 2nd Essex gained their objective fairly easily, at zero plus 9 hours the Dukes and the King's Own will go right through to a further objective about 1000 yards ahead.

The Battalion left Wolfe Camp the night 7/8th October and marched by Cos. to the line, to relieve the Hampshire Regt. 11th Brigade.

The weather since the 4th had been simply poisonous and as the line simply consists of posts in shell holes, it will be awfullybad for the men until the attack comes off. It stopped raining at about 5 p.m. on the 7th.

"A" Co. moved off at 6:30 p.m.

"C" Co. Moved off at 6:45 p.m.

"B" Co. moved off at 7 p.m.

"D" Co. moved off at 7:15 p.m.

Watkins and Martin left at about 8 p.m. with headquarters.

October 8th was a fine day with a strong westerly breeze. A good drying wind. Towards the evening however it began to rain again which will make the ground very bad going for the troops. The creeping barrage however only goes 100 yards in the first ten minutes and 100 every 6 minutes afterwards. Besides this pace the attackers wait 1½ hours on the first and second objectives. Zero hour is 5:20 a.m.

October 9th 1917.

Attack on enemy positions North of Poelcappelle. Final of objectives about 1500 yards into the enemy territory. General direction of the attack 6° Magnetic bearing.

The following account of the fighting is written from accounts given by officers who went into the attack with the Battalion.

The night preceeding zero hour 8/9th October the Battn assembled for the attack. Tape had been put out by Major Hodgett of the 9th Field Co. R.E. for the assaulting Companies "A" & "C" to line up on. The Support Cos. "B" & "D" formed up behind. One platoon of "B" Co. No.5. under 2nd Lt. Elliott was mopping up platoon for "A" Co, No.16 platoon of "D" Co. under 2nd Lt. L.Shipman was mopping up party for "C" Co.

The men carried two days rations with them and their water bottle full.

At zero Hour 5:20 a.m. on the 9/10/17 the battalion was ready. The barrage opened on time and from all account was the most extraordinary sight. It consisted of 18 pund shrapnel and H.E. up to 9.2

The first 10 minutes the Battalion moved 100 yards The enemy barrage came down on the Support line 3 minutes after the attack started. The attackers were scheduled to reach the first objective at about 5:45 a.m. and were up to time. Major Watkins, Capt.Martion,M.C. the Adjt. Capt.S.Clarke the Intelligence Officer and 2nd Lt.R. Gilmour the Signalling Officer comprising Headquarters were up on 19 Metre Hill before the attack commenced and went over practically with the first wave, which position they maintained till the end of the attack.

The first ½ of an hour of the show may be described by the remarks of an officer and a private, Pte.Olive, 2ndLt. Elliott's Servant brought Elliott down the line after that officer was hit, and having seen him off to the C.C.S. reported to the Transport. When asked how the show was going he said "It was grand, Sir; the first 5 or 6 minutes was just like a practice attack on parade".

The other description was by 2nd Lt. W.H.Riley. This officer was hit just beyond the first objective, but when he got to the C.C.S. he refused to go down the line, and came back to the Battalion, and was only stopped going back to join the Battalion in the line with the greatest difficulty. When asked what he thought of the show he said "That it was the finest mornings outing he'd ever had in his life". He admitted at the same time that he had been wounded before the worst part of the fighting began.

The worst fighting began according to all accounts at the Light Railway on the Poelcappelle - Conde House Road. The Division on the right had been held up in Poelcappelle and Machine Guns enfiladed this road. In addition to this enemy snipers who had escaped the barrage were very active round Landing Farm and Compromise Farm and isolated shell holes. By the time the Battalion had crossed the Farm the advance had turned from walking behind our barrage, to rapid jumping from shell hole to shell hole. Capt. Lowe, Essex Regt. att. Lan. Fus. was killed crossing the road. 2nd Lt. Worrall and Thicknesse were also killed. Capt. Elkington had been badly wounded in the right arm, by a shell very early and in addition Daglish, Shipman, Elliott, Dodson and Faragher were all wounded. This left the Battalion at this part of the proceedings as follows at about 11 a.m.

"A" Co.   Lloyd and Dunlevy
"B" Co.   No Officers.
"C" Co.   Judd, Blewes.
"D" Co.   Macdonald & Riley.
Hd. Qrs. As at the beginning.

The first serious check came to the left of the Battalion from Millers House. The Essex on the right had already been held up by the right Division failing to advance. This caused a temporary standstill.

The Germans had not been giving themselves up very willingly and appeared to be very numerous around Landing and Compromise Farms, Millers Houses.

The result of this standstill was that our barrage got right ahead of us.

Major Watkins and Capt. Clarke, seeing how things were going immediately got up to the front line and reorganised things. By this time men of the Dukes and King's Own and one or two of the Essex had got middled up with the Battalion. Besides them men of the Royal Fusiliers and 1st. Battalion Lan. Fus. from the 29th Division were in amongst us, so that proceedings were rather disorganised. Also owing to the extraordinary state of the ground which was cut to pieces with shell

holes it was almost impossible for an officer or N.C.O. to handle more than half a dozen men.

Major Watkins and Capt. Clarke however collected a party of all Regiments and went for Millers Houses. Parties went round either flank and the enemy eventually surrendered. This side show produced about 40 prisoners.

After this the advance was very slow and finally came to a standstill on a line about 400 yards in front of the main road. From all accounts the reason of the advance stopping was the awful condition of the ground. It was absolutely cut to bits and impossible for the officers to handle the Companies and they had got disorganised. Also the stoppage at Millers Houses had brought the Battalion in Support in amongst us and these together with units from the Division on the left completed the disorganisation.

Major Watkins, therefore, determined to dig in where he was. This was at about 12 noon. Touch was gained with the 29th Division and the Essex and a line of posts put out.

The Battalion was in the line all that night and conditions were very bad. Shell holes were half full of water. The men had no cover and it was bitterly cold. Towards morning Major Watkins was wounded by a stray bullet through the right arm and went down. This left Captain Martin in command. He was wounded about four hours later by a piece of shrapnel in the back and Captain Clarke took over command of the battalion.

The Bosche for some reason made no counter attacks at all, but was very active with his snipers. The only method of movement was series of kangaroo like leaps from shell hole to shell hole which meant landing in about a foot od muddy water every time.

The Battalion were still in the front on the morning of the 10th inst. but were relieved the night of the 10th/11th by the Warwicks and came right out of the line to Redan Camp. The Rifle Brigade went right up to the line to take our places and were attached to the 12th Brigade, thus repaying their debt to us from Pilkem July 1915. We were attached to the 11th Brigade meanwhile. The 1st arrivals at Redan Camp were Gilmour and Clarke at about midnight and the Battalion began to come into Camp at about 2 a.m. The officers who came out with the Battalion were Capt. Clarke and Judd, Lt. Macdonald M.U. 2nd Lts. Gilmour, Lloyd, Blewes, Dunlevy, and Capt. Buxtable M.C. the Doctor.

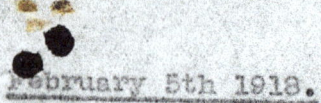
February 5th 1918.

About this time a new organisation came into being. Three Battalions per Brigade. This led to numerous Battalions in the B.E.F. being split up and other Battns. being transferred. The Dukes were taken from the 12th Brigade and put into the 10th Brigade.

Organisation of the 10th, 11th and 12th Brigades is now :-

New.	Old.
10th Brigade.	Seaforths.
Seaforths.	Warwicks.
Warwicks.	Household Battalion.
Dukes.	3/10th Middlesex Regt.
11th Brigade.	
	Hants.
Hants.	R.B's.
R.B's.	Somersets.
Somerset Light Inf.	East Lancs.
12th Brigade.	
	King's Own.
King's Own R.L.Regt.	Lan. Fus.
2nd Lan. Fus.	Essex.
2nd Essex.	Dukes

Operations on March 28th 1918.

Fampoux Ridge.

Prior to the commencement of the enemy's offensive on March 21st the 4th Division had for some time been holding the line South of the Scarpe. After a period of rest the Division relieved the Guards Division. On March 19th the Battalion relieved the 1st Bn. Scots Guards at St. Laurent-Blangy; one Company "D" Co. (Capt. G.H.Strange) going forward to Lemon Trench. When two days later, the battle opened on the 5th Army front all ranks felt that the enemy would attempt to retake the Fampoux Ridge and everyone, whether they had taken part in its capture on April 9th 1917, or no, felt confident in stopping him. The stand which the Battn. made on March 28th will always be famous and will rank with the greatest achievments of the Regiment. The German attack was launched on both banks of the Scarpe; it was preceeded by an intense bombardment and it was pressed bravely with great determination. Its object was the capture of Arras and the Vimy Ridge.

In the following brief account it is well nigh impossible to name many individual heroes and it is equally impossible to do justice to the fallen. The heroism of Cassidy and his Company and the subsequent resistance which "B" Co. under Howarth and "D" Co. under Stange offered - aided as they were most gallantly in the thick of the fight by "C" Co. 1st King's Own Regt (Capt. T.Pritchard,M.C.) were entirely responsible for the bloody repulse which the enemy sustained.

It is hoped that the accompanying map will make the account clear.

On the morning of March 28th the 2nd Essex Regt. held the Front line; no pen can do justice to their heroic stand which completely broke up the first waves of the

23.

attack and made possible the subsequent defence. The Battalion was in Support and the 1st King's Own Regt. in Reserve. At 3 a.m. an intense bombardment opened of both artillery and trench mortars. At about 5:30 a.m. the 56th Division on our left flank sent up the S.O.S. and at 6:30 a.m. the enemy was reported to be cutting the wire on our Brigade front. Our Front Line extended from Civil Avenue - Costa Alley some thousand yards in front of the 2nd System. At about 7:30 a.m. the attack was launched. The Bosche made slow progress and suffered heavy losses but by 9 a.m. the Essex were overwhelmed by sheer weight of numbers and the enemy with our front system in his hands, at once pressed his attack upon our Second which fell soon afterwards - Line Cadiz - Calf - Chalk - Chicken.

The dispositions of the Battalion were :-

"A" Co.   Humid and Civil Trenches.
"B" Co.   Hudson and Hyderabad Trenches.
"C" Co.   Trent Trench.
"D" Co.   Harry and Hussar Trenches.

This was a switch line and had been constructed for Right flank defence; consequently the full force of the attack now fell upon "A" Co. It was entirely owing to their splendid resistance that the enemy was unable to turn the left flank of the Division.

Up to this time the enemy had succeeded largely owing to the fact that our Artillery were occupying fresh positions, necessitated by our withdrawals, South of the Scarpe, and were unable to provide an effective barrage and the Germans were able to bring up reinforcements and Field Guns in full view over the top of Greenland Hill.

Finding that he could make little headway/the open he now took every advantage of our numerous communication trenches and worked his way up Chili, Caledonian and Civil Avenues in large numbers. By about 10 a.m. he bombed his way into the junction of Humid and Harry Trenches taking "A" Co. in the rear and separating them from "D" Co.

Cassidy had already suffered heavy casualties - his supply of bombs was almost exhausted and he could not re-establish touch with Stange and in addition large numbers of the enemy were coming up on his left flank. At about 10:30 a.m. he was practically surrounded and he saw that he could only extricate his Company by a withdrawal across the open to the line Trent - Hyderabad Trenches. He went up and down the line cheering and encouraging his men and fell whilst organising this movement. Heron was seen to fall a few minutes later and lastly, Butler-Bowden. Not more than 6 of the Company escaped unwounded. The enemy made repeated strong bombing attacks up Hussar Trench which were all repulsed by "B" and "D" Cos.

The 11th Brigade on our right had fought with great gallantry but were compelled to fall back owing to the situation South of the River. At Noon the Line was established in Trent - Hyderabad - Havana Trenches. At dusk in order to conform with the 11th Brigade we re-established ourselves on the line Trent - Hudson - Stoke Trenches.

The dispositions of the Regiment were now :-
"C" Co. and about 50 survivors of the Essex Regt. Trent Trench.
"D" Co.   ....   Tripoli Trench.
"B" Co. and "C" Co. 1st King's Own Regt. Hudson & Stoke Tr

At dawn on the 29th the enemy made a further determined bombing attack on Hudson Trench. He was repulsed by "B" Co. who captured one prisoner of 189th I.R.Regt. and one Machine Gun. Another Machine Gun was captured by "D" Co.

Capt. S. Clarke M.C., joined with 10% reinforcements.

On 30th the enemy repeated his bombing attack with great determination and with no better success. For 48 hours these two gallant Companies withstood his repeated efforts and he was unable to make a yard of progress.

On the night 30/31st the 1st King's Own Regt. relieved the Battalion in the Front Line and the Regiment moved into Support Missouri - Mississippi Logic and Lemon and Effie Trenches.

One Company of the Essex Regt. joined the Battalion on 31st under 2nd. Lt. Stenderwick. This Company relieved "B" Co. in Mississippi Trench and later held Stoke Trench most gallantly.

Brigadier General E.A. Fagan, D.S.O. had much against his will been forced to move his Headquarters from Lemon Trench to the Railway Embankment at St. Laurent-Blangy. On the night of the 28th the Regiment formed a joint Headquarters with the 1st King's Own Regt. at the old Brigade Headquarters and during the following days of inter Battalion relief until the Brigade was relieved by Regiments of the 1st Canadian Division on 7th April. The 1st King's Own Regt. showed kindness and consideration such as it will be impossible for any one of us ever to forget. The Signallers were beyond all praise as also the Headquarters and Company Runners and communication was maintained to Companies throughout the operations. The thanks of the Battalion are once again due to Major. W. Bowes, D.S.O. Lieut. A.R. Topping and the N.C.O's and men on their respective staffs. Rations were brought up under severe conditions and under heavy shell fire with unfailing regularity.

Much regret is felt at losing our Medical Officer, Capt. L. Little, M.O.R.C., U.S.A. His work and that of the Battalion Stretcher Bearers, especially No. 34906 Pte. Jones, M.M., was simply magnificent. We wish the former a speedy recovery.

The following Officers were present with the Battalion :-

Headquarters.

Lt.Col.J.W.Watkins, D.S.O./M.C.
Lieut E.Hartley, A/Adjutant.
2nd Lt. R.Gilmour. Signalling Officer.
2nd Lt. W.H.Riley. Intelligence Officer.
Capt. L.Little, M.O.R.C., U.S.A. Medical Officer.

"A" Co.	"B" Co.
2nd Lt.B.M.Cassidy,V.C.	2nd Lt.A.Howarth,M.C.
2nd Lt.J.Heron.	2nd Lt.H.W.Everett.
2nd Lt.B.J.B.Butler-Bowden.	2nd Lt.J.W.Keightley.
	2nd Lt.W.F.Lilley,M.M.

"C" Co.	"D" Co.
Capt. T.H.Robinson.	Capt.G.N.Stange,M.C.
2nd Lt.W.S.Gilbert.	2nd Lt.E.de B.Cantrell-Hubbersty.
2nd Lt.A.W.B.Potter.	2nd Lt.G.R.Willans.
2nd Lt.W.G.Wilding.	2nd Lt.S.H.Hope.

List of Decorations awarded :-	Award.
2nd Lt.B.M.Cassidy.	V.C.
Lt. Col.J.W.Watkins,M.C.	D.S.O.
Capt. G.N.Stange.	M.C.
2nd Lt.A.Howarth.	M.C.

"B" Coy.

660.	C.S.M.,E.A.North.	D.C.M.
242243	Pte.W.H.Roscoe.	D.C.M.
34906	" T.Jones,	M.M.
7421	" J.Bennett.	M.M.
33602	" H.Blackledge,	M.M.
27058	L/Cpl.F.T.Howarth.	M.M.
40554	Cpl. A.Carter.	M.M.

"C" Coy.

306801	L/Cpl.	H. Airey.	D.C.M.
2873	Cpl.	C.B. Clayton.	D.C.M.
24013	Pte.	E.J. Wooldridge.	M.M.
24294	"	W. Booth.	M.M.
42419	"	H.C. Pontet.	M.M.
39794	"	R. Wood.	M.M.

"D" Coy.

1314	C.S.M.	J. Baines.	D.C.M.
26291	L/Cpl.	R. Kenyon.	M.M.
7152	Pte.	T. Lackey.	M.M.
201335	"	A. Walker.	M.M.
18074	L/Cpl	R. Sladdin.	M.M.
235901	Pte.	J. Jesse.	M.M.
7034	"	T. Johnson.	M.M.
45167	"	S. Wood.	M.M.

28.

COPY OF

RAID ORDERS.
―――――――――――――

6/7/18.

LANCASHIRE FUSILIERS ORDER No. 17.

Ref. Map. Sheet 36A. S.E. 1/20,000

Field 3/7/18.

1. The Battalion will carry out a raid on shell holes held by the enemy at Zero Hour 6/7/18.

2. **Objectives.** Shell Holes at Q.34.c.60.75 and Q.34.c.70.65.

3. **Object.** 1. To obtain identification.
   2. To damage and destroy the enemy's position
   3. To raise the morale of the troops.

4. **Strength.** The Raiding Party will consist 1 Officer and 21 Other Ranks of "B" Coy.

5. **Dress.** Rifle and Bayonet.

   2 Bombs per man.

   All means of identification are to be removed

   Equipment and Box Respirators will be left in the trench, at Point of Exit and picked up on return.

   Steel Helmets will be worn.

6. **Support.** The raid will be covered by Artillery and Machine Gun barrage, neutralisation of rear areas and flanks by heavy Artillery and Machine Gunfire.

   Lewis Guns in the Front Line, 6" Newton and 3" Stokes will co-operate.

7. **Method of Attack and Withdrawal.** The Raiding Party will leave the Front Line at Q.34.c.7.4. at Zero Hour - 20 minutes and crawl through the crops to area Q.34.c.70.42., where they will form up in line of sections in file 2 yds interval between sections. From Zero Hour to Zero plus 1, Party will lie flat, from Zero plus 1 to Zero plus 3 party will creep towards the objectives whilst artillery barrage is on objectives. At Zero plus 3 minutes barrage will left and party will rush the objectives, killing or taking prisoners any of the enemy and destroying his works. The barrage on flanks and in

rear of the objectives will continue till Zero plus 15 minutes

Withdrawal. The signal for the return to our line will be a blast on the whistle at the discretion of the Officer in charge of raiding party. This must be within the period Zero plus 15 minutes. The raiding party will crawl back to our line down the ditch on the East side of the road running from Q.34.c.25.25 to Q.34.central, and will re-enter our line at Q.34.c.25.25. rendezvousing at Front Company Headquarters Q.34.c.85.35.

8. Artillery Programme. Appendix A.

9. Machine Gun Programme. Appendix B.

10. 6" Newton Programme & 3" Stokes Programme.
Appendices C?D.

11. Lewis Guns. Two Lewis Guns with teams of 5 men each from "B" Co. will accompany the raiding party. One will occupy a shell hole at Q.34.c.52.54 and give covering fire on the Left Flank. The other will take up a position at Q.34.c.70.55 and give covering fire on the Right Flank.

12. "C" Co. will detail picked marksmen and rifle grenadiers to rifle grenade and keep down any movement East of a line Q.34.c.7.4. -- Q.34.d.4.9. paying special attention to area Q.34.d.5.6. and West of a line Q.34.c.3.0.-- Q.34.c.3.9. and the E. edge of Pacaut Wood.

13. "C" Co. will detail 1 N.C.O. and 3 men to collect any prisoners in the Front Line. These will be brought back direct to Bn.H.Q. by the raiding party.

14. 2 Stretcher Bearers will accompany the Raiding Party.

15. The Raiding party will leave L'Ecleme evening 5/7/18 and spend night 5/6th in the Front Line. On completion of operation raiding party will return to L'Ecleme.

16. Acknowledge.

(sgd) V.F.S.Hawkins, Capt & Adjt.
2nd Lan. Fus.

Watches will be synchronised at Battalion Headquarters W.8.d.1.6. at 7 a.m. 6/7/18.

Zero hour will be at 9:30 a.m.

Officer i/c   Lt. H.H.Barker-Jones.

N.C.O.   Sgt. Wiggin.

Result.   3 Prisoners.   3 8 R.I.R.
                                   12 R.Div.

        1 Slight casualty.

        12 Huns killed.

Copy No.3.

12th Infantry Brigade Operation Order No.139.

Reference Map. Sheet 36A. S.E. 1/20,000.

4th July 1918.

---

1. The 2nd Battalion, Lancashire Fusiliers will carry out a raid on enemy's posts in the immediate neighbourhood of Q.34.c.50.71 and Q.34.c.80.65 on 6th inst.

2. <u>Object.</u>   To capture a suspected machine gun.
   To obtain an identity.
   To destroy enemy's moral.

3. <u>Strength of Raiding Party.</u>   1 Officer, 26 Other Ranks including two Lewis Guns.

4. Party will be told off in 4 groups, with one Lewis Gun to guard either flank.

5. <u>Zero Hour,</u> 9:30 a.m.

6. Artillery (including 9.45 Trench Mortars and 6" Newton Mortars) Machine Guns, and Light Trench Mortars will co-operate.

Barrages as on attached Tables "A", "B", and "C".

<u>Note.</u>   The Infantry must keep flat from Zero to Zero plus 1, while 106 Fuze ammunition is being fired.

6. O.C. 2nd Lan. Fus. will arrange for telephonic and visual communication from the Front Line, so that he can report result of Raid as early as possible to Brigade Headquarters.

8. Any prisoners taken will be sent back to Brigade Headquarters without delay.

9. No papers, identification discs or distinguishing marks (other than Raid identification discs will be carried by the Raiding Party).

10. Watches will be synchronised by Right Group R.F.A 4th Battn.M.G.Corps, 12th L.T.M.Batty. at headquarters 2nd Lan. Fus., W.8.d.1.6. at 7 a.m. on the 6th inst.

11. Acknowledge.

                    (signed) J.J.M.Cunningham, Captain,
                        A/Brigade Major, 12th Infantry Brigade.

Issued through Signals at .....

Copies to :-   9. C.R.E.

1. B.G.C.   10. 10th Infantry Brigade.
2. 1 King's Own.   11. 11th   "   "
3. 2nd Lan. Fus.   12 76th   "   "
4. 2nd Essex R.   13 4th Bn. M.G. Corps.
5. 12 L.T.M.Batty. 14 Staff Captain.
6. Right Group R.F.A. 15 Bde I.O.
7. D.T.M.O.   16 File.
8. 4th Division.   17 War Diary.

TABLE "A".

Artillery Support for Raid by 2nd Lancashire Fusiliers.

(1) 18 pdrs.

(a) Tasks.

Battery	Time From.	To.	Objective.			
27th	Zero plus 3.	Zero	Shellholes 50yds. radius of Q.34.c.64.68.	Zero plus 3	Zero plus 15	Road Q.34.c.8.9. to Q.34.b.1.2.(3 guns) Hedges about Q.34.a.95.20. (3 guns)
134th (2 guns)	"	"	Q.34.c.75.67 to Q.34.c.95.77.	"	"	Q34.b.6.1. and 25.35.
135th (2 guns)	"	"	Shellholes at Q.34.c.45.66.	"	"	Shellholes at Q.34.c.40.85
A/104th (2 guns)	Zero plus 15	"	Enclosure Q.33.d.95.95 to Q.34.a.2.2.	"	"	
B/104th	"	"	Line of Shellholes Q.34.a.75.20 to Q.34.a.3.5.			
C/104th (Forward Section)	"	"	Shellholes Q.34.c.13.68 to 25.85.			
C/104th (4 guns)	"	"	Shellholes and House in area 50 Yds radius from Q.34.d.47.60.			
504th	"	"	Edge of wood Q.28.c.0.0.- 50.15.- Q.34.a.70.95.			

3rd D.A.

6th	"	"	Shellholes 25 yds radius from Q.34.c.35.70.
49th	"	"	Shellholes Q.34.c.97.65.- Q.34.d.25.50.
1 Battery	"	"	Shellholes Q.34.d.55.60.-95.60.

(b) Rates of Fire.

	From	To.	
27th,134th,135th,6thBtys.	Zero	Z.Plus 3	4 R.P.G.P.M.
	Z.plus 3	Z." 8	3 " " " " "
	Z. F	8 Z." 12	2 " " " " "
Remainder	Zero	Z " 3	3 " " " " "
	Z plus 3	Z " 12	2 " " " " "

TABLE "A" Continued.

All Batteries ... Z Plus 12 Z plus 15 ... 1 r.p.g.p.m.

(1) 18 pdrs. (contd).

(c) Ammunition.

5th Battery
    zero   Z.plus 1   H.E. 106 fuze
    Z.plus 1   Z.plus 3   Time Shrapnel.
    Z " 3   Z " 12   Percussion Shrapnel
    Z " 12   Z " 15   Time Shrapnel

27th, 134th 135th Battys.
    Zero   Z " 1   H.E. 106 Fuze
    Z.plus 1   Z " 3   Time Shrapnel
    Z " 3   Z " 16   75% T.S. 25% H.E.

504th & Forward Section
C/104th Bde   Time Shrapnel throughout
    75% Time Shrapnel 25 % H.E.

Remainder

TABLE "A" Contd.

3. 4.5. Hows.

(a) Tasks.

Battery.

	Time From	To		Objective.
86th	Zero	Zero plus 15.		1 How. on each Q.34.d.35.80., 30.85 Q.34.b.3.0., 3.1., 25.25., 45.45.
D/104th	"	"	" "	House Q.34.b.0.2. (Hows) Enclosure Q.33.d.95.95. to Q.34.a.2.2. (2 Hows). Edge of Wood Q.34.a.05.55. to 10.65 (2 Hows).
1 Battery 3rd D.A.	"	"	" "	Copse Q.34.d.70.85. (2 Hows) Shellholes about Q.34.b.75.00 (2Hows) Shellholes about Q.34.b.95.20 (2Hows)

(b) Rate of Fire.

    Zero to Zero plus 4 mins. .... 3 r.p.g.p.m.
    Zero plus 4 to Zero plus 12 .... 2 r.p.g.p.m.
    Zero plus 12 to Zero plus 15.... .... 1 r.p.g.p.m.

(c) Ammunition.

    H.E., 106th Fuze.

(3) 6" Hows.

    2 Hows. each on (a) Shellholes at Q.34.a.75.86.
                   (b) Shellholes at Q.34.a.85.22.
                   (c) Old Rifle Butt at Q.28 .c.45.15.

Rate of Fire.

    Section fire 30 secs. from Zero to Zero plus 15 minutes.

Ammunition.

    H.E. 106 Fuze.

(4) Trench Mortars.

    1 - 9.45" T.M. will fire at enclosure and houses in Q.28.d.
    1 - 6" Newton will fire on House Q.35.b.65.60.

(5) Counter Batteries will be requested to neutralise hostile Batteries from Zero plus 3 minutes until hostile fire ceases.

TABLE "B".

3" Stokes Mortars. (3 Guns)

Rate of fire.

Zero to Zero plus 12 minutes.
   1 gun at Q.34.c.65.35. will fire on junction
of Roads at Q.34.d.40.65.
   2 guns at Q.33.d.75.40 will fire on edge
of wood from Q.34.c.10.75 to Q.34.c.1.6.
include small out building at Q.34.c.10.75.

8 r.p.g.p.m. from Z to Z plus 5 mins.

5 r.p.g.p.m. from Z to Z plus 5 to Z plus 12.

TABLE "C".

Machine Guns.

(a) Two guns firing from Front Line trench about Q.34.c.80.35. direct on to shellholes Q.34.c.8.7.

(b) Two guns firing from Front Line Trench about Q.34.c.15.40 direct into shellholes Q.34.c.35.70.

(c) Six guns in position in Hill Trench to barrage area in Q.33.b. and Q.34.a.

(d) 3rd Battalion Machine Gun Corps are arranging to place a barrage of four guns on to neighbourhood od Road junction Q.34.b.3.4.

Enemy withdrawal from Pacaut Wood. August 5th-15th 1918.

The Battalion went up into the Pacaut Sector on the night of the 3rd/4th August by march route from Gantraimne and Busnettes to take over from the Rifle Brigade.

"B" Coy.   Front Line.
"C" Coy.   Support Line.
"D" Coy.   Canal Bank.
"A" Coy.   In Reserve.
H.Q. was at Stink Inn.
Map Sheet 36A. S.E. 1/20,000.

The relief started at 10;30 p.m. and was finished at 1:30 a.m. Aug. 4th. The Rifle Brigade told us on taking over that it was suspected that the enemy were going to withdraw as their patrols on the last two nights had found no trace of him. Accordingly Cos. were notified and told to pay special attention to patrolling. Accordingly on the night of the 4th strong patrols were pushed out and report enemy line unoccupied. On the early morning of the 5th however the enemy put down a heavy barrage on the front Co. and the King's Own lasting about 15 minutes at the same time attempting to raid the posts held by the King's Own in Pacaut Wood. The rest of that day was fairly quiet. At dusk fighting patrols were sent up from "C" Co. and pushed out into the enemy advance line which they occupied. Patrols continued to creep forward. The night 5/6th and all day the 6th and in the evening of the 6th "C" Co. was in possession of La Pannerie and the King's Own and Essex were half way through Pacaut Wood. Posts were established on the N. edge of La Pannerie for the night and the line ran back from there to the original line held by the Division on our right. At 1 a.m. on the morning of the 7th "C" Co. captured two prisoners of the R. Grenadier Guards. The prisoners were Alsations and talked French preferable to German. On being questioned at Bn. H.Q. they said that the enemy were still holding the N. edge of Pacaut Wood but were to withdraw during the night. They were immediately sent on to Brigade H.Q. and at 4:30 a.m. orders were received from Brigade for the pursuit which was to take the form of "peaceful" penetration. Orders were at once issued to Cos. to assemble. Zero hour being at 8 a.m.

"C" Co. under Capt. A.D.Macdonald, M.U. was to be the leading Company and was to assemble in the posts held during the night 6/7th. "B" Co. under Capt. T.H.Robinson was to assemble in Front Line and became Support Co. "A" Co. under 2nd Lt. C.Dunlevy M.C. moved up from Brigade Reserve Line to the Support Line, and became Bn. Reserve. "D" Co. under Capt. S.Clarke M.C., remained on the Canal Bank and became Brigade Reserve. Two objectives were laid down by the Brigade. - 1st and 2nd Yellow Lines. At 8 a.m. "C" Co. in touch with the King's Own on the left but with their right in the air moved forward followed closely by "B" & "D" Cos. The opposition consisted mainly of scattered enemy snipers and an occasional Machine Gun Team. By 9:30 a.m. the first Yellow Line had been reached with only a few casualties which included 2nd. Lt. P.Deschamps who had joined the Battalion about 3 weeks previously. At 9 a.m. the enemy artillery came to life and put down a very nasty barrage of 4.2 H.E. and Whizz Bangs on La Pannerie which fell right into the midst of "A" Co. However "A" Co moved forward and only lost one or two wounded. This went on till about 10 a.m. when it stopped. Meanwhile the Division on the right who had only come into the line on the night of the 6/7th had not moved and apparently knew nothing about the proceedings. This left "C" & "B" Cos. right flanks very much exposed and accordingly 2nd. Lt. J.E.S.Malpass with a platoon of "A" Co. was sent up to form a defensive flank and get in touch with the Division on the right. This was carried out successfully and Brigade was informed at 11 a.m. that the first Yellow Line had been reached.

At 10 a.m. an advanced Bn. H.Q. consisting of C.O., or Adjt. percentage of Signallers and a percentage of Orderlies was formed at Burke Farm. At 4 p.m. Bn. H.Q. proper moved up to Halfway House and joined Bn. H.Q. with the King's Own.

Except for occasional snipping the enemy was fiarly quiet all day. At 11 p.m. however his artillery got on to Burke Farm and the original Front Line and dosed it for an hour with H.E. and Blue Cross shell (Gas) without however doing any damage. The casualties for the 7th were 2nd Lt. P.Deschamps and 6 O.R's wounded.

The line at dawn on the 8th was much the same as the previous night. During the mornings orders were received to try and establish a line of posts on the Turbeaute River which was the 2nd Yellow Line. Accordingly patrols were pushed out and followed up. On the right of the line the 19th Division should have been up and established posts in Vert Bois Farm. As however they had not yet moved the right of the line swung back a bit and patrols reported Vert Bois Farm held by enemy Machine Guns and the "peaceful" penetration move on that flank was held up. On the left however the movement was continued for about 200 yds when another Farm was run into. Now the orders received up to date was that no fighting was to be carried out, but only Farms etc. vacated by the Hun were to be occupied. Accordingly no attempt was made to encircle or capture this farm. Brigade however on being told suggested that we try and take it, which suggestion was passed on to Macdonald who in his turn passed it on to 2nd Lt. C.C.Bracewell, a boy of 19 years, one of his platoon commanders. This Officer - however - could only pass it on to one person - i.e. the Hun, which he proceeded to do. He made his dispositions - pushed a section off to the right - another to the left which he personally led, and left his 3rd section to worry the occupants from in front whilst the other two worked their way round. In a very short space of time the Hun saw what was happening and "buzzed". Bracewell occupied the Farm and came back to Bn. H.Q. to report - wounded. The little effort was extremely well carried out and the Farm became known as Bracewell Farm. The line now ran - 5 p.m. 8th. practically parallel with the river about 200 yards short of it from Bracewell Farm - to just N. of Le. Vert Bois Farm, from where it ran back to get touch with the 19th Division.

At the same time as Bracewell was wounded, Cocker also of "C" Co. was hit and sent back. This left Macdonald with no officers. "C" Co had now been on the go since the night 4/5th. The enemy artillery had been putting down spasmodic barrages throughout the operations - wherefore the whole Company was about played out. "A" Co. in Reserve meanwhile had moved back to the original Front Line and except for nightly shelling had not had a hard time. Accordingly "A" Co was sent orders to relieve "C" Co. in what was to become the outpost line "B" Co. would remain in Support. 2nd Lt. Longlands, A/CSM Brown of "A" Co. and 2 N.C.O's were sent up to take over the Front from "C" Co. prior to the relief The party not knowing the country walked right through the outposts line and apparently on to an enemy post. 2nd Lt. Longlands gave the order to clear out but only the two N.C.O's got back and neither Langlands or Brown were seen or heard of since. Patrols were sent out to look for them but no trace of them was found.

OPERATION ORDER - LAN. FUS.

Map. Ref. Trench Map. Monchy Sector.

1. **OPERATIONS.** The Battalion will carry out a raid on the enemy's trenches on the night 15/16th November.

2. **OBJECT OF RAID.**
   1. To take prisoners.
   2. To obtain identifications.
   3. To harass the enemy.

3. **STRENGTH.** The raiding party will consist of one officer and 20 Other Ranks from "A" Coy. (2nd Lt. R. Walden).

4. **OBJECTIVE.** Long Trench between O.2.b.4.5. - O.2.b.5.0.

5. **POINT OF ENTRANCE.** O.2.b.4.3.

6. **PLAN.** The Raiding Party will form up for the raid at the Lewis Gun post in Twin Copse O.2.b.05.20. Supported by Artillery, T.M., and M.G. fire the party will cross "No man's land" in file. The general direction from starting point to point of entrance to enemy's lines is due EAST. The Officer leading the raid will carry the beginning of a 200 yards length of tape, each man of the raiding party holding this tape. This will ensure no straying or loss of direction. On reaching the enemy's lines the party will branch alternatively man North and South, moving up the trench 50 yards in each direction. The head of Poodle Trench will be held by a bombing party, to be told off by the officer in charge of the raiders.

The officer will remain at the point of entrance and give the raiders eight minutes in which to take prisoners and kill any enemy resisting and bomb dugouts if any. In the event of no prisoners being taken identifications must be brought back off any dead. Shoulder straps or letters which are usually found in the pocket in the tail of the coat. At the end of eight minutes, Officer will give the signal to retire and raiding party will make their way back as they went finally rendezvousing at Battalion H.Q. Artillery, M.G. and T.M. will co-operate with this movement. A time table is attached.

45.

7. **EQUIPMENT.** Raiding party will carry rifle and fixed bayonet, full magazine and one round in the breach, 2 bombs per man. All marks of identification will be removed before starting i.e. badges, letters, pay book, red and green identification discs. Special discs will be issued. The officer will carry a compass and a whistle. Men will wear white arm bands. Steel helmets and gas respirators will be worn.

8. **PRELIMINARY OPERATIONS.** **Artillery.** Wire cutting will be carried out by daylight in conjunction with other normal shoots. The area of "No man's land" will be patrolled every night and reconnoitred by the officer and N.C.O. and picked men of the Raiding party. Special attention is to be paid to the state of enemy wire; his manner of holding the line i.e. if forward posts. The raiding party will practise the assembly crossing "No man's land" and the attack by day and by night with and without leaders. Track from Canister to Twin Copse will be taped night 15/16th.

9. **MACHINE GUN BARRAGE.** 4 guns of the 12th Machine Gun Co. situated in East Reserve Trench will give covering fire with Western edge of the Bois du Sart as target. The M.G. Officer will arrange rates of fire in conjunction with the movements of the raiders. 2 guns of the Divisional M.G.Co. situated in Spade Reserve R.1. and R.2. will fire on their S.O.S. lines on the Bois du Vert. 1 gun of Divisional M.G.Co. will fire on Cigar Copse during the operations. Lewis Guns in the front line will co-operate.

10. **STOKES MORTARS.** Will fire according to Time Programme and as shewn on the map. Newton 6" Mortars will fire during the operation on Foal Trench and the Mound. Arranged by the Artillery.

11. **ARTILLERY BARRAGE.** One minute after zero, Artillery will put down a light barrage on Hen Foal and to the North as shown on the map. 15 minutes after zero their barrage

will change to part of trench raided. Raiding party will be clear. Barrages on two other fronts will be put down at the same time as a blind.

12. TO INDENT FOR:-   White Armlets   42.
　　　　　　　　　　 Mills Bombs   42.
　　　　　　　　　　 Identity discs, Special, will be
　　　　　indented for by "A" Co.
　　　　　　　　　　 500 yds of Tape.

N.B. 200 yds of tape to be sent direct to "A" Co. in the Brown Line. Remainder and other articles to be sent to Bn. H.Q.

　　　　　　　　　(Signed) V.F.S.Hawkins, Capt.
　　　　　　　　　　　　 Comdg. 2nd Lan. Fus.

AMENDMENT.

PLAN. Insert at end :-

COVERING PARTY.   The Lewis Gun post at C.2.b.01.01. will be advanced 50 yds. into "No man's Land" to act as covering party on the flank of the attack.   4 Stretcher bearers will accompany the Raiding party, remaining at the point of entrance to help any wounded back. These will be detailed by the Medical Officer. Any prisoners captured/will at once be sent back via the tape under escort to Battalion H.Q. The party will report to Bn. H.Q. by Zero minus 2½ hours and will be assembled by Zero minus ½ hour on night of 15/16th.

TIME PROGRAMME.

Zero hour minus 1 min.	Stokes Mortar barrage as shown lasting 1 min.
Zero hour.	Raiding Party advance M.G. Open rapid fire.
Zero plus 1 min.	Artillery barrage and medium T.M.
Zero plus 5 mins.	M.G. slow rate of fire.
Zero plus 10 mins.	Raiding party retire.
Zero plus 15 mins.	M.G. open rapid and artillery barrage on Raided trench. Stokes Mortars fire for one minute, as shewn on Map.
Zero plus 20 mins.	Cease fire.

SECRET.

32nd Brigade No. H/2135.

27th Battery.
434th Battery.
135th Battery.
86th Battery.

RAID BY LANCS. FUS. ON NIGHT 15/16th NOVEMBER.

(1) Strength of Party:- One Platoon.

(2) Forming up Point:- O.2.b.20.25.

(3) Enter in single file at O.2.b.45.23.
Party divides and moves out to O.2.b.50.00 and O.2.b.35.35.
Party returns by same route.

(4) Artillery support (proposed).

(a) <u>18 Pdrs.</u> At Zero plus 1.

Barrage.	Guns.	Battery.	Objective.
A	5	134	Front Line O.2.d.60.75. - O.2.d.53.93.
B	5	135	Front Line and Sap O.2.b.30.45. - O.2.b.30.60.
C	4	27	Hen and Trench O.2.d.6 O.80.- 85.95.
D	5	29th Bde	Foal Trench O.2.d.85.95 - O.2.b.75.20
E	5	15th D.A.	Trenches in area O.2.b.75.20.-O.2.b.80.35-62.40-60.35.
F	5	15th D.A.	O.2.b.65.40-30.65.

At Zero plus 3 mins.

G   A Barrage will lift to Front Trench from O.2.d.60.80 to Infantry Land.
H   B Barrage will lift to Front Trench from O.2.b.30.50 (including Sap to O.2.b.15.80.
K   C Barrage will left off Hen Trench in O.2.d.

At Zero plus 20 mins all Batteries of 32nd Brigade will fire 3 rounds per gun on S.O.S. Lines.

Rate of Fire.

Zero to Zero plus 3 mins. ... 3 rounds per gun per min.

Zero plus 3 to Zero plus 16 mins 2 " " " "

Ammunition.

A?B?C?G.H.K. Shrapnel throughout.

Remainder 75% H.E. Fuze 101E 25% Shrapnel.

(b) <u>4.5" Hows.</u> Zero plus 1 min. to Zero plus 16 mins.

Barrage	Guns.	Battery	Objective
L	2	86	Trench elements O.2.b.45.70-70.75.
	3	86	Poodle Trench in O.3.a.
M.	4	15th D.A.	Trench Mortar positions and

Barrage.	Guns.	Battery.	Objective.
M (contd)			Trench I.33.c.40.10 - 20.00 - 05.30.
M.	2	29th Bde.	O.9.a.70.90.
	1	" "	O.9.a.20.90.
	1	" "	O.3.c.35.50.
	1	" "	O.3.b.10.15.

Rate of Fire.

2 Rounds per gun per minute throughout.

(c) 6" Hows. Zero plus 1 min to Zero plus 16 mins.

As for M Barrage. As many rounds as possible.

(d) 9.45" T.M. Most active T.M. positions in Bois du Vert

(e) 6" Stokes. Active T.M. positions near the mound, O.3.c and O.9.a.

(f) Counter Batteries to fire if requested.

(g) Heavy artillery fire to be directed on portions of front line or flank to detract attention from actual front of attack.

(5) Following Liaison Officers will be found :-

(a) At left Battalion H.Q. Senior Subaltern from 135th Battery.

(6) 6" Stokes Mortars will cut wire from O.2.d.55.80 to O.2.b.20.30. with particular attention to wire in front of point of entry, of Raiding Party.

(7) A 3" Stokes Barrage will operate on the Front of Attack

(sgd) J.E.Nichols.
Lt. R.F.A.
13/11/1917. Adjutant, 32nd Brigade, R.F.A.

LEGEND.

———— Stokes Mortars. Zero minus 1 min to Zero and Zero plus 15 to Zero plus 16.

———— Light Artillery Barrage. Zero plus 1 to Zero plus 20 mins.

———— Machine Guns. Zero to Zero plus 20 mins.

———— Medium Trench Mortars. Zero plus 1 to Zero plus 20 mins

———— Artillery.

◁ Lewis Guns firing bursts.

4th Div. No.G.A.3/19.

XXII Corps.

I forward herewith report on the establishment of Bridgeheads across the Trinquis Brook. It was difficult to establish Bridgeheads as the ground was commanded and the Germans seemed anxious to prevent our crossing. I think great credit is due to the Lancashire Fusiliers who got across by surprising the enemy and established and held the bridgeheads under almost continual artillery fire, and frequent attempts to oust them, also to the Engineers who showed great perseverance in putting the bridges over and repairing them when destroyed.

We have thus :-

(a) got a good base for any further operations.
(b) got a footing across the obstacle which caused the Germans to be apprehensive of attack and to detain troops in the neighbourhood.
(c) caused casualties to the Germans.

Our casualties have in all been about 24.

                        (signed) L.J.Lipsett, Maj. Gen.
7/10/18.   Commanding 4th Division.

XXII Corps No.G.3400.

4th Division.

The Corps Commander has read with much interest the report forwarded with 4th Division No.G.A.3/19 of 7th October.

He considers that much credit is due to all concerned for the determination and energy shown in establishing a footing on the further side of the Trinquis. The work done has greatly facilitated the maintenance of contact with and pressure on the enemy, and has led up to the successful minor operation by the 1st Canadian Division today.

He wishes that his appreciation of their work should be communicated to all concerned.

                        (signed) C.W.Gwynn,
8/10/18.   B.G., G.S., XXII Corps.

12th Inf. Brigade. No.B.M.1/57/4.

1st King's Own.
2nd Lan. Fus.
2nd Essex Regt.
12th L.T.M. Battery
9th Field Co. R.E.

The Brigadier has much pleasure in forwarding the attached letter from XXII Corps. Will you please see that the Corps Commanders appreciation is communicated to all concerned.

(sgd) GGGGGGGGGGGGGG   Captain.
Brigade Major, 12th Inf. Brigade.

11/10/18.

50.

Report by Capt. A.Howarth, M.C. Commanding "D" Coy. 2nd Lancashire Fusiliers, on enterprise 5/6th October 1918.

The Company relieved the Centre Company King's Own on the night 2/3rd October 1918.

On the morning of the 3rd the Brigadier visited Co.H.Q and expressed his wish that we should cross the Trinquis Brook. He explained the situation and the difficulties to be overcome and asked if I, as a Company Commander, had any suggestions on a scheme for making the crossing. He pointed out that bridging material was at hand and the R.E's were at our disposal, also the Artillery, T.M's & M.G's if necessary. I asked for a little time to appreciate the situation and decided on the method of action, whereupon he left it to me to let him know my decision.

I had a conference with my Platoon Commanders, 2nd. Lt. D.Blore and 2nd Lt. E.J.H.Orchard and after a careful study of maps and aeroplane photos, we thought it necessary to reconnoitre the place in daylight. After explaining to the Company Scouts Cpl.Beggs and Pte. Lackey,M.M. they with 2ndLt. D.Blore reconnoitred the approach to the River. 2nd Lt. E.J.H.Orchard and myself observing the progress from Company O.P. Seeing the river edge gained without opposition, I decided to attempt a crossing.

Lt. E.J.H.Orchard and myself went over the river and while 2nd Lt. D.Blore and the Company Scouts kept a look out, 2nd E.J.H.Orchard waded waist deep into the river and secured two planks to the dam. That done Cpl. Beggs and Pte. Lackey,M.M., crossed to the N.E. side followed by 2nd Lt. E.J.H.Orchard, 2ndLT.Blore and myself. Time 3:15.

We hurriedly reconnoitred the far bank and found a gun pit and dug out entrance full of water. The two covering L.G. Sects. then moved across and took up positions on the flanks with the Scouts covering the front.

C.S.M.Baines, D.C.M. observing the progress from

Co. H.Q. and with Orderly previously arranged, sent two platoons to take up positions on the S.W. side of the river. I then returned to Company H.Q. to inform Bn. H.Q. of the situation. Almost immediately the Adjutant came into H.Q. having been up to see the situation and in comjunction with him I informed Brigade H.Q. of the situation and arranged for the present S.O.S. Lines for the Artillery to be altered. At the same time I arranged with the Adjutant to let me have two extra Signallers who were sent up that evening and visual established with the forward posts.

The posts as then established were one at J.26.c.5.6., one in the old gun pit at J.26.c.7.6. and the third in the A.A. Post at J.26.c.9.5.

When the posts were well established I ordered patrols to reconnoitre right and left. An enemy post was found at the sluice gate.

Pte. Taylor opened fire on the position with a L.G. and set fire to a Very Light Dump. The Hun immediately cleared in disorder. By this time many Huns were on the move and afforded some good targets for the Artillery. At the same time C.S.M. Baines, D.C.M. collected the men at Co. H.Q. and carried out overhead fire with success.

By this time the light was failing so we prepared to resist counter attacks but the night passed quietly. 2nd. Lt. D.Blore being on duty throughout the night. Before daybreak I relieved the men forward with two platoons from Co. H.Q. and 2nd Lt. E.J.H.Orchard relieving 2nd Lt. D.Blore

At daybreak the enemy raided the left post but 2nd Lt. E.J.H.Orchard with Sgt. Williams successfully dealt with it, killing one Hun, the rest being put to flight. 2nd E.J.H. Orchard then occupied the sluice gate Pill box, and found the Bosch that was killed. All identification had been removed but a torn up message was found and sent to Bn.H.Q.

At 10 a.m. 2nd E.Halstead from "A" Co. relieved 2nd Lt

E.J.H.Orchard and all went well during the day. 2nd Lt. D. Blore relieved 2nd Lt. E. Halstead at 3 p.m. and at 7:30 p.m. the enemy raided the left post for the second time but was driven off with L.G. fire. The enemy persistently threatened the left flank and I asked the Adjutant for support from "C" Co. as owing to the flood they could not render any assistance from the S.W. side of the river. At 8 p.m. Capt. G.N.Stange M.C., sent a patrol across the bridge at J.26.c.65.40 and they patrolled during the night from my left post at J.26.c.5.5. to the sluice gate at J.26.a.3.3. This patrol was withdrawn at daylight.

2nd Lt. E.J.H.Orchard relieved 2nd Lt. D.Blore at 8 p.m and 2nd Lt. E.Halstead relieved 2nd E.J.H.Orchard at 3 a.m. the 5th. At 5:15 a.m. a heavy bombardment started and at 5:45 a.m. the barrage lifted and the right post was raided, but was successfully repulsed, the Bosche scuttering before our L.G. fire in disorder, leaving behind rifles equipment and an automatic raiding gun.

In repelling this attack Pte. Turner showed great coolness when about to be bayoneted, grasping the bayonet with his hand and warding off the point. One man threw bombs with good effect from A A Post. Pte. Beardmore got his L.G. into action by climbing out of his post and placing his gun on the bank side.

The above was an attempt by the Hun to cut off the post by attacking from under the bank. 2nd Lt. D.Blore relieved 2nd Lt. E.Halstead at 8 a.m. At 9 A.m. a steady bombardment started and was kept up throughout the whole day. At 2 p.m. 2nd Lt.E.J.H.Orchard relieved 2nd Lt. D. Blore and from 3 p.m. to 7 p.m. the bombardment was increased to drum fire. During this period all communication between the forward positions and Company H.Q. were cut off Judging from the intensity of the bombardment I thought an attack was imminent, so ordered a stand to at Company H.Q. and prepared to deal with any attack.

At 7:15 p.m. the barrage lifted into Meadow Lane. 2nd Lt. E.J.H.Orchard thinking the time had come, stood to, and had no sooner done so, when two Huns were seen approaching from the wire around Sailly. Fire was opened on them and directly after an enemy M.G. opened fire from our right flank, at the same time a party of Huns were seen approaching under cover of the bank.

Another party was observed creeping forward with the intention of a frontal attack, they were in extended order. 2nd. Lt. E.J.H.Orchard fired the S.O.S. and instantly the artillery put down a good barrage. All L.G.s opened fire and 2nd Lt. D. Blore with 15 Platoon moved across the valley in extended order, having a heavy barrage to pass through. He successfully reinforced 2nd. Lt. E.J.H.Orchard on the far side of the river. 2nd Lt. E.Halstead with 13 Platoon moved across the valley and took up a position in shell holes in close support to 2nd Lt. E.J.H.Orchard and 2nd Lt. D.Blore.

During this attack Pte. Boyd, 2nd Lt. Orchard's runner did very good service, and though badly shaken and suffering slightly from gas, he refused to leave his Officer, finally he brought a message back to Co.H.Q. reporting that the attack had been repulsed, without the enemy having gained a foothold in the positions.

After the attack when things had been reorganised, the forward positions were held by three platoons and on our left Capt. G.N.Stange, M.C. sent 2nd Lt. D.A.Nickson with No.9 Platoon to establish posts on either side of the sluice gate. When in position the 9th Field Co. R.E. endeavoured to erect a bridge across the sluice gates, but owing to the rough state of the sluice walls and the depth of the water it was found impossible to complete the work that night. At daybreak the posts were withdrawn by the bridge at J.26.c.65.40.

I also had one L.G. Section sent from Capt. G.N.

54.

Stange, M.G. and placed them on the road at J.26.d.3.2. They were to deal with any of the enemy approaching under the bank at J.26.d.2.4. to d.5.6.

When things had quietened down 2nd Lt. D.Blore and 2nd Lt. E.Halstead took over.

The bombardment ceased after the attack, but during the night enemy patrols twice attempted to raid the left post, but were driven off.

My men having had little rest and also sleep during the tour and having suffered terrific bombardments were very fatigued, so I asked H.Q. for a relief. The Adjutant's cheery reply was to hang on for that night as we knew the situation and it would not be any good putting new troops into that position in the dark, - he would send up two platoons from "A" Co. to help next day.

At 5 a.m. 6th 2nd Lt. E.J.H.Orchard and W.E?Ashley from "A" Co. along with two fresh platoons from "A" Co. relieved 2nd Lts. D.Blore and E.Halstead.

At 7:30 a.m. the Brigadier visited the forward posts and expressed his appreciation for the way the men had held on to the position.

At 8 a.m. 2nd Lt. E.J.H.Orchard crawled out and secured identification from a Bosche N.C.O. who had been killed during the attack.

At 11 a.m. 2nd. Lts.D.Blore and E.Halstead relieved 2nd Lts. E.J.H.Orchard and W.E.Ashley. At the same time a heavy bombardment started and it was not until two hours later that they were able to cross the bridge and then at great risk.

At 11:30 a.m. 2nd Lt. D.Blore was severely wounded and only with great difficulty and risk was he safely taken to the aid post.

The bombardment was kept up until 7 p.m. when it ceased The intensity of the bombardment can be judged from the number of shells all of a heavy calibre.

From 1 - 1:30 p.m.   76 shells burst.
From 1:30 - 2:5 p.m.   119   "   "
From 2:5 - 4 p.m.   140   "   "

The heaviest concentration was 35 in 5 minutes.

2nd Lt. E.Halstead during the bombardment showed great coolness and cheerfulness, and throughout kept communication by visual with Company H.Q.

At 7 p.m. 2nd Lt. E.J.H.Orchard relieved E. Hastead and successfully handed over the outposts line to the Canadian Scottish.

During the three days in this position the bridges were damaged repeatedly and much can be said for the way in which the R.E's carried out their work under such trying conditions.

4th Div. G.A. 38/26.

12th Infantry Brigade.

The following wire was received from XXII Corps on 6th October 1918 :-

"The Corps Commander wishes you to convey his congratulations to all Officers, N.C.O's and men of the posts which have been established North and East of the Trinquis Brook Canal on their successful repulse of various enemy attacks AAA Their bold action and tenacity in sticking to these posts has been of the greatest value in deceiving the enemy as to our intentions."

(Signed) J. Stanley Rogers, Capt.
for Lt. Colonel. General Staff, 4th Division.

6th October 1918.

MOJO (2nd Lancashire Fusiliers.)
Q.137 6th.

Following received from ZIZO timed 1115 begins AAA Following addressed G.O.C. ZIZO timed 0920 has been received from Corps.AAA The Corps Commander wishes you to convey his congratulations to all Officers N.C.O's and men of the posts which has been established N.and E. of the Trinquis Brook Canal on their successful repulse of enemy attacks AAA Their bold action and tenacity in sticking to their posts has been of the great value in deceiving the enemy as to our intentions AAA ends. Addressed Units Peno.

Quake (12th Infantry Brigade). 1310.

MOJO. (2nd Lancashire Fusiliers).
G.130. 5th.

Please convey to all ranks concerned Brigade Commanders congratulations for splendid endurance and defence shown by the garrisons of the posts North of the Trinquis Brook.

Quake. (12th Infantry Brigade).

4th Div. No.G.C. 7/25.

12th Infantry Brigade.

Please convey to the O.C. 2nd Lancashire Fusiliers and those who took part in establishing posts across the river in J.26.c. my appreciation of their good work.
It is a very valuable position to gain and showed very considerable enterprise on the part of those concerned.

4th October 1918. (signed) G. Lipsett, Major General.
Commanding 4th Division.

2.

2nd Lan. Fus.

The Brigade Commander has much pleasure in forwarding the above message from the Divisional Commander.
(signed) D.McCallum, Capt. Bde. Major,
12th Infantry Brigade.

5/10/18.

Raid Orders
By
Lieut Colonel F. E. B. Freeth. C.M.G. D.S.O.
Commanding 2nd Bn Lancashire Fusiliers.

(1) DETAIL. A raiding party of 2 Officers. 1 Sergeant and 30 men will enter the German Trenches at K.35.C.21.35 at 12-30 a.m. on the night of the 9th July.

(2) DISTRIBUTION OF PARTY. The party will be divided into 3 groups:-
"A" Group -   2 Lieut Waghorn and 10 men.
"B"   "   -   Sergt Wetherall and 10 men.
"C"   "   -   Lieut Greaves and 10 men.

The latter group will be in support.

(3) DETAIL.
(I.) The party will assemble at midnight in Trench 2, near BEET Street.

(II.) At 12-30 a.m. Groups A + B will go out over the parapet and move to a disused trench EAST of our line.

(III.) At 12-35 a.m. Groups A + B will advance and enter the enemy's trenches, each party leaving two men at the point of entrance, and turning outwards will raid down the front line trench for a distance of not more than 50 yards in each direction.

Group C will move from our front line trench to the disused trench and will remain there.

(IV.) If possible prisoners will be made of any Germans that are met. Any Germans found in dug-outs who refuse to surrender will be bombed.

(V.) Directly either party has made as many prisoners as it can control, it will return to the point of entrance and take the prisoners back to the supporting group, the 2 men originally left behind remaining at the point of entrance until the other group returns.

(VI) Neither party will remain longer than 10 minutes in the German Trenches.

(VII) Communication Trenches will be blocked until the parties have returned.

(VIII) On return, the party will re-assemble at Batt'n Head Quarters.

(4) EQUIPMENT. Rifle and Bayonet, one bandolier, and haversack slung on the right side by one brace with 8 Mills grenades, the other brace round the waist to keep the haversack in place. Steel Helmets. Tube helmets will not be taken.

All identity discs and other means of identification will be left behind.

(5) ENGINEERS. 2 Royal Engineers will accompany each of Groups "A" and "B", carrying explosives, in order to blow in any mine shafts that may be encountered.

(6) MACHINE GUNS. The raid will be supported by Lewis Gun fire on both flanks. Special attention will be paid to the mine craters East of the REDAN. The guns will be so sited as to bring cross fire on the enemy's line adjacent to the point of entrance, after the raiding party has left the German trenches on their return journey.

(7) AID POST. An aid post will be established in "B" Coy's Headquarters, FREDDY STREET.

(8) WATCHES. All watches will be synchronised at 11-0 pm at Batt'n Head Quarters.

(9) INSTRUCTIONS RE. ARTILLERY. Instructions regarding Artillery and Stokes Gun support will be issued later.

(Sd) G. Freeth. Lt Col.
Comd'g 2 Lancs Fus'rs

4th Division
War Diaries
12th Infantry Bde
2nd Lancs Fus.

August to December
1914

12th Brigade.

4th Division.

2nd BATTALION

THE LANCASHIRE FUSILIERS

AUGUST 1 9 1 6

WAR DIARY
or
INTELLIGENCE SUMMARY.
(Erase heading not required.)

Army Form C. 2118.

2 Lancs Fus

VOl 23

Place	Date	Hour	Summary of Events and Information	Remarks and references to Appendices
Field Camp O/C A 30 d.2.9.	August 1st		Ref: Map Belgium Sheet 29.N.W. 1/20,000	
			Anniversary Minden Day - G.O.C 12th Inf Bde inspected Bn. in the morning. Company - Platoon Purries in camp.	
	2nd		In camp during the day.	
	3rd		Moved by night Hqrs. B. 2 platoons of C and D in to Chateau De Trois Tours B.26.d.7.1 and A.C and 2 platoons of C in to Canal Bank C.25.d.8.3	
Ad Reserve				
	4th		Relieved 9th Seaforth Highlanders in trenches in C.15.c & d	
Trenches			Hqrs on Right 1st Bn. East Lancashire Regt on left	
	5th		Quiet day. Machine gun activity at night. Casualties - Nil.	
	6th		Occasional bursts of shell fire. Little damage. Casualties - 4 O.R. Wounded	
	7th		Quiet day. Casualties - Nil	
	8th		Enemy seemed to be registering on different places in and behind the line. 10 p.m. Heavy bombardment of trenches with shell fire and French mortars began. Enemy Support Brigades was done to the trenches by the bombardment. French damage considering the fact that the bombardment on our right and left. Casualties small considering the fact that Pleeshinge and Royal Rance in Regt were blowing up at the time the bombardment commenced and were all in the trenches with us. Casualties Killed 2 O.R. Wounded 4 O.R.	

Army Form C. 2118.

WAR DIARY
or
INTELLIGENCE SUMMARY.
(Erase heading not required.)

Instructions regarding War Diaries and Intelligence Summaries are contained in F.S. Regs., Part II. and the Staff Manual respectively. Title pages will be prepared in manuscript.

Place	Date	Hour	Summary of Events and Information	Remarks and references to Appendices
Furnes	August 8th		On relief Major A.C. & 2 Platoons 1st Bn went to Chateau de Trois Tours and Bn 2 Platoon 1st Bn to Canal Bank.	
"	9th 10th 11th		In billets as above. Day and night working parties.	
Rifle Reserve				
"	12th		Relieved 1st Bn K.O.R. Lanc Regt in Furnes. Intermittent shelling during the day. Hq Bn Wings damaged at night. Casualties 1 O.R. wounded.	
Furnes	13th		Quiet day. Hour communication trench wings banged. Casualties 2 O.R. wounded.	
"	14th		Quiet day. Casualties 2 O.R. wounded.	
"	15th		Enemy bombed one of our isolated posts. Casualties 2 O.R. killed 2 O.R. wounded.	
"	16th		Bn. relieved at night by 1st K.O.R. Lanc Regt. Hd. Qrs A&B Bns to H.S. (H.S. Central) C&D Bns to Canal Bank.	
Rode Reserve	17th		Bn in Bde Reserve.	
"	18th 19th		Relieved by 17th R.W. Fus. in Bde. Reserve. Proceeded by train to POPERINGHE. Lt. Harris accidentally wounded.	

WAR DIARY
or
INTELLIGENCE SUMMARY.
(Erase heading not required.)

Army Form C. 2118

Place	Date	Hour	Summary of Events and Information	Remarks and references to Appendices
	August			
Trenches	20-22nd		In Billets at Poperinghe. Co. training. Relieved 2nd Canadian Mounted Rifles in trenches.	
"	23rd		Casualties. 1 O.R. wounded.	
"	24-27th		Enemy Artillery, Trench Mortars and Machine Gun active. Casualties 3 killed 6 wounded. Casualties I 34.b. and I 30 g.d.	
"	28th		Relieved by 1st K.O.R. Lanc Regt. On relief moved into OTTAWA Camp. C 24 c.8.5 In Camp. Co. training.	
Div Reserve 29 A 30			G.O.C. II Div presented decorations to Officers and Men than of 12th Bde. Battalion paraded.	
"	31st		Relieved in Camp by 5 Australian Infantry, and moved into Billets at POPERINGHE.	

E.M. Wilson

P. Col.

Commdg. 2nd Lancashire Fusiliers

12th Brigade.

4th Division.

2nd BATTALION

THE LANCASHIRE FUSILIERS

SEPTEMBER 1916

WAR DIARY or **INTELLIGENCE SUMMARY**

Army Form C. 2118

2 Lowes Ins

Place	Date	Hour	Summary of Events and Information	Remarks
	September 1916			
	1st 2nd 3rd		In billets at POPERINGHE La Lovie.	
	4th		Hd Qr A+D Coy moved to ELVERDINGHE B+C Coy " " to BRANDHOEK	
	5-15th		In billets as above. A+D Coy found day working parties on ELVERDINGHE Defences. B+C Coy " " night " " near ST JEAN	
	16th		G.O.C. VIIIth Corps spoke to Hd Qr A+D Coy and informed them that the IVth Div had been selected to go down South again. At 6 p.m. moved to billets in POPERINGHE	
	17th	9.14 am 10 p.m.	Bn entrained at HOUT POUTRE Detrained at SALEUX. Marched to billets at COISY. arriving at 2.30 AM	
	18-21st		In billets at COISY. Coy Training.	
	22nd		A Coy moved to BERTANGLES, otherwise as above.	
	23rd 24th		As above	
	25th	3 p.m.	Bn moved to billets in ALLONVILLE at 5 p.m.	

WAR DIARY
or
INTELLIGENCE SUMMARY.

(Erase heading not required.)

Army Form C. 2118.

Place	Date	Hour	Summary of Events and Information	Remarks and references to Appendices
	September			
	26th		Battalion moved to St CORBIE	
	27th	10.30	In billets as the above. Coy: training. Bn: training (Attack practice).	

F.R.Willis Lt. Col.
Commanding: 2 Hamp: Regm:

12th Brigade.

4th Division.

2nd BATTALION

THE LANCASHIRE FUSILIERS

OCTOBER 1 9 1 6

Appendices attached :-

Reports on Operations 12th & 23rd Oct 1916.

Messages during operations.

WAR DIARY or INTELLIGENCE SUMMARY

Army Form C. 2118.

2 Royal Fus
Vol 25

24 V
Azehielo

Place	Date	Hour	Summary of Events and Information	Remarks and references to Appendices
ALBERT Centred Sheet 1/40,000 57D NE 57C NW 57D SE 57C SW	7/10/16 to 7/10/16		Battalion in billets at CORBIE. Company Battalion and Brigade training in the attack was carried out.	
	8/10/16		Battalion marched from CORBIE to CITADEL camp F.21.A.2. via CROSS country track. Battalion in huts and hutments.	
	9/10/16		Marched from CITADEL camp to trenches halted at TRONES WOOD took over SPECTRUM and DONALD trenches from QUEENS WESTMINSTER RIFLES. March was on all cross tracks. (Like) Commenced 12 o'c at night. Casualties in taking over. Wounded 1 officer. 6. O.R.	
	10/10/16		In trenches Enemy shelled front line heavily. Left of line blown in and working parties busy but but on general rebuilding as it got dark. Communication trench and GAMALIM H.Q. also shelled forward dug out SPECTRUM Heavy shelled. Casualties killed 12. O.R. wounded 1 officer 19. O.R. missing 3. O.R.	
	11/10/16		In trenches. Enemy shelled heavily around Bk. No Out relieved 6 [illegible] bk. Supplement continuing 16% of Battalion left the trenches for but Brigade. Reserve trenches. Forward dugs continued and connected up. Embarking advance trench measurably. Casualties killed 4 O.R. wounded 19 O.R.	
	12/10/16		In conjunction with 8th Divi an attack the Battalion was ordered to attack at 2.25 h.m. formed up in according trenches by 3.20 am. Very little hostile shelling during the morning. Our heavy artillery became active towards midday. The Battalion attacked at 2.25 h.m.	

2449. Wt. W14957/M90 750,000 1/16 J.B.C. & A. Forms/C.2118/12.

WAR DIARY
or
INTELLEIGENCE SUMMARY

Army Form C. 2

Place	Date	Hour	Summary of Events and Information	Remarks and references to Appendices
	12/10/16		The attack failed with heavy casualties. Report on attack. appendix (i) Important message received ___ (iiA) + (iiB) Important message despatched ___ (iii) Casualties Killed 4 officers 62 O.R. Wounded 6 officers 162 O.R. Missing 1 officers 100 O.R.	(i) (iiA)(iiB) (iii)
	13/10/16		In original trenches. Enemy shelled heavily all day. One Company went to support trench DONALD. 10% reinforcement returned to Battalion. Two patrols went out at night to reconnoitre ZENITH TRENCH and found it occupied by the enemy. Relieved by 2nd Essex Regt. Relief completed by 3·0 am 14/10/16. Marched to Brigade Reserve trenches BERNAFAY WOOD. Casualties Killed 2 O.R. Wounded 2 O.R.	
	14/10/16 15/10/16 16/10/16 17/10/16 18/10/16		In Brigade Reserve trenches. Working parties up to 200 strong out daylight and digging at night.	
	19/10/16		In Brigade Reserve trenches. Reinforcement of 176 O.R. joined the Battalion. 200 O.R. Battalion (less 30 officers and 120 O.R.) marched to Reserve trenches. JOHN BULL + COW arrived in trenches 11·30 pm. Battalion H.Q. situated at 72.R. Major BURKE D.S.O. R.I. Rif. took over command	

WAR DIARY or **INTELLIGENCE SUMMARY**

Army Form C. 2118.

3

Place	Date	Hour	Summary of Events and Information	Remarks and references to Appendices
	19/10/16		3 officers and 120 o.r. attached to 2nd Duke of Wellington (West Riding) Regiment in front line BARNABY - THISTLE TRENCHES. Remainder of Battalion went up to dig a trench from BARNABY to WINDY trench.	
	20/10/16		Same disposition as 19/10/16. Two working parties out at night 60 m communication trench. 80 m new trench from WINDY TRENCH	
	21/10/16		Same disposition as 20/10/16. Working Party 80 men on THISTLE TRENCH. Casualties Wounded 2 O.R. Missing 1 O.R.	
	22/10/16		JOHN BULL TRENCH heavily shelled. Battalion moved to assembly trenches THISTLE + WINDY. Sunken Road T.2.d 6.6 All troops in position by 1.30 am 23/10/16. Battalion HQ to dugout in Casualties. Killed 2 O.R. Wounded 2 O.R	
	23/10/16		In conjunction with the general attack the battalion was ordered to attack and consolidate DEWDROP TRENCH from the Sunken road, from LES BOEUFS to LE TRANSLOY, to where that trench curls back, about 250 yds South of this Sunken road. Included in the line the elements of trenches surrounding DEWDROP, including RAINY TRENCH. The Battalion was ordered to attack at 11.30 am, but owing to fog this was postponed till 2.30 pm. Report on attack appendix (IV)	Officers list (iv)

WAR DIARY or INTELLIGENCE SUMMARY

Army Form C. 2118.

Place	Date	Hour	Summary of Events and Information	Remarks and references to Appendices
	23/10/16		Important message received from O.C. 4 Battalion Appendice V & B. Important message to the attack was totally received. Our fire was advanced 150 yds a small trench being dug at that point and held. Casualties Killed Officer. 10 OR Wounded 49 OR Missing 1 – 85 OR	Appendices V A B VI
	24/10/16		The Battalion took over BURNABY TRENCH from 2nd Seaforth Highlanders at 11.0 am. Many mortars until about 3.0 pm when heavy bombardment was opened and trench badly blown in in places. Battalion relieved in trenches by 1st Middlesex Regt. Relief complete at 2.0 am. marched to dugouts at Briquetere A4 b 65. Casualties. 1 Battalion. 1 OR wounded 49 OR	
	25/10/16		Handed on at 9.50 am by 53rd security track to CITADEL CAMP. Arrived at 12 noon. Battalion in huts and tents. Reinforcement 1 OR joined Battalion	
	26/10/16		In camp at "CITADEL"	
	27/10/16		Marched to VILLE SUR ANCRE Battalion in billets. In billets at VILLE SUR ANCRE. Reinforcements 1 OR joined Battalion.	
	28/10/16		Marched to MERICOURT L'ABBÉ Station at 10 am. A Train battalion entrained at 12 noon for MÉZIÈRES. Detrained at AIRAINES and marched to billets at DREUIL. Transport marched at 6.0 am by road to DREUIL.	

Army Form C. 2118.

WAR DIARY
or
INTELLIGENCE SUMMARY

(Erase heading not required.)

Instructions regarding War Diaries and Intelligence Summaries are contained in F. S. Regs., Part II. and the Staff Manual respectively. Title Pages will be prepared in manuscript.

Place	Date	Hour	Summary of Events and Information	Remarks and references to Appendices
In Indiah DEBUR	30/10/16		Transport reported at H.Q from Rainforcement 137 O.R joined Battalion	
In Indiah DEBUR	31/10/16		Company training	

C J Burk
Lieutenant Colonel
Commanding 2nd Battalion Lancashire Fusiliers

APPENDIX

(1)

Report of the operations on Oct 12th

The LANCASHIRE FUSILIERS assembled for the attack in Spectrum Trench. Four companies were in the front line A.B.C.D from the right. We were the left assaulting Battalion of the Brigade with the Dukes on our right and the 6th Div. Yorks and Lancs on our left. Only one objective was finally laid down, the Brown line N 29 c 33 to N 28 b 81.

The Battn were to attack in 8 waves. The first 4 waves with a distance of 50ˣ between each were to take the objective, push patrols forward and dig in. The last 4 waves following at a distance of 200ˣ behind the first four, each with a distance of 50ˣ between them, were to dig a support trench 200ˣ in rear of the objective.

The LAN. FUS. were ordered to advance at .20 as the Dukes on our right had to take Spectrum before we could advance.

As regards when to leave our trenches we were ordered by the C.O. to use our discretion whether we left our trenches at zero and laid out in shell holes or leave at the appointed time for attack. 20 after zero, taking into consideration our own barrage and the enemy's barrage and Machine Gun fire.

Up to zero the enemy's machine guns were silent and very little sniping was done. All his shell fire was directed well behind our lines. Ten minutes before zero about 20 Germans left Zenith trench and ran towards us with their hands up. They seemed very demoralised. Ten of them succeeded in reaching us the remainder were killed. A small number were also seen to leave their trenches and run back. I think this is a ruse on their part as on each attack the same thing has happened and they may have some secret signal.

Two German Aeroplanes flew very low along our lines 10 mins. before zero and then made right away to the rear of their lines. All our men were kept well down in their trenches but I think they must have seen our trenches were full.

The two Right Companies decided it was best to leave their trenches at zero and lie out and at zero this was done. Very few casualties were suffered in doing this. The two left Companies left at .20 and by this time the machine guns were well going and immediately on leaving they were caught by them.

The whole Battalion left the trenches together and were caught in mass, very heavy losses being sustained. Immediately the Battalion got over the top, "C" Company Commander noticed that a small piece of trench in front of Zenith was manned by about 20 Germans with 2 Machine Guns. This piece held up the advance as they poured enfilade fire along the right Companies and prevented advance on the left.

Small isolated parties of the two centre Companies got past this trench and pushed forward 200 yards where they dug in. Unfortunately they were afterwards cut off and either captured or killed. This was at about 1 hour after Zero. From this time no advance was made and what few men were left hung up in shell holes and waited until dusk when they withdrew to our original line.

I think that the whole attack on the left failed through this small trench being quite overlooked as it was quite undamaged.

The Brigade Machine Guns rendered good assistance with their overhead fire

The German snipers were very good and I think more attention should be paid by us to sniping.

Our bombers unfortunately did not get into action as no part of the enemy's trench was taken.

The Lewis Guns advanced with the 2nd wave and with the exception of one could not get forward. One gun succeeded in pushing through with one of the isolated parties and got into position in a shell hole where it did considerable damage before it was eventually knocked out.

The Stokes Guns did not get into action at all. The would have been the greatest assistance to us had they remained in SPECTRUM and after observing the machine guns in the previously unobserved trench in front of ZENITH have poured a rapid fire on them this would have enabled the remaining men to push forward some distance.

Our Artillery barrage was very good but I think a F.O.O. should be in our front line and be in direct communication with the batteries. Several of our shells fell very short and caused us casualties in our own trench prior to the attack. The German barrage, chiefly with 5.9s was wholly directed well behind our lines and practically no casualties were sustained through it; the barrage on our front line was all by machine guns.

Suggestions

Lewis Guns should I think always advance with the last wave where they stand the least chance of being knocked out and are then ready to take up position immediately the objective is taken

Stokes Guns

These should render very great assistance if properly placed and a competent Officer actually in the trench. I think they should stay in our front line and observe where the advance is held up by machine guns and then direct their fire on that spot. The Officer in charge should act entirely on his own initiative and not wait for orders from the Company Commander to fire. It is very difficult to get messages to these detachments during heavy shelling.

Equipment

The method of carrying equipment was I think quite satisfactory.

The feeding arrangements could not I think have been improved upon

Communication was entirely by runner and this I think is the only way, it is very difficult for either discs or flags to be used during the actual attack.

APPENDIX (ii). A.

Important Messages received from 12th Brigade

Appendix (iiA)

To 2nd Lancashire Fusiliers

(1) Are you holding ZENITH AAA Brigade on left are held up AAA 10th Brigade have no information of their left Battalion but they have progressed as far as HAZY and 35 D AAA reports say DEWDROP is held by us AAA addressed RECORD repeated REDAN.

From 12th Brigade 4-50 p.m. Oct 12th/16.

To 2nd Lancashire Fusiliers

(1) Endeavour to push patrols into ZENITH and establish post co-operating with REDAN who should bomb down towards you. Addressed RECORD repeated REDAN.

From 12th Brigade Oct 12th 1916.

To 2nd Lancashire Fusiliers

Ref. your G.M.29 you will consolidate ground captured and organise your defences AAA M.G.Co have guns near you to support you AAA your 10% reinforcements have been ordered to reinforce AAA Report your disposition as soon as possible.

From 12th Brigade 5-30 p.m. 12th Oct/16.

To 2nd Lancashire Fusiliers

ZENITH Trench will be taken and held tonight AAA O.R. units with no one a combined raid on the part that is in front of our sector AAA RECKON will send 2 Companies to help to consolidate captured ground, they will report at the Windmill N33D at 9-30 p.m. where O.C. Lancashire Fusiliers and Dukes will meet them with guides AAA Acknowledge

From 12th Brigade 7-30 p.m. Oct 12th/16

To 2nd Lancashire Fusiliers

14th Corps wire AAA. It is essential that we should clear up situation tomorrow, contact aeroplanes will push out tomorrow at 8 a.m if weather is suitable not at 10am AAA. Troops will show their positions by flares, mirrors, etc AAA ends AAA O.C. Units will clear up situation as far as possible tonight and arrange to dig in on captured ground straightening the line as far as possible by pushing out patrols A.A.A. The 10th Brigade are reported on the BROWN LINE so no ground on our front should be given up and every opportunity should be taken to gain more ground during the night by patrols being pushed out to dig in.

From 12th Brigade 7-10 pm. 12th Oct/16.

To 2nd Lancashire Fusiliers

Aeroplane report reads confidently that we have troops in ZENITH. Patrols will be sent out by RECORD and REDAN to verify this and ammunition should be dug to them tonight by REFORM AAA. They are probably men of REDAN or right Company of 2nd Lancashire Fusiliers AAA Acknowledge.

From 12th Brigade 5·50 pm. 13th Oct/16.

APPENDIX (ii) B.

Important Messages received from Companies.

___

Appendix (ii) B.

To Adjutant 2nd Lancashire Fusiliers

"B" Company are in serious situation. All Officers are killed or wounded.

Reinforcements are required

From R. W. Anderson 2/Lt. B Co.

Octr 12th/16 3-30 pm

___

Progress Report.

A to C

To O.C. A Coy 2nd Lancashire Fusiliers 4010

ADDRESS 100 yards in front of our sector of trench

12th October 1916.

No 1

1 Situation reached Shell hole
2 Strength of Platoon (remaining) by Ranks:-

Cpl. J. Hall
Pte. G. Benson
 "   F. Maddox
 "   A. Hamer
2/Lt. S. W. Howarth
2/Lt.   Jones

7 General Remarks

We are in a Shell hole and have a Lewis Gun and two rifles.

From S. W. Howarth 2/Lt
2nd Lancashire Fusiliers C010
Sent by "Runner" at 5-25 P.M.

To Adjutant, 2nd Lancashire Fusiliers

A number of men are at present holding out in Shell holes about 100x in front of our trench. Enemy seems to have settled down again.

Have got Mr Hawkins and Mr Greaves in our trench.

From J. R. Laverick C.S.M. "B" Co/
Time 5-25 P.M.

To O.C. 2nd Lancashire Fusiliers

Have brought "D" Co to first line. No Officers or N.C.O's about 40 men whom am I to report to.

From W. Russell, Sgt. 2nd L.F.

Time 5-30 p.m.

To O.C. 'D' Coy.

I am awaiting orders about 80 yds in front. Germans have been reinforced. I have about 11 with me.

From W. Russell Sgt. 14 Platoon
Time 6 p.m. Oct 12th 1916.

To 2nd Lancashire Fusiliers

Attack failed, on left flank heavy Machine Gun fire enfiladed my Company. Odd parties have got forward about 200 yards but are outflanked and will have to retire or be surrounded.

I have crawled back to our line. Odd parties of each Coy have crawled in.

Have only found 6 of 'C' Coy up to present.

Casualties are very heavy. Am manning front line. Very lights required. Please advise me anything you know. Stretcher bearers badly needed. "C" Coy.

Place Spectrum
From J.W. Watkins Lt.
Time 6-10 P.M.

Progress Report

B. Co. 2nd Lancashire Fusiliers 4010.

Address   Original Front line trench
12th October 1916.

No 2

1 Situation, unaltered. See previous report
2 Strength of Company (remaining) by Ranks :—

2 Lt. S. W. Howarth
Sergeants   Nil
One Corporal
Two Lance Corporals
15 Rank & File.

3 General Remarks

This is as much as I am able to give you at present. There is every hope that several are in shell holes in front of our line and may come in anytime now.

From S. W. Howarth 2 Lt. O.C. B Co.
2nd Lan Fus

Time 9-50 P.M.

To 2nd Lancashire Fusiliers

Present strength of "B" Company. 1 Officer
1 C.S.M. 2 Sgts, 1 Cpl, 4 L. Cpls. 27 Men
3 Sigs. and 1 Orderly.

We are holding SPECTRUM and

the advanced saps. All the men having returned to SPECTRUM when I arrived.

When the Kings Own Companies move up, the whole of remainder moves down to "A" Company's old position.

From R. H. Higson 2 Lt B Coy
Time 8 p.m. Oct 12th 1916.

To 2nd Lancashire Fusiliers

B Company about 20 strong holding advanced saps.

About 80 men of the DUKES are in our trench.

From R. H. Higson 2 Lt "B" Coy
Time 8-10 P.m. Oct 12th 1916.

To 2nd Lancashire Fusiliers

Will arrange re Stores &c aaa Patrols from us and ESSEX gone out aaa Can you supply any stretchers, we are blocked up with serious cases. We can arrange carrying.

Place SPECTRUM Time 2-15 A.M.
From J. W. Watkins Lt

To 2nd Lancashire Fusiliers

Position as follows. "A" Coy about 20 strong "B" Coy about 30. C Coy 34 D Coy 54, about 134 in all and 1 Coy of Essex about 120 strong are in SPECTRUM trench AAA Trench is too crowded and I have ordered D Coy to occupy support trench formerly occupied by A Co AAA The Dukes hold DEWDROP and connection is now being established by digging AAA. No line is held beyond line dug by C Co twenty yards in advance of SPECTRUM AAA. It is possible that one or two isolated posts exist in front of this but surrounded by GERMANS AAA. Officers remaining in Battalion Lieut Watkins 2Lt Howarth 2Lt Higson AAA Capt Mansell killed, shot through heart AAA Patrols report ZENITH strongly held AAA.

From C Coy   Place SPECTRUM Time 5 am.

To 2nd Lancashire Fusiliers

The DUKES are in SPECTRUM not in DEWDROP as they thought AAA. They are now sending Patrols to ascertain if DEWDROP is held by Germans or not AAA. When the Dukes came back after the attack they occupied SPECTRUM thinking that it was DEWDROP AAA

From C Coy. Place SPECTRUM. Time 5-20 am.

To 2nd. Lancashire Fusiliers

The Germans are in DEWDROP aaa. The DUKES are now sapping through the gap and intend to re-take DEWDROP bombing. aaa. I have sent A Co back to support trench as well as D to relieve congestion aaa. Wounded are being evacuated as quickly as possible and communication trench is being deepened aaa. I am sapping out to the front but work is slow as not much can be done by daylight aaa. Will send approximate casualties as soon as possible. Will let you

From B Coy Place DECTRUM. Time 7-15 am.

APPENDIX.(III)

Important Messages Dispatched

Appendix (III)

To 12th Brigade.

Patrol Report.

Object

To reconnoitre ZENITH Trench.

Result

Trench was found to be practically a continuous line from N 28 d 52 – N 34 b 87. This line was held by 1 rifle every 50ˣ as far as could be seen. There was some wire out just in front of the parapet but of very little importance. This would not have been noticed but that a very light went up and showed what appeared to be a one strand fence.

From G.C. Martin. Lieut. 2nd Lanc: Fus.

Time 5 A.M.

To Companies.

1. We have now only one objective the Brown line which will be taken by the first four waves. The second 4 waves will dig a support trench

about 200ˣ in rear of the Brown line. This must be carefully sited.

II. As the Barrage in front of the Dukes will take sometime to straighten, the Battalion will not start until 0-20 or 20 minutes after zero

III During this 20 minutes every man to be absolutely flat and the whole should spring up at 0.20' like one man

From G. C. Martin. Lieut. 2nd Lanc: Fus
Time 7-50. A.M.   Octr. 12th 1916

To Scatter

Our artillery dropping short into Spectrum Trench AAA Some men buried AAA

From G. C. Martin. Lieut. 2nd Lanc: Fus
Time 11-10 A.M.   Octr 12th 1916

To 12th Brigade

One under-Officer and 7 Privates have just given themselves up to our C Coy AAA 70th Regt AAA They are being sent in now AAA

From G. C. Martin Lieut 2nd Lanc: Fus
Time 11-30 AM   Octr 12th 1916

NOTE. Prisoners came from East in front of Spectrum

To R.A.M.C.

Use your discretion about leaving trench after observing position of our barrage AAA We are going to crump the Hun trench S of Spectrum so close off to the N & lie doggo AAA Watch out for your right when you advance as you will have 4 waves in hand.

From R.R Willis.   2nd Lanc: Fus:
Time 11-34 AM.   Octr 12th 1916

To 12th Brigade

Captain Robertson wounded reports that Lancashire Fusiliers were held up by Machine Gun Barrage and have suffered heavily AAA He remained for some time but was unable to report any progress AAA He reports Lieut Hawkins wounded.

Time 3-30 PM

To 12th Brigade

Two Coy Commanders wounded and no reports received except verbal from Capt Robertson already sent in AAA Please send up supports AAA Have asked for Barrage to be increased as

3

1 p't reports enemy have been reinforced AAA

From 2nd Lancashire Fusiliers.

Time 4-15 P.M.   Oct 12th 1916

To 12th Brigade.   Oct 12th 1916

Have asked Region to send up two Companies to hold SPECTRUM pending receipt of your orders AAA Enemy show signs of taking advantage of our losses

From G. C. Martin, Lieut, 2nd Lanc: Fus.

To 12th Brigade.   Oct 12th 1916

Estimated casualties up to 7 P.M.
2nd Lancashire Fusiliers. 10 Officers, 300 OR

Lieut W. N. Fortescue   Killed
Lieut V. F. S Hawkins ⎫
  "   T Greaves   ⎬ Wounded
  "   Addison   ⎪
Capt   M. Robertson   ⎭

From G. C. Martin. Lieut 2nd Lanc: Fus.

To O. C. "C" Coy   Oct 12th/16

Have had no news yet about the Kings Own. Will you make all efforts to hold any bit of ground that may have been taken.

4

The C.O wishes you to organize small
parties to go out and relieve the men at
present in the shell holes and dig in
making Posts.

Take no notice of what Regiment
they are. Any news of anybody and
the situation will be most welcome.

From Adjutant. Oct 12th 1916

To. 12th Brigade.   Oct 12th/16

Your B.M. 20. Am I to capture
ZENITH TRENCH tonight with 2 Officers
and 80 men which is all I can lay
hands on at present AAA Suggest the
disorganization resulting from 50%
Officers and 70% men is unlikely to
produce desired result AAA The two Coÿs
Reckon can probably produce the required
result if employed as I suggested.

From 2nd Lancashire Fusiliers. 8-50 P.M.

To Lieuts Watkins & Hygson.   12/10/16

One Coÿ Essex Regt has arrived to
reinforce AAA For the present they will
take over "D" Coÿs Sector (left). Will you
with the men you have, take over "C" Coÿs
Sector (right) AAA The R.E are making

strong points behind you, and two Co's
Kings Own are coming to consolidate
captured positions. Will you state what
portions if any of ZENITH, i.e. the trench
just in front of SPECTRUM, were captured.
A covering party from Kings Own would
I expect be sufficient for the remainder
to work behind.

From R.K. Wilks, 2nd Lancashire Fusiliers

To Capt. Ward (Reform) Thro' Lieut Watkins.

It is reported by wounded that
ZENITH is a good trench and untenanted
AAA If this is so it seems a pity not to
take it over AAA Please send 1 Patrol each
to ascertain this fact AAA If correct send
1 covering party each and take over the
trench AAA Report early AAA

From Adjutant, 2nd Lancashire Fusiliers
Oct. 12/16

To Lieut Watkins   Oct 13th 1916
Have got stores of bombs, sandbags
flares and Very lights AAA Please relieve
a carrying party of one Sgt and 14 men
from Essex Regt and detail them to draw
from dump opposite Bn Head Quarters what
you require AAA Don't overdo the trouble
about ZENITH but it would be too for

6

our wounded AAA Salt is relieving you soon AAA Arrange for stores with Essex Coy on left as well AAA Any report by bearer

From R. R. Willis Lt Col. 2nd Lanc. Fus.

To 12th Brigade Octr 13th/16

My patrols reported this morning ZENITH held in strength by Germans AAA Suggest the Germans deceived the aeroplanes by the expedient of wearing our helmets AAA It is improbable men of 2nd Lanc. Fus. or REDAN would fail to report

From R. R. Willis. 2nd Lancashire Fusiliers
Time 6-30 P.M.

To 12th Brigade

Patrols confirm previous report AAA Enemy is making strong point in right of ZENITH AAA

From 2nd Lancashire Fusiliers.
Time 9-55 P.M.   Octr 13th 1916.

Report on operations carried out by
2nd Bn Lancashire Fusiliers
on October 23rd 1916.

1/ The objective allotted to the 2nd Lancashire Fusiliers was DEWDROP trench from the sunken road from LES BOEUFS to LE TRANSLOY to where that trench curls back about 250 yards to the south of the sunken road. Included in this were the elements of trenches surrounding DEWDROP there. This included a small trench called RAINY.

On the left were the KINGS OWN, and on the right the ESSEX who had also to take some of DEWDROP.

On these battalions moving on to the second objective the LANCASHIRE FUSILIERS were to take over DEWDROP entirely and consolidate the position, as well as completing any mopping up necessary.

To carry this out four companies of LANCASHIRE FUSILIERS were told off. They comprised two hundred and fifty men and this was the whole battalion and included such men as Lewis Gunners but 48 men were retained as Battalion reserve.

The front was about 250 yards and the attack was to be made in four waves. This meant that the waves were extended to over four yards a man

P.T.O.

2

The task of the Battalion as I understood it was:-

(1) In conjunction with other units to capture the trench line of which DEWDROP was a part and in the actual taking of DEWDROP the ESSEX were to take the part on our right.

(2) To clear and consolidate DEWDROP and its elements and to remain in it where the other battalions had gone on.

For the first portion of our task there were the four assaulting companies.

For the second portion there would be such men as had got in to the hostile trenches and possibly the Battalion reserve.

What I conceived to be the difficulty with regard to the second objective was to have some control in the captured positions and to meet this difficulty I arranged for Captain Salt not to go over with the assaulting companies but to remain behind in the front line trenches until he saw our men go into the hostile trenches. He then was to work his way across to DEWDROP six runners were to go with him to enable him to direct the consolidation on arrival.

Before the attack 25 men of the battalion reserve were placed under his orders in order that he should have a body of men to direct on a portion of trench where the Germans might be holding out or carry out some definite work.

3

The Lewis Gunners were placed in the front assembly trench as the weight of the gun makes the Gunners move more slowly than the other men in an assault. Though some had to be recovered from No-Mans Land none were lost and this position of assembly would certainly ensure that on leaving the position the Lewis Guns would be with the waves they were assigned to.

From a hole about in headquarters I endeavoured to follow events before and after Zero hour and I noticed the following.

The guns appeared to me to be warming up as Zero hour approached but I ascribed this to the fog in the morning not having permitted them to range or get off the allotted number of rounds, as I had not noticed a similar state of affairs on October 12th.

Some batteries seemed to open the barrage a minute before Zero.

The German S.O.S. practically went up at Zero hour. The arrangements for sending it up must have been made excellently as it went up all along the line.

The German Machine Guns opened at once and were well in action before the German barrage commenced.

A heavy barrage was placed W of the village of LES BOEUFS and along the LES BOEUFS–GINCHY road for a distance of two hundred yards. This latter was allowed to die down after about

4

a quarter of an hour. The shelling on other parts of our line was not so intense as on the 12th of October and there was no artillery barrage on the front line.

From these observations it would seem that a vertical artillery barrage is placed behind our assaulting troops to prevent reinforcements going forward while a horizontal machine-gun barrage deals with the assaulting troops.

The assaulting troops got well clear of our trenches but in front of the front line the machine guns cut them down.

The men passed from the second to behind the first assembly trench with extremely few casualties and nearly all the men who were killed lie behind the front line.

For some time no reports came in and no wounded. Some ESSEX wounded reported that the assault had failed and this was confirmed by watching the lights the Germans were sending up and these did not recede at all in our neighbourhood.

The first report that was received at 5.10pm was from Lieut Watkins and this reported the failure of the assault and that he was hanging on in front of RAINY. He also mentioned that the troops on his right had failed and gone back. This message was written at 3.30pm.

From what I had seen of the German lights there appeared to have been no change since that time and I endeavoured to

collect some information as to the situation
While doing so I received a message
at 6 p.m. urging the supreme need of capturing
DEWDROP.

I had spoken to the C.O. of the Essex and he told me that two Companies of his were digging in on the further objective, another was about to attack DEWDROP from as I understood the EAST by returning from where they had advanced to. His information very much surprised me but I gave orders for every available man

to be put in to an attack on DEWDROP.

As far as I could then make out our battalion was placed as follows:-

Lieut. Watkins and fifteen men were in a newly dug trench in front of RAINY. Captain Scott with thirty men in the front line. This included all the unwounded men he could collect.

The battalion reserve close by which had now dwindled to twenty owing to losses.

This made two officers and 65 men remaining out of six officers and 298 men present a few hours before. All were tired and some exhausted.

This is apparently a true estimate of the situation because our numbers were not increased by even twenty five by men rejoining during the next forty eight hours.

6

I determined however to make an effort with what I had especially in view of the situation as understood by the O.C. ESSEX and at 5-50 p.m. issued orders for attack. Append X.

Soon after this I found that the situation was quite different to what was reported to O.C. ESSEX. Wounded men spoke of returning across empty front line trenches, and that there were no troops in front of these trenches. While going into these points I was handed a message directing me to clear the situation and reform in conjunction with ESSEX and KINGS OWN for capture of DEWDROP. The Seaforth Highlanders were to assist.

At 6-15 p.m. I stopped the arrangements previously made to push for DEWDROP and went out to see for myself how things stood.

There was a good deal of debris & units about some of the men not even belonging to the South Division but on getting to our front line I found Captain Salt had collected nearly all the unwounded men and had them extended to connect up with troops on right and left. The gap on the right behind the sunken road had been filled by the Seaforths who had apparently come in on our right

7

The men under Captain Salt were in a very much better condition, as regards morale than I expected and that point reflects great credit on this Officer and Lieut Watkins.

A patrol of 15 men under Lt Watkins had gone out to find if there were any British troops in RAINY or DEWDROP and while awaiting their return the C.O. of the Seaforth Highlanders arrived. He wanted to hear the report the patrol brought in and what the situation was with us.

I informed him of the last message I had received in which it mentioned that his battalion would assist in the attack. I could not give him a copy as I purposely carried no papers at all on myself.

He told me he had clear instructions not to take part in the attack on DEWDROP. I informed him that I intended to see the other C.O's in accordance with my instructions.

After various efforts to get information Lieut Watkins returned with definite information that both DEWDROP and RAINY were held by the enemy. I went on and saw the O.C. Dukes and O.C. Kings Own, on my way passing a good number of the KINGS OWN dead and wounded.

From the two C O's I learnt that they were going to try and collect as many men as possible and bomb the Germans out of what they held of SPECTRUM. If successful they would continue in to DEWDROP. Any assistance I could give would be by pushing from in front.

From what I had seen I thought it would be some time before these men could be collected. I decided to return to my own front line by way of my headquarters. There I got the order that the Dukes, Seaforths and Essex were to move back.

I gave orders to extend our holding of the trenches up to the Brigade boundary from where O.C. Kings Own fixed his right flank.

This meant over three hundred yards of trench would be held by eighty men.

In view of the obvious condition of the enemy and the presence of five Lewis guns I considered that I should hang on to the trench in front of RAINY and dig a communication trench out to it

9

and gave orders for this and the improvement of this advanced trench.

APPENDIX. V. A.

Important messages received
from Companies and Battalions.

To 2. Lan. Fus.

Have seen Lt Watkins. He has collected 15 men and has dug a small trench about 12 yds long parallel to UNION. TR. 120 yds out. We have 12 men in one end of trench believed to be RAINY. Lt Watkins is now taking patrol of 15 men to find out.

① If Germans are in DEWDROP. TRENCH
② If   "   "   " RAINY. TRENCH.

I have only about 20 men here including unwounded that I have collected.

FROM. Capt. SALT.
Place. UNION. TR.
TIME   7.15 p.m.

To. Capt. Salt 2. Lan. Fus.

Am in front of RAINY. Our people advanced over RAINY. But right have retired and advance is at a standstill at present. Am trying to collect men.
Some Bosch still in RAINY.
    2Lt. WATKINS.
3.30 p.m.

To 2" Lan. Fus.

My right is about 30 yds from Sunken Road in SPECTRUM. Am now using every means to secure up to Sunken Road. 2" Seaforths say 2" Essex are in DEWDROP right. Only very few Lan Fus wounded passed here. I think if I carry on shoving down and you fellows make a rush for it we shall have all DEWDROP without difficulty.

1st K.O.R.L. Regt.   Time 9.40 pm.

To 2" Lan Fus.

I have just received enclosed from Watkins. I shall wait half an hour to see if you have any later news, and then go out to look for him when it is dark. He does not ask for help or I should have gone now. 2/Lt Parry with 10 men of A Co is in Burnaby, and I am going to join up with him.

From Capt. Salt.

Time. 4.55 pm.

To Lan. Fus.

I fix the boundary as UNION street inclusive to 1st K.O.R.L.

From.   1st K.O.R.L.

Time 3.40 am.
24/10/16.

To 2 Lan. Fus.

2Lt. Watkins has 15 men.
There are still the 23 men in Thistle
Trench, if the C.O has not already used
them.   I will report immediately on
return of 2Lt Watkins, as it may be
necessary to make bombing attack on
RAINY.
   From.   Capt Salt.
   Place   UNION.
   Time   7.15 pm.

To 2 Lan. Fus.

   Your G.m. 51 received.
2Lt. Watkins left 20 minutes ago to patrol
DEWDROP, will report immediately on return.
and will get all available men into new
position.   Wounded man reports 2Lt WATSON
is dead.
   I am bringing up Cpl Sheridan with the CO's
reserve, as I suppose this is meant by
every available man.
   From.   Capt Salt.
   Time.   8.12 pm.

APPENDIX VI b.

Important messages received from Brigade.

To 2. Lan. Fus.

4th Divn urges the supreme need of capturing DEWDROP.
11th Bde. making good progress.

From. 12. Bde
Time. 4.55 p.m.

To 2. Lan. Fus.

Get situation cleared and reform in cooperation with Seaforths and King's Own. for capture of DEWDROP.
Seaforths will help.

From. 12. Bde.
Time. 5.40 p.m.

APPENDIX VI

Important message dispatched.

To Capt. Salt.

All the men of the Ran. Jus to be collected and join the support which is with you. aaa Take all the support and the men you collect and endeavour to join up with 2 Lt. Watkins and a push into RAINY TR. at least aaa. From RAINY push must be made to take DEWDROP. aaa

ZENITH is reported to be in our hands aaa. Two Cos of the Essex are on the Brown line and one Co. of the Essex which did not reach the Brown line is returning to attack DEWDROP from the other side. aaa

Division place greatest importance on capture of DEWDROP. aaa.

Your attention is drawn to the possibility that other units may have got into DEWDROP. aaa. If you find this to be the case, organise defence of DEWDROP and surroundings from 2. Lan Jus.

Time 5.50 p.m.

(Sgd) G. C. Martin. Lt Lodgitant

To 12th Brigade.

Lieut. Watkins reports at 3.30pm that he was in front of RAINY also our people advanced over RAINY but right have had to retire, and advance is at a standstill at present. aaa Am trying to collect men aaa. Some Germans still in RAINY aaa. Ends aaa. This officer is in command of our left Co. aaa. Capt. Salt reports Lieut Parry and 10 men in BURNABY aaa. Have directed Capt Salt to collect everyone and with Btn. Reserve of 48 men to join Lt. Watkins and push on.

From. 2. Lan. Fus.
Time 6.0pm.
(Sgd) G Martin. Lt & adjutant.

12th Brigade.

4th Division.

2nd BATTALION

THE LANCASHIRE FUSILIERS

NOVEMBER 1 9 1 6

Army Form C. 2118.

WAR DIARY
or
INTELLIGENCE SUMMARY
(Erase heading not required.)

Vol 26

Place	Date	Hour	Summary of Events and Information	Remarks and references to Appendices
FIELD	November 1st & 2nd		The Battle of DREUIL	
	3rd		Bn moved from DREUIL to MORIVAL and VISMEUILLE C10 July in latter	
	4 & 5		to week as above.	
	6th		HQ & A, B & D Coys turned from MORIVAL to MAIGNELLE	
	7		Battalion in billets above — Coy Parades and Platoon training	
	8, 9, 10, 11, 12		Battalion training	
	13, 14, 15, 16, 20		The whole month was devoted to refitting and training absence	
			During the month 13 Officers and 390 O.R. reinforcements arrived	

Lieutenant Colonel
Commanding 1st [illegible]

25-V.
1 sheet

12th Brigade.

4th Division.

2nd BATTALION

THE LANCASHIRE FUSILIERS

DECEMBER 1916

SECRET.

WAR DIARY.

of

2nd Bn. Lancashire Fusiliers.

From : 1st December 1916
To : 31st December 1916.

VOLUME

Date.   E.L. van Someren Lt.Colonel,
                        Commanding,
                2nd Bn. Lancashire Fusiliers.

WAR DIARY

or

INTELLIGENCE SUMMARY.

(Erase heading not required.)

Army Form C. 2118.

Place	Date	Hour	Summary of Events and Information	Remarks and references to Appendices
MAIGNEVILLE	1st		Bn Training	gen.
"	2nd		Bn Training	gen.
OISEMONT	3rd	4.30pm	Bn ENTRAINED at OISEMONT at 4.30p.m. having waited since 10.30 a.m.	gen.
		10.30pm	Detrained at MERICOURT L'ABBE at 10.30 p.m.	
		11 p.m	@ 11p.m. left Station for Camp 112 (L.2.b)	
L.2.b.	4th	5.15 A.M.	Arrived at Camp 112.	gen.
		9.45 A.M.	Travelled off from Camp 112 for Camp 107 (A.26.a.30) throughout this [strike] inche [/strike] route the transport and cyclists moved by Road	
A.26.a.30	5th		Bn in Camp 107.	
"	6th		Bn in Camp 107. C.O and 1 rep: parco went up to line to see new trenches.	
Trenches Close Support	7th		Bn took over trenches in Close Support from the 20th Regt: of FRENCH gen. Trenches situated in proximity to BAPAUME - PERONNE main Road about ½ a mile South of SAILLY.	

[sketch map showing roads between BAPAUME, SAILLY, PERONNE, and FREGICOURT]

WAR DIARY
or
INTELLIGENCE SUMMARY.
(Erase heading not required.)

Army Form C. 2118.

Place	Date	Hour	Summary of Events and Information	Remarks and references to Appendices
Trenches Close Support	7th		Trenches were in very bad condition. Full of mud and water. No shelter in trenches for men at all. The weather was very bad the whole time.	9am
- do -	8th		In close support trenches. Chief work:- Extending and improving trenches — Erecting shelters.	9am
- do -	9th		As on 8. Capt. RAVENSCROFT, 2nd Lieut HOWARTH Rejoined d/f leave. 1 O.R. killed & wounded 9am.	9am
- do -	10th		Enemy shelled A Coy slightly. 2nd Lieut FALLOWFIELD - COOPER 9am. Admitted to Hospital Suffering from SHELL SHOCK. 1 O.R. wounded. LIEUT COL BURNE Rejoined d/f leave.	
- do -	11th	4.15pm	Enemy of 11th relieved through our Right & 1st K.O.R. Lanc. R. in Trenches	9am
		9 a.m.	LEFT FRONT SUB SECTOR. Relief complete about 2 a.m. The relief took so long owing to the difficulty of moving men over the mud to get them to the front line. Many men stuck in the mud and consequently throughout the night men were occupied pulling others out of the mud. 2nd Bn. ESSEX REGT on Right — IRISH GUARDS on left.	

Army Form C. 2118.

WAR DIARY
or
INTELLIGENCE SUMMARY.
(Erase heading not required.)

Instructions regarding War Diaries and Intelligence Summaries are contained in F.S. Regs., Part II. and the Staff Manual respectively. Title pages will be prepared in manuscript.

Place	Date	Hour	Summary of Events and Information	Remarks and references to Appendices
FRONT TRENCHES LEFT SUB SECTOR	11th		Major R. HENCOWE. M.C. admitted to Hospital. 2. O.R. wounded	
	12th		Trenches in very bad condition also all the ground around them – Trenches impassable and falling in fact all round. Collapse tried to be prevented but was quicker than the men could dig. Disposition front line Left Co: C Centre Co: B Right Co: A Support Co: D	[sketch map showing "A Co", "B Co", "C Co" positions and "B'Wagon"]
-do-	13th		The trenches seen through the remains of SAILLISEL South End U.14.d and for over 24 hours. 1. O.R. wounded. 2. O.R. Died of Exposure having been stuck in the mud for over 24 hours. 3. O.R. killed. 4 wounded. Capt. G. RAVENSCROFT and 2nd Lieut G. WATSON admitted to Hospital in same trenches.	
-do-	14th		2. O.R. killed 1 wounded. 7. O.R. Rejoined.	

2353 Wt. W3141/1454 700,000 5/15 D.D.&L. A.D.S.S./Forms/C. 2118.

WAR DIARY
or
INTELLIGENCE SUMMARY.
(Erase heading not required.)

Army Form C. 2118.

Place	Date	Hour	Summary of Events and Information	Remarks and references to Appendices
FRONT TRENCH LEFT SUB SECTOR	15th	8.40pm	Relieved in trenches by 1st K.O.R.LANC.R. Relief Complete. Relief made easier by a pathway of Duck-Boards having been laid from Close Support trenches almost to FRONT LINE.	JCW.
FREGICOURT Bde RESERVE	16th		On Relief Bn. moved back into Bde RESERVE near FREGICOURT. Trenches a trifle more comfortable - still plenty of mud. Work commenced to improve Shelter Accommodation.	JCW.
-do-	17th		In same trenches.	JCW.
-do-	18th		In same trenches.	JCW.
-do-	19th		In same trenches. Enemy dropped a few shells near H.Q.	JCW.

Army Form C. 2118.

WAR DIARY
or
INTELLIGENCE SUMMARY.
(Erase heading not required.)

Instructions regarding War Diaries and Intelligence Summaries are contained in F. S. Regs., Part II. and the Staff Manual respectively. Title pages will be prepared in manuscript.

Place	Date	Hour	Summary of Events and Information	Remarks and references to Appendices
	19th	5.30pm	Left FRECICOURT to relieve 1st K.O.R. Lanc. R. in front line (Left sub Sector) A and D left for and right front Coys respectively. B in close Support. HQ in Reserve in BETTIE TRENCH. Killed 1 O.R. Capt. R.H. PARKINSON admitted to Hospital.	9th
FRONT TRENCH LEFT SUB SECTOR	20th		Hard frost - much work done to improve trenches for defence and for comfort. Killed 1 O.R.	9th
	21st		Frost continued until about 3 pm. Thaw then set in. Rained and snowed intermittently during the night. Lieut Col. C. I. BURRE admitted to Hospital. 2 O.R. killed 2 O.R. wounded.	9th
	22nd		Bad weather continues. All work done on 20th and 21st quickly disappeared. Lieut A.S. CHAPMAN admitted Hospital.	9th
	23rd	8.45	Relieved in evening by 2nd SEAFORTH HIGHLANDERS. Relief complete.	9th

Army Form C. 2118.

WAR DIARY
or
INTELLIGENCE SUMMARY.
(Erase heading not required.)

Instructions regarding War Diaries and Intelligence Summaries are contained in F.S. Regs., Part II. and the Staff Manual respectively. Title pages will be prepared in manuscript.

Place	Date	Hour	Summary of Events and Information	Remarks and references to Appendices
Camp 107	23rd		During the Som. 2/5 4 O.R. were admitted to Hospital.	qu.
	24th		After Relief Bn was conveyed in motor lorries to Camp 107.	qu.
	25th		In Divisional Reserve.	qu.
	26th		"	qu.
	27th		"	qu.
Camp 124	28th		Bn marched back to Camp 124 (S.35. c.6.3)	qu.
"	29th		In Camp 124 Co Training	qu.
"	30th		"	qu.
"	31st		"	qu.

4th Division
12th Infantry Bde.
2nd Lancs. Fus.

January - December
1917

Secret

War Diary

of

2ⁿᵈ Bn Lancashire Fusilier Regt

From: 1st Jany 1917
To: 31st Jany 1917

Volume

Date.   C/ Burke   Lt Colonel
            Commanding
       2 Bn Lancashire Fusiliers Regt

Army Form C. 2118.

WAR DIARY
or
INTELLIGENCE SUMMARY

(Erase heading not required.)

Ref: Map FRANCE. ALBERT (Enlarged Sheet) 1/40,000.

Place	Date	Hour	Summary of Events and Information	Remarks and references to Appendices
Camp 124 (J.35.b.9.0.) LE PLATEAU. F.20.	January 1st		B.C. & Tors and Hd Qrs in Camp 124 (J.35)(F.20) training. A Co at Le Plateau (F.20) unloading ammunition.	G.Ch.
	2nd		Co as 1st. Working party of 65 men found by Bn at Camp 124.	G.Ch.
	3rd		Major General FRAMPTON, G.O.C. Division inspected Camp 124. 2nd Lieuts H.T. INGLETON, T. JUDD, H. BROWN and 4 O.R. joined Bn.	G.Ch.
	4th		2nd Lieuts C. GREGORY, C.J. YATES, H. CARDWELL, G.H. YAPP, C.S.M. WILLIAMS and 4 O.R. joined Bn.	G.Ch.
	5th		In Camp 124.	G.Ch.
	6th		" "	G.Ch.
	7th		43 O.R. joined Bn.	G.Ch.
	8th		In Camp 124.	G.Ch.
	9th		" " A Co returned from Le Plateau. Lieut YAPP and 21 O.R. proceeded to CORBIE for work under Field Supply Depot. A.S.C. Lieut MACDONALD returned and 2nd Lieut L.S. ORRELL joined.	G.Ch.
	10th		Bn. celebrated Christmas. Untrained and very small. In Camp 124.	G.Ch.
	11th			G.Ch.

Army Form C. 2118.

WAR DIARY
or
INTELLIGENCE SUMMARY

(Erase heading not required.)

Instructions regarding War Diaries and Intelligence Summaries are contained in F. S. Regs., Part II. and the Staff Manual respectively. Title Pages will be prepared in manuscript.

Place	Date	Hour	Summary of Events and Information	Remarks and references to Appendices
Camp 124	12th		In Camp 124 — 2ND LIEUT. A. CLARKE and 3 O.R arrived joined Bn	See
	13th		" — Capt. J.S. RENSHAW and 2ND LIEUTS H.C. TOLLER & A. WARREL joined Bn.	See
	14th		" — Co Training	See
	15th		" —	See
	16th		" — 19 O.R. Reinforcements joined	See
	17th		" —	See
	18th		" —	See
	19th		" — Major A.D. CARMICHAEL (9th Royal Highlanders) joined Bn	See
	20th		" —	See
	21st		" — 250 O.R. Reinforcements joined	See
			" — Lieut Col. C.T. BURKE D.S.O. and 2ND LIEUT R.S. THICKNESSE joined Bn. Lieut G.R SPENCER rejoined from Hosp.	See
	22nd		" —	See
Camp 112 L.2.b	23rd	1.20 pm	Bn moved to Camp 112 (L.2.b), leaving in 124 at 9.35AM and arriving at Camp 2ND LIEUT G.S.T. WRIGHT joined Bn	See

WAR DIARY
or
INTELLIGENCE SUMMARY

(Erase heading not required.)

Army Form C. 2118.

Instructions regarding War Diaries and Intelligence Summaries are contained in F.S. Regs., Part II. and the Staff Manual respectively. Title Pages will be prepared in manuscript.

Place	Date	Hour	Summary of Events and Information	Remarks and references to Appendices
SUZANNE	24th		Bn. moved to SUZANNE, leaving 112 at 11.40am and arriving at 1.45pm	9 Che
"	25th		In SUZANNE. Co. Training. — 7 O.R. Reinforcements joined	9ch
"	26th		" " " "	9ch
"	27th		" " " "	9ch
"	28th		" " " "	9ch
"	29th		" " " "	9ch
"	30th		" " Party returned from CORBIE	9ch
"	31st		Lieut General Sir T.P. Du Cane K.C.B. G.O.C. XV Corps presented following Officers, N.C.Os, and men with their ribbons	9ch
			Major W. BOWES D.S.O.	
			# Lieut (Temp Capt) E. GREGORY M.M.	
			6663 R.Q.M.S. BIRSBY "	
			19489 C.Q.M.S. ASHWORTH "	
			7451 C.Sgt. VOWLES "	
			7174 Sgt. TAYLOR "	
			999 S/Sgt. DIGGLE "	
			3945 Pte. KEATING "	

Secret

War Diary

of

2nd Bn Lancashire Fusiliers

From 1st February 1917
To 28th February 1917

Volume No 2

Date 3/3/1917

C G Tiffin Lt Colonel
Commanding 2 Lancashire Fus

Army Form C. 2118.

WAR DIARY
or
INTELLIGENCE SUMMARY
(Erase heading not required.)

Instructions regarding War Diaries and Intelligence Summaries are contained in F. S. Regs., Part II. and the Staff Manual respectively. Title Pages will be prepared in manuscript.

FEBRUARY.

Place	Date	Hour	Summary of Events and Information	Remarks and references to Appendices
SUZANNE	1st	7.30 p	B'n in SUZANNE. B'n relieved 1st B'n. RIFLE BRIGADE in Close Support trenches in 'BOUCHAVESNES Sector. 1st B'n. K.O.R. Lanc. R. Right front B'n. 2nd W. Rid. R. Right front B'n. Essex R. in Reserve.	9ch
BOUCHAVESNES	2nd		Working parties found by day and by night on support line.	9ch
"	3rd		3 O.R. killed. 2 O.R. wounded.	9ch
"	4th		Working Parties found.	9ch
"	5th		" " "	9ch
Left front Sector	6.		4 O.R. found. Relieved 1st B'n. K.O.R. Lanc. R. in Left Sector. CAPTAIN HEATON ARMSTRONG and 12 O.R. wounded.	9ch
"	7th		Artillery Active.	
"	8th		Our heavy guns shelled left and left centre in badly. 4 O.R. Killed 5. O.R. wounded.	9ch
"	9th		Quieter day. Aeroplane activity.	9ch
"	9th		1. O.R. wounded	9ch
Junction Wood	10th		Relieved by 1st K.O.R. Lanc. R. in line. B'n Relief B'n proceeded to Junction Wood in Bde. Reserve.	
"	11th		15. O.R. Reinforcements arrived. Night working parties from B'n. Rest by Day. Working Parties found by night.	9ch

Army Form C. 2118.

WAR DIARY
or
INTELLIGENCE SUMMARY

(Erase heading not required.)

Instructions regarding War Diaries and Intelligence Summaries are contained in F.S. Regs, Part II. and the Staff Manual respectively. Title Pages will be prepared in manuscript.

Place	Date	Hour	Summary of Events and Information	Remarks and references to Appendices
Tune Wood	12th		Moved Daily slightly working Parties	9ch
Left Sub Sector 'B'	13th		Bn relieved 1st Bn. K.O.R Rane R in left front Sector	9ch
	14th		Quiet day. Aeroplane activity	9ch
	15th		Capt. FANNER returned from Hospital	9ch
	16th		Quiet Aeroplane activity on both sides.	9ch
			1.O.R. wounded	9ch
			Relieved in trenches by 1st Bn. E. Lan. R	9ch
			On Relief Bn moved back to Camp 17. Arrived about 9 a.m.	9ch
Camp 17.	17th	9am	Bn arrived at Camp 17.	9ch
	18th		5. O.R. Reinforcement. Bn. cleaned up & refitted	9ch
	19th		Camp 17	9ch
	20th		Bn moved to Camp 112	9ch
Camp 112	21st		Bn moved to CORBIE. 2nd Lieut DAVENPORT. 2nd Lieut GILMOUR joined Bn.	9ch
CORBIE	22nd		Reorganization. Co Training	9ch
	23rd		5. O.R. Reinforcement	9ch
	24th		Co Training	9ch
	25th		" " 5. O.R Reinforcement	9ch
	26th		" "	9ch
	27th		" "	9ch
	28th		" " Capt. Douglas HAMILTON joined	9ch

Commdg 1 Cam: Hrs;

Vol 30.

29.V
3 sheets

Secret

War Diary

of

2 Bn Lancashire Fusiliers

From 1st March 1917
To   31st March 1917

Volume 3

9/4/1917

C. J. Griffin /Colonel
Commanding 2 Lanc Fus.

Army Form C. 2118.

WAR DIARY
or
INTELLIGENCE SUMMARY
(Erase heading not required.)

Instructions regarding War Diaries and Intelligence Summaries are contained in F.S. Regs., Part II. and the Staff Manual respectively. Title Pages will be prepared in manuscript.

MARCH

Place	Date	Hour	Summary of Events and Information	Remarks and references to Appendices
CORBIE	1st		Co. Training	geh.
"	2nd		Co. Training.	geh.
"	3rd		Orders received to be ready to move in 48 hours.	geh.
VILLERS-BOCAGE	4th		Moved to Villers Bocage leaving Corbie at 8.35 AM. Arrived at 3.0 pm	geh.
BEAUVAL	5th		Moved to Beauval. Left Villers Bocage 9.20 am Arrived 1 pm	geh.
WAVANS	6th		Moved to Wavans. Left Beauval 8 am Arrived 3.30 pm	geh.
VAULX	7th		Moved to Vaulx. Left Wavans 9.30 am Arriving 12 noon	geh.
"	8th		95 O.R. Reinforcements arrived	geh.
"	9th		Co. training. 61 O.R. Reinforcements arrived	geh.
"	10th		" "	geh.
"	11th		" "	geh.
"	12th		Sunday.	geh.
"	13th		Co. Training	geh.
"	14th		" "	geh.
"	15th		" "	geh.
"	16th		" "	geh.
"	17th		" "	geh.
"	18th		Sunday.	geh.
"	19th		Bn Training	geh.
"	20th		" "	geh.
"	21st		" "	geh.

Army Form C. 2118.

WAR DIARY
or
INTELLIGENCE SUMMARY

(Erase heading not required.)

Place	Date	Hour	Summary of Events and Information	Remarks and references to Appendices
OSTREVILLE	22nd		Bn. moved to OSTREVILLE in busses.	9am
	23rd		32 O.R. Reinforcements obtained	6am
	24th		Co. training	9am
	25th		Sunday.	9am
	26th		Co. training	9am
	27th		" "	9am
	28th		" "	9am
	29th		21 O.R. Reinforcements joined	9am
	30th		Bn. training	9am
	31st		" "	9am

C.J.Griffin Lieut Col
Commdg 2 Can: Inf.

No. 1

Operation Orders

by

Lieut Colonel C.J. Griffin D.S.O.

Commanding 2ND Lancashire Fusiliers

In the Field   Ref Map. 51 B N.W. $\frac{1}{20000}$

Original	Filed
No. 1	War Diary
No. 2	War Diary
No. 3	Headquarters
No. 4	A. Coy
No. 5	B. Coy
No. 6	C. Coy
No. 7	D. Coy
No. 8	2ND Lt. R. Gilmour

Appendix B

Time Table of Creeping & Protective Barrages.

	ZERO +	to ZERO +	RATE OF ADVANCE	REMARKS.
Protective barrage 300 yds E. of BROWN LINE	8.00	9.40	Stationary	
Advance till parallel to 4th GERMAN TRENCH SYSTEM	9.40	9.50	100 yds per 2 mins	Barrage remains stationary S. of the FAMPOUX ROAD
Advance along whole front	9.50	10.6	100 yds per 2 mins	
Lift off 4th GERMAN SYSTEM.	10.6			
Barrage on W. and N. edge of FAMPOUX. Concentrated fire on Road Junction H.17.c.9.6 Road Junction H.17.d.6.9 HYDERABAD REDOUBT Trench Junction H.17.b.6.9	10.6	10.42	Stationary	
Lift off W. edge of FAMPOUX and H.17.c.9.6	10.42			
Concentrated fire on road junction H.17.d.6.9 trench junction H.17.b.6.9	10.42	10.50	Stationary	See Special How. creeping barrage for FAMPOUX.
FAMPOUX. Special 6" How. Barrage Lift from W. edge of FAMPOUX.	10.42			
Advances	10.42	11.14	100 yds per 4 mins	
Lifts to protective positions in front of GREEN LINE	11.14		Stationary	

APPENDIX A.

TIME TABLE.

MOVES	9th DIV.	12th INF. BDE.
LEAVE Y CAMP		+ 0
REACH ASSEMBLY AREA		+ 2.30
HALT		2 HOURS
LEAVE ASSEMBLY AREAS		+ 4.30
REACH AREA BEHIND BLUE LINE	+ 2.43	+ 6.40
LEAVE BLUE LINE	+ 6.46	+ 7.40
REACH 3RD TRENCH SYSTEM W. OF BROWN LINE	+ 7.32	+ 8.40
ARRIVE IN OR PASS OVER BROWN LINE (N. OF FAMPOUX ROAD)	+ 8.00	+ 9.40
(S. OF ROAD)		+ 9.50
REACH 4th GERMAN TRENCH SYSTEM		+ 10.12
LEAVE 4th GERMAN TRENCH SYSTEM		+ 10.42
REACH GREEN LINE		+ 11.14

General Idea

1. The Battalion is taking part in an attack, made by the XVII Corps at an hour ZERO on Z day, immediately North of the R. Scarpe.

 6th Corps is attacking South of R. Scarpe.
The 9th Division is to capture the Black, Blue and Brown lines.
The 4th Division will pass through the 9th when they reach the Brown line, capture the German 4th System, FAMPOUX and consolidate on Green line.

Disposition IV Division

(b) The 12th Infantry Brigade will be on the right, 11th Brigade on left and 10th Brigade in Divisional Reserve.

Disposition Brigade

(c)
RIGHT	1st Kings Own
CENTRE	2nd Lan Fus
LEFT	2nd Essex Regt
RESERVE	2nd West Riding Regt

12th Brigade M.G.Co.

(d) 3 Machine Guns will be allotted to each of Assaulting Battalions and the Remainder to the Reserve Battalion.

(e) 12th T.M.B
2 Stokes Mortars will be allotted to each of 2nd Lan Fus and 2nd Essex and 4 to 1st K.O.

Boundaries

(f) B'de and Bn Boundaries are shown on tracing.

Battn Boundaries

(g) 1. ATHIES–FAMPOUX Road as far as curve at H.16.c.3.5 – trench junction H.16.c.9.0 along communication trench to H.22.b.35. 95 (trench inclusive to Kings Battn)

Cross Roads H.17.C.3.5 - Fampoux-Plouvain Road to H.18.a.9.2 on green line (Rgt. inclusive to   Bn)

(h) H.15.a.30.55 - H.15.b.3.4 - H.16.d.5.8 - H.12.c.7.0 on green line.

2. (a) <u>Battn Dispositions</u>

Bn will attack in four waves. The 1st and 2nd wave being composed of (Bn+ left) C on right.ˣ Both companies will detail 1 Platoon each as Moppers up, who will move between 1st and 2nd Wave. The 3rd and 4th wave being composed of (A on+ left) D on right.ˣ The 3 Machine Guns and 2 Trench Mortars will move in rear of the Bn near Bn Hd Qrs These may be called on by Cos. if required for any special work

(b) <u>Battn Objectives</u>

(1) German 1st System from H.16.d.10.05 to H.16.d.70.96

(2) H.18.a.9.2 to H.12.c.7.0

N°(1) is allotted to B & C Cos
   (2)   "   "   "   A & D Cos.

<u>Moves Preparatory to attack:-</u>

Prior to Z day the Bn will be accommodated in Y huts near ETRUN

On Z day the Bn will move to its Assembly area in G.15.d

There will be a halt of approximately two hours in the Assembly area where a hot meal will be issued.   Bn will then move to Brown line by following route.

Track from G.15.b.9.1. to road junction G.16.a.1.1 - Cross Rds. G.16.c.6.9 - road junction G.16.c.5.7 - G.17.c.10.65 - Track North of Oil Factory G.18.a.0.0

On reaching the Brown line Bn will form up as follows:-

Approximate line of trenches from (1) H.15.a.9.5.6. H.15.a.1.6. - (2) H.15.b.6.5 to H.15.b.7.6
C & B take up position on (1)
D & A   "   "   "   "   (2)

Attack
The attack will be carried out according to attached time table

Direction
C. Coy will direct with its right on Bn Boundary
As soon as 2nd German System has been captured, Posts will be pushed forward as follows by C and B Cos.

(1) To Sunken Road from H.17.a.9.0 to H.17.a.8.9
(2) C. Coy will send out if possible posts to the N.E of FAMPOUX to cut off German retreat from this village.

Lewis Guns will be sent forward with these posts

No troops to enter FAMPOUX

There will be a halt of about ½ an hour on German 2nd System

On continuing the advance:-

D & A Cos will pass through C & B Cos (D Coy deviating) to Green line,

The West Riding Regt will pass through Kingsbeam and attack FAMPOUX

C & B Cos will consolidate German 2nd System.

On capturing Green line, Strong Patrols will be pushed out to capture any Artillery, and to keep in touch with enemy

The organization of a defensive line approximately along the Green line, will be taken in hand at once by D.R.L.S.

The line will be on the Western slopes of the ridge, but posts will be pushed forward to obtain observation East of the Ridge

Cos must be prepared at anytime during the attack to form a defensive flank, and to push on and try to turn the obstacle which is holding up their right or left flanks

Strong Points

B & C. cos. will, directly the Green line has been taken, send up 20 O.R. each under reliable N.C.Os to H.18.a.5.5 where they will build a strong point under supervision of and with aid of ½ a Section of 71st Field RE.

Artillery

Artillery table attached.

Rocket and light signals will be used for communication with Artillery

Succession of Green lights .... OPEN FIRE
" - Red " .... SHORTEN RANGE
" - White " .... LENGTHEN RANGE

One Yellow and Black flag will be carried by each platoon to indicate the position of assaulting troops

Areoplanes

Contact areoplanes will receive signals from Bn H.Q. by means of (1) Ground Signal Panels
(2) Lamps

from attacking Infantry by (3) Flares.

Signals

(a) A Cable is being taken by Brigade to Fampoux. A trench wireless set will be about H.11.6.6.1 and another about H.13.6.8.9

Signals

There will be an amplifier about H.17.b.1.
Batt'n will have a Power Buzzer.

(b) Two pigeons will be issued to Batt'n.

(c) Brigade will establish a visual station on the
Blue line about H.7.d.9.0 and intermediate
also about H.16.c.9.1.
Signalling Officer will arrange to maintain
communication with one or other of these stations.

(d) Bde Pig. H.Q. at Zero hour will be at C.17.b.1.5.
        Later at   G.17.a.70.05
        Later at   H.13.b.8.9

Prisoners

Prisoners will be sent to L'ABBAYETTE H.14.b.8.2
where they will be handed over to A.P.M.
Attention is drawn to S.S.135 Para XXVI.

Medical arrangements

Aid Posts, collecting station and times of
evacuation will be notified later.

                  [signature]
                  Lieut & Adjt
                2nd Lan Fus.

Ref Para. I

	A		B		C		D	
	NCO	OR	NCO	OR	NCO	OR	NCO	OR
Add. Party of Batln Carriers	1	15	1	15	1	15	1	15

Additions to Operation Orders issued 29-5-17.

1. The following Carrying Parties and other details will be furnished by Companies for the forthcoming Operations:—

	A		B		C		D	
	N.C.O.	O.R.	NCO.	OR.	NCO.	OR.	NCO.	OR.
A. Carriers for 12/M.G.Co	-	-	-	-	-	6	1	6
B. " " 12/T.M.B.	-	8	-	8	-	-	-	-
C. Runners for B'de Sigs	-	1	-	1	-	1	-	-
D. Men for detonating Bombs etc at B'de Dump	-	-	-	1	-	1	-	-
E. Repair of Roads from H17.C.3.5 to H17.D.6.8 and from H16.C.7.2 to H16.D.5.3 under C.R.E.	1	12	1	12	1	12	-	12
G. Men for detonating bombs etc. at Div'n Dump	-	1	-	-	-	-	-	1
H. Runners for Div'n Signals	-	1	-	1	-	1	-	1
I. B'de Intelligence Personnel	-	-	-	-	-	-	-	2
Total	1	23	1	23	1	21	1	22

Parties A. B. H & I have already proceeded.
Party C will report to Orderly Room at 5-30 P.M. on Y. day
  " D " " " " " 7.0 A.M. " 3rd inst
Rations for 3rd Full Equipment and blankets will be taken
  " E. Further instructions will be issued later
  " G " " " " "
  " J. B.N Carriers further orders will be issued

Dress

See Chapter XXXI S.S. 135 para 2

Section (VI) delete from Cap Comforters ——— the flap
Insert Iron Ration.

Section (VII) delete Bombers, Scouts, Lewis Gunners and carrying parties

Section X for three, read four.
  delete carried under braces at back.

Para 3. Further orders will be issued re surplus kit

Section III All men will carry either a pick or a shovel.
  50% of each will be carried

Verey's Pistols. 1ˢᵗ Pistols will be taken by assaulting troops
  1½" will be sent up at night

See Chapter XXXII
  "   "   XXXIII

10% Reinforcements
See Chapter XXX
and Amendment

C.S.M. Duckers and C.S.M. Cole will not go into action with Battⁿ.

Signallers will be arranged by Signalling Officer.

Gas Instructor   A Coy
Bombing   "   B "
Lewis Gun   "   C Coy (Sgt Vernon)
  "   "   "   D Coy

Bayonet Fighting
& Physical Training } A & B. Cos.

Further instructions will be issued later as to when and where these parties will be left.

Nominal Rolls

Nominal Rolls of Cos should be forwarded to Orderly Room as soon as possible, under following heading
  A. Those who will accompany Coy in assault
  B.   "   "   "   "   Bn H.Q.   "
  C. 10%
  D. Bn Hd Qrs Stores & Transport
  E. Drummers
  F. Courses
  G. Employed away from Bn

Secret

War Diary

of

2nd Bn Lancashire Fusiliers

From 1st April 1917

To 30th April 1917

Volume
No 4

J W Watkins Capt / Major
Comdg 2 Lan Fus

WAR DIARY or INTELLIGENCE SUMMARY

Army Form C. 2118.

April

Place	Date	Hour	Summary of Events and Information	Remarks and references to Appendices
OSTREVILLE	1		Co training preparatory to Offensive Action. Lieut HARTLEY and 62 O.R. Reinforcements arrived.	gen.
	2		Co training	gen.
	3		Bn training. Attack Practise	gen.
	4		Co training	
	5		Pde: practise attack	gen.
	6		Pde: practise attack	gen.
	7		Bn: moved to Y Huts before Attack.	gen.
	8		Last preparation. Bombs, Grenades, Bombs &c issued.	gen.
"Y" Huts	9	3.30AM	Reveille	
		4.30AM	Bn moved to Assembly Area in G.15.d.	
		7.25AM	Bn arrived at Assembly Area	
		9.30AM	Men had a hot meal. The Assembly area was near a prisoners cage and the sight of so many prisoners made the men cheerful and made them forget the rain and the coming attack	
		10.20AM	Bn moved off from Assembly Area, by platoons at 100x distance, behind the Essex. Route: track from G.15.b.9.1 to Road junction G.16.a.1.1 — Cross Roads G.16.d.6.2 — G.16.d.3.7 — track N. of Oil Factory to G.16.d.0.0	

Army Form C. 2118.

WAR DIARY
or
INTELLIGENCE SUMMARY
(Erase heading not required.)

Instructions regarding War Diaries and Intelligence Summaries are contained in F. S. Regs., Part II. and the Staff Manual respectively. Title Pages will be prepared in manuscript.

Place	Date	Hour	Summary of Events and Information	Remarks and references to Appendices
	9th		From this point Bn moved by a water track in N.W.ly Outskirts of ST. LAURENT BLANGY making from Railway Bridge across BLANGY - ATHIES Road at H.14.Z.①.⑪③.	
		12.50 p.m to 1.30 p.m	Bn arrived under cover of Railway Embankment they formed up into Artillery formation "C" on Right with Right on Main Road. "B" on left. (C.W. directing) "D" on Right in Support to B w; "A" on left in Support to B w; Bn HdQrs line got into touch with HdQrs K.O.R. Lanc. R. South of the Road	
			Casualties up to 12.30 p.m estimated at 1 Officer wounded 15 O.R. killed and wounded, caused by Shell fire in vicinity of Cemetery about G.15.d.5.5.	
		1.30 p.m	Bn moved on to BROWN LINE or trenches in G.14.b.	
		2 p.m	Arrived at BROWN LINE C + B Coys assembled in trenches from approximately H.14.b.9.3 to H.15.a.1.6. A + D Coys 6.3 to H.14.c.7.6	

Army Form C. 2118.

WAR DIARY
or
INTELLIGENCE SUMMARY

(Erase heading not required.)

Instructions regarding War Diaries and Intelligence Summaries are contained in F.S. Regs., Part II. and the Staff Manual respectively. Title Pages will be prepared in manuscript.

Place	Date	Hour	Summary of Events and Information	Remarks and references to Appendices
	9th	3.15pm	Bn moved off in rear of B'avage to attack German 4th System and to push on and dig in on Green Line. Part of Objective allotted to Bn: H.16.d.10.05 to H.16.d.70.95. H. System from H.16.a.9.2 to H.17.c.7.0. Green line from H.16.a.9.2 to H.17.c.7.0. Bn reached except for a few shells and wild rifle fire the 4th German System without any difficulty. Casualties 1 Officer wounded, 1 O.R killed 3 O.R wounded. The greater part of the Germans came out and surrendered but a few stated to run away, many of which were accounted for by Lewis Gun fire. At this period the Germans dropped many shells amongst the trenches composing the 4 System. This added to the discomfort of the German Prisoners but evidence did no damage to us. The Number of Prisoners taken is doubtful estimated at 2 Officers and about 50 O.R.	

Army Form C. 2118.

WAR DIARY
or
INTELLIGENCE SUMMARY
(Erase heading not required.)

Instructions regarding War Diaries and Intelligence Summaries are contained in F. S. Regs., Part II. and the Staff Manual respectively. Title Pages will be prepared in manuscript.

Place	Date	Hour	Summary of Events and Information	Remarks and references to Appendices
	9th		9 Small Guns were captured in 4th German System (Wing Lang?) 5 at G.16.d.4.5. four at G.16.d.5.6. CoPs were pushed out patrols to their front.	
		3.50 pm	At about 3.50 pm posts were pushed out on to Sunken Road in G.17.a. The L/F pots took four guns (approximately 4.2's) on SUNKEN ROAD.	
		4.12 pm	T & A Coy passed through CoB in and pushed on to Green Line. On reaching line of Roe. FAMPOUX - GAVRELLE ROAD they came under heavy machine gun fire but finally had to dig in just East of the Road. Touch was maintained with the Duke of Wellington. W. Rid. R. and Essex R. on Right and Left respectively and a continuous trench dug. As a counterattack was evident a defensive position was soon built.	

2449 Wt. W14957/M90 750,000 1/16 J.B.C. & A. Forms/C.2118/12.

Army Form C. 2118.

WAR DIARY
or
INTELLIGENCE SUMMARY

(Erase heading not required.)

Instructions regarding War Diaries and Intelligence Summaries are contained in F. S. Regs., Part II. and the Staff Manual respectively. Title Pages will be prepared in manuscript.

Place	Date	Hour	Summary of Events and Information	Remarks and references to Appendices
	9th		Enemy were seen to be massing and advancing in Artillery formation, his attack however took place. Casualties:-	Gen.
			Officers Wounded. 2ND LIEUT C. STM. WILLIAMS	
			2ND LIEUT PARKES	
			O.R. Killed. 6	
			Died of wounds 2	
			Wounded 53	
			Missing 1	
	10th		The weather throughout the day was very changeable at the Assembly Area. It rained hard during the day. It rained occasionally. At night it showed hard. During the morning the Enemy were active. Sniping and shelling. In the afternoon the Cavalry came up to attack. We were going to advance in support to them. Objective the ROUVAIN - GAURELLE Road and GREENLAND HILL, no action took place.	

WAR DIARY or INTELLIGENCE SUMMARY

Army Form C. 2118.

Place	Date	Hour	Summary of Events and Information	Remarks and references to Appendices
	10th		Casualties. Officers Wounded. Capt. W.R. TANNER. Lieut. E.L. HARTLEY. 5 O.R. Killed. 2 Died of Wounds. 64. Wounded. Aeroplane Artillery and Aircraft Active	Gen.
	11th	12 noon	Bde. attached. B and C Coys were in support to the K.O.R. Lanc. R on the right. A and D Coys remained in Reserve.	
		2pm	An attack was held up on Right by machine gun fire D Coy was sent up to support to O.E. K.O.R. Lanc. R to come under his orders	
		1.20pm	Cavalry attempted to break through, but owing to machine gun fire did not succeed.	

WAR DIARY
or
INTELLIGENCE SUMMARY
(Erase heading not required.)

Army Form C. 2118.

Place	Date	Hour	Summary of Events and Information	Remarks and references to Appendices
	11th		At night B, C and D Coy were in front of line K.O.R. Lanc. R. on their Right. Dukes in Original line A Co was still on green line on left of some Irish Fusiliers who were next to the Dukes, with Essex on their Rgt. Reorganisation was then taken in hand. After warning the necessary people on Right and left of A Co, the Company was moved to get in touch with B & D. on this was accomplished without much difficulty. Cas. altr. Officers wounded 2nd Lieut. G.L. WILKINS. O.R. Killed 6, Wounded 12, missing 4.	
	12th	5pm	Enemy shelled TAMPOUX heavily and parts of "Gunners" & "Oyster" South of the Road. the 9th Division, after a preliminary bombardment attempted to force through and attack on to the ROEUX-GAVRELLE ROAD.	

Place	Date	Hour	Summary of Events and Information	Remarks and references to Appendices
	12th		The 26th Inf. Bde was coming up through us and the Bn Hqrs and C. Coy was going to move back to the Brown line, the remainder was going to move back when it was ascertained that the 9 Dunin were well dug in. On the 26th Inf Bde did not move up the Bn stayed in the line until relieved by the 8th Black Watch and part of 15th Argyle and Sutherland Highlanders	
		5 AM	Relief complete. Bn. moved to Brown line	
			Casualties. O.R. Killed 2, Wounded 6	
	13th	6pm	Bn moved to trenches in approximately G.11.c.	

Army Form C. 2118.

WAR DIARY
or
INTELLIGENCE SUMMARY
(Erase heading not required.)

Instructions regarding War Diaries and Intelligence Summaries are contained in F. S. Regs., Part II. and the Staff Manual respectively. Title Pages will be prepared in manuscript.

Place	Date	Hour	Summary of Events and Information	Remarks and references to Appendices
G.11.b.	14th		Bn in Square G.11.b. Resting	gen
	15th		"	gen
	16th		" Reorganising Preparatory to Attack	gen
	17th		"	gen
	18th		"	gen
	19th		"	gen
Monteniscourt Manin	20		Bn moved to Monteniscourt	gen
	21st		Bn moved to Manin	gen
	22nd		Co Training	gen
Etrée Wamin	23rd		Bn moved to Etrée Wamin	gen
	24th		Co Training	gen
	25th		" "	gen
	26th		" "	gen
Beaufort	27th		Bn moved to Beaufort	gen
Lauresset	28th		Bn moved to Lauresset	gen
G.17.	29th		Bn moved to 5 tents Camp in G.17.	gen
	30		Bn Relieves 22nd Bn M.F. in line from Railway Embankment (inclusive) to I.13.2.9.6.	gen

Vol 32

12/4 81.V.
10 sheets

Secret

War Diary

of

2ⁿᵈ Bn. Lancashire Fusiliers Reg't

From 1ˢᵗ May 1917

To 31ˢᵗ May 1917

Volume 5

June 3ʳᵈ 1917

J.W. Watkins Major
Commanding
2ⁿᵈ Bn. Lancashire Fusiliers Reg't.

WAR DIARY
INTELLIGENCE SUMMARY

Place: [blank]

Date	Hour	Summary of Events and Information	Remarks and references to Appendices
MAY 1st		On the night of 30/1st May Bn relieved 22nd NORTHUMBERLAND FUSILIERS in trenches due East of FAMPOUX.	app.
	2 AM	Relief complete. Artillery active. Casualties A.O.R. killed 4 O.R. wounded.	
2nd		Artillery short. Clinic Cave hit in the evening. Enemy retaliated fairly heavily. Casualties 3 O.R. wounded.	app.
3rd		During the early hours Bn moved into assembly position preparatory to attack. (Operation Orders attached) B + C in trenches South of Railway Embankment, D + A Co in trenches North of Railway Embankment, B + D in front C + A in support respectively.	app.
	3.45 AM	Zero Hour Bn left trenches in rear of a moving barrage. Owing to the large [?] and darkness the two Cos North of the Embankment did not progress. The two Cos South of the Embankment pushed ahead and took all their objectives. Owing to the height of the embankment the two Cos on N.S. of Railway were unable to keep in touch this difficulty was added to by the darkness, no one on their R + L advanced with them thus forming two lines on either flank. The enemy closed in to these two who were informed through works and returned and RO Box.	

Place	Date	Hour	Summary of Events and Information	Remarks and references to Appendices
	3rd		Casualties. Officers. WOUNDED: 2nd Lieut J.E. Trimmer " H. Cardwell " W.E. Collins Capt C. Gregory 2nd Lieut T.E. Slater " J.H. Stott " R. Davenport " O James WOUNDED & MISSING " J. Concannon " J. Allen " G.S.T. Wright " A.E. Rogers MISSING " P. Norris " E.M. Briggs O.R. Killed. 17 Wounded. 84 Missing 174	

Army Form C. 2118.

WAR DIARY
or
INTELLIGENCE SUMMARY.
(Erase heading not required.)

Instructions regarding War Diaries and Intelligence Summaries are contained in F. S. Regs., Part II. and the Staff Manual respectively. Title pages will be prepared in manuscript.

Place	Date	Hour	Summary of Events and Information	Remarks and references to Appendices
	4th		Bn. working in trenches N of Entrenchment. Artillery and snipers active. 10 O.R. wounded. 7 O.R. reinforcements arrived.	See
	5th		Quiet day. Snipers still active. Reinforced in trenches by 1st Bn. K.O.R. Lanc. R.	See
	6th		On completion of Relief Bn. moved back to 4th German System. Enemy shelled trenches occasionally. 2 O.R. wounded. 2/Lieut. A. Thomas joined Bn. Depot.	See
	7th		Artillery active. Enemy moved Headquarters particularly shelled, about 12 noon. 2/Lieut STANGE and 170 O.R. joined Bn Depot. As right Bn (Camerons & Coys) relieved 1st K.O.R. Lanc. R. & 2 Cos. 1st Bn. in front trenches near CHEMICAL WORKS.	See
	8th		1 O.R. wounded. Artillery active especially on H.Q. Street. 1 O.R. wounded.	See
	9th		Artillery very active. Our Chinese Barrage drew a very heavy fire on Bn. HQrs.	

WAR DIARY
or
INTELLIGENCE SUMMARY

Army Form C. 2118.

Place	Date	Hour	Summary of Events and Information	Remarks and references to Appendices
B'tn in RIDGE	9th		Bn. relieved in Trenches by 7th YORKS. R. On completion of Relief Bn went back to RAILWAY Embankment East of ATHIES. 3. O.R's wounded.	Appx
	10th		Bn in Div. Reserve in Embankment on 9th 10th & 11th Bdes attacked CHEMICAL WORKS — ROEUX Cemetery & trench system around Rlme. Bde in Div Reserve.	Appx
Bn in Embankment	11th		Bn. moved up to 4th German System to come under orders of 72nd and RIDGE	Appx
	12th	12 mn 2pm	B.G.C. 11th Bde. sinuded into support to Rifle Brigade Bn moved 32 mn RIDGE East of FAMPOUX in support to Rifle Brigade with orders to keep in touch with them and Essex and move forward as they did. 2. O.R's wounded to a cellar in FAMPOUX. Bn. HQrs Enemy shelled continuously all day. 1000 hrs wounds. 2nd Lieut C. DUNLEVY crossed Casualties 2. O.R. wounded to old English front line. As soon as it was dark Bn. withdrew to in G. 17.	Appx

Army Form C. 2118.

WAR DIARY
or
INTELLIGENCE SUMMARY.
(Erase heading not required.)

Instructions regarding War Diaries and Intelligence Summaries are contained in F. S. Regs., Part II. and the Staff Manual respectively. Title pages will be prepared in manuscript.

Place	Date	Hour	Summary of Events and Information	Remarks and references to Appendices
PENIN	13th		Bn. moved to PENIN in busses.	gcu
"	14th		Reorganisation	gcu
			4 O.R. Reinforcements	gcu
"	15th		Reorganisation	gcu
			Army Commander inspected & spoke to Bn.	gcu
"	16th		Div. Commander addressed Bde.	gcu
"	17th		60 Training	gcu
"	18th		15 O.R. Reinforcements	gcu
"	19th		60 Training	gcu
"	20th		Sunday	gcu
"	21st		7 O.R. Reinforcements	gcu
"	22nd		60 Training	gcu
"	23rd		" "	gcu
"	24th		" "	gcu
"	25th		7 O.R. Reinforcements } and 7 O.R. Rein/forcements	gcu
"	26th		4 O.R " 2nd LIEUT HOWARTH A	gcu
"	27th		BARON J.H.	gcu
			CORNETT E.H.	
			CAIN R.K.	
			GUY	
"	28		Sunday Training	gcu

Army Form C. 2118.

WAR DIARY
or
INTELLIGENCE SUMMARY.

(Erase heading not required.)

Instructions regarding War Diaries and Intelligence Summaries are contained in F. S. Regs., Part II. and the Staff Manual respectively. Title pages will be prepared in manuscript.

Place	Date	Hour	Summary of Events and Information	Remarks and references to Appendices
PENIN.	29		Co. training	App.
	30	"		App.
	31	"		App.

JShatRue for Lieut. Col
Comdg 2 Lancashire Fusiliers
Majr

Operation Orders
by
Major H.W. Glenn
Commanding 2nd Lancashire Fusiliers

Field   2nd May 1917

1. The Bn is taking part at an hour Zero on May 3rd in a general attack on the enemy's position covering FRESNES-LES-MONTAUBAN and PLOUVAIN.

2. **Divisional Scheme**

   The Division is attacking with the 10th Brigade on the Right, 12th Brigade on the left and 11th Bde in Reserve.

3. **Brigade Scheme**

   Brigade Boundaries

   South. Cross Roads H.1.d.55.10 – Chemical Works (inclusive) – thence straight line to SOUTHERN edge of PLOUVAIN I.16.d.0.0

   North.
   Hyderabad Redoubt – Clyde – Cut (all inclusive to 9th Div:) thence straight line from Junction of CUBA and CASH to Station in I.9.c

   Objectives.

   (a) CHEMICAL WORKS, STATION BUILDING and CEMETERY, thence to track from I.8.c.3.3 to I.14.c.5.5 and Buildings at Eastern end of ROEUX. (BLACK LINE).

   (b) Woods in I.8.d – CANDY, CYPRUS and CARROT Trenches. (BLUE LINE)

(c) Trenches WEST of PLOUVAIN from the Station to I.16.a.0.0 – thence through Guns positions along the track, running to I.21.b.5.0 (RED LINE)

(d) After reaching the RED LINE a further advance may be made by Reserve Division and 11th Bde.

4. (a) The attack on the 1st Objective will be carried out by the 2nd LAN FUS on Right and 2nd ESSEX Regt on Left.

Dividing Line :- CAM to the ROEUX-GAVRELLE Road thence – RAILWAY JUNCTION I.13.b.8.2 – along Railway (inclusive to Essex.)

The 2nd W. RIDING REGT follow the 2nd LAN FUS and the 1st Kings Own the 2nd W. RIDING R.

(b) The 2nd ESSEX on being squeezed out during advance on 2nd and 3rd Objectives will form a defensive flank along the Railway.

(c) On the 1st Objective, the 2nd W. RIDING REGT. will form up on the Right of the 2nd LAN FUS either in line with them or failing that, Slightly in rear.

For the attack on the 2nd Objective, the boundary between 2nd W. RIDING R. and 2nd LAN FUS will be a line from the JUNCTION of Trench and Road at I.14.c.4.9 to point I.15.b.2.1 where trench cuts Road.

(d) The 1st KINGS OWN will pass through the 2nd LAN FUS on the 2nd Objective to capture the 3rd Objective.

Battalion Scheme

(a) Order of attack

    B on RIGHT
    D on LEFT
    C in Support on RIGHT
    A in Support on LEFT

Battalions will attack in 4 WAVES B. and D. forming first two and C. & A. the second two.

B. Co. will assemble in 120 yards of CEYLON TRENCH with left on Railway Embankment

D. Co. will assemble in NEW TRENCH joining CAWDOR and OAIL.

C. Co. in combination of CAWDOR South of Pivot.

A Co. in Cawdor with Right on Railway Embankment.

Until both Companies are on the South of the Railway Embankment the Cos will move with their flanks on the Railway Embankment

When D. Co. crosses at Railway Junction B. will move to its Right and march by the left. D. Co directing with left flank on Railway.

Same applies to C & A. Cos.

On reaching BLACKLINE C & A Cos will pass through B & D. Cos. and move on to the BLUE LINE, A Co. directing.

B & D Cos will consolidate BLACKLINE.

G. Churston Lieut & Adj
2nd Lancs Fusiliers.

<u>Secret.</u>

War Diary

of

<u>2ⁿᵈ Bn Lancashire Fusiliers Regt</u>

From: 1ˢᵗ June 1917
To: 30ᵗʰ June 1917

VOLUME

Date 2/7/17

[signature] Lt Colonel
Comdg: 2ⁿᵈ Bn Lancashire Fusiliers Regt

WAR DIARY or INTELLIGENCE SUMMARY

Army Form C. 2118.

(Erase heading not required.) Ref. Map 51.B.N.W. 1/20,000

JUNE

Place	Date	Hour	Summary of Events and Information	Remarks and references to Appendices
PENIN	1st		Co. training Lieut L.G.C. CHAPMAN and 2ⁿᵈ Lieut R. NISBET joined Bn	9cu
	2nd			9cu
	3rd		Sunday	9cu
	4th		Co. training	9cu
	5th		2nd Lieut H.S. ELLIOTT and 5 O.R. joined Bn	9cu
	6th			9cu
	7th		8 O.R. Reinforcements arrived	9cu
	8th			9cu
	9th			9cu
ARRAS	10th	8.15AM	Bde Rifle meeting	9cu
		1.30pm	Moved in busses to ARRAS	
			Arrived	
FIFE CAMP	11th	10AM	Moved to FIFE CAMP (200x east of St NICHOLAS) = Bde. Reserve. 4 O.R. Reinforcements	9cu
"	12th		Physical training and Bathing	9cu
"	13th		"	9cu
"	14th			9cu
Trenches	15th		Bn. relieved 1st K.O.R. Lanc. R. in trenches East of Chemical Works, North	9cu
			of FAMPOUX - PLOUVAIN RAILWAY q.r.	
			Essex on Right, 34th Divison on left front. D in SUFFOLK B in Bn. Reserve	
			C Co on Right front, A Co on left front. 5 O.R. Reinforcements	
E of CHEMICAL WKS N. of FAMPOUX - PLOUVAIN RLY.	16		1 O.R. Wounded. Shell Shock. Artillery active on both sides 4 O.R. Wounded.	9cu
	17th		Enemy very quiet Enemy Artillery active 1 O.R. wounded	9cu

Army Form C. 2118.

WAR DIARY
or
INTELLIGENCE SUMMARY.
(Erase heading not required.)

Place	Date	Hour	Summary of Events and Information	Remarks and references to Appendices
In trenches	18th		Enemy Artillery and Aircraft active. Trench mortars active at night. 2/Lieut C.M CORBETT wounded SHELLSHOCK and 1.O.R. wounded.	9cm
	19th		Enemy Quiet. Bn: Relieved in trenches by 2nd Bn. Seaforth Highlanders. 1.O.R. K. 3 O.R. wounded.	9cm
			(On the 16th 1 Co of 3/4th Queens were attached to Bn for instruction)	
DINGWALL CAMP	20th	3.30am	Bn arrived at DINGWALL CAMP (Map: N.W of BLANGY) 2nd Lieut D.H RILEY REINFORCEMENT Officer	9cm
"	21st		Bn in DINGWALL CAMP. Day and night working parties found	9cm
"	22nd		" " "	9cm
"	23rd		" " "	9cm
"	24th		" " "	9cm
"	25th		" " " 5 OR Reinforcements	9cm
"	26th		" " "	9cm
"	27th		Bn. relieved 1 Co. HAMPSHIRE Regt in RESERVE TRENCH DUE SOUTH OF FAMPOUX H.29.B. and SCARPE RIVER	9cm
Trenches S of TEUCHY N of GERMAN SYSTEM H29 a central	28th		(Bn: less Bn relieved 9th Essex Regt. in trenches in vicinity of ORANGE HILL (South of SCARPE) Bde. RESERVE. 1 OR wounded	9cm
	29th		Bn. found night working parties for K.O in front line	9cm
	30		" " " 1 OR wounded	9cm
			1.OR. KILLED 1 OR wounded.	

J.H./Cunn Lieut Col
Comdg 2 Ham Rn

<u>Secret.</u>

War Diary

of

<u>2nd Bn Lancashire Fusiliers</u>

From 1st July 1917

To 31st July 1917

Volume 7

Aug 3rd 1917

GAlmaster Cmdt NSL
for Lt Colonel
Commanding 2 Lancashire Fus

Army Form C. 2118.

WAR DIARY
or
INTELLIGENCE SUMMARY.
(Erase heading not required.)

Instructions regarding War Diaries and Intelligence Summaries are contained in F. S. Regs., Part II. and the Staff Manual respectively. Title pages will be prepared in manuscript.

JULY.

Place	Date	Hour	Summary of Events and Information	Remarks and references to Appendices
HIMALAYA TRENCH	1st		Bn. in Bde. Reserve	6pm
	do	10pm	Relieved 1st K.O.R. Lanc. R. in Left Sub Section	
LEFT SUB SECTION FRONT TRENCHES	2nd		1st Bn. holding the River Scarpe. 2nd W. Rid R. on Right	9am
	3rd		Casualties 1 O.R. Killed 1 O.R. Wounded 2nd Essex Relieved W. Rid R. on Right	9am
			Both Artillerie active	
			2 O.R. Killed. 2nd West Ridden F. and 1 O.R. Wounded	
	4th		Quiet day 1 O.R. Wounded	9am
	5th	10pm	Bn. Relieved in position by 1st K.O.R. Lanc. R.	9am
HIMALAYA TRENCH	6th		Proceeded in relief to HIMALAYA TRENCH	9am
			In Bde. Reserve	
			At night found working Parties for front and support lines	
	7th		do	9am
	8th		do	9am
	9th	10pm	Relieved 1st K.O.R. Lanc. R. in front trenches. Disposition as on 1st July	9am
LEFT SUB SECTION FRONT TRENCHES	10th		1 O.R. Wounded	9am
	11th		2nd Lieut J.M. Thompson while visiting his advanced listen ones in nomans land. It is believed that he was wounded by a German Patrol and taken Prisoner	9am
			General activity. 3 O.R. Killed 1 O.R. Wounded	
	12th		1 O.R. Killed 2 O.R. Wounded	9am

Army Form C. 2118.

WAR DIARY
or
INTELLIGENCE SUMMARY.
(Erase heading not required.)

Instructions regarding War Diaries and Intelligence Summaries are contained in F. S. Regs., Part II. and the Staff Manual respectively. Title pages will be prepared in manuscript.

Place	Date	Hour	Summary of Events and Information	Remarks and references to Appendices
Front Line Trenches	13th		1 O.R. Killed	
REST SUB-SECTOR		10pm	Bn. Relieved by 11th Bn. The Rifle Brigade	Apx
BAROSSA CAMP G 13	14th		On Relief Bn. moved back into Divisional Reserve at Francois Camp. Reorganisation and Preparations for Bn. training. 2Lieut V.F.Stowers M.C. 2Lieut B.W. Jones, 2Lieut Dodson joined Bn.	Apx
"	15		Bn. training	Apx
"	16		"	Apx
"	17		"	Apx
"	18		"	Apx
"	19		"	Apx
"	20		"	Apx
"	21		"	Apx
"	22		Bn. found Working Parties by day and larger work on front line and lines of communication	Apx
"	23		do	Apx
"	24		do	Apx
"	25		do	Apx
"	26		do	Apx
"	27		do	Apx
"	28		do	Apx
ARMENTIERES CAMP G 13	29	6pm	Bn. should have proceeded to HIMALAYA TRENCH but were allowed to stay out so as to be able to celebrate "MINDEN DAY" on the 1st Aug. Ceremonial Preparations to MINDEN DAY Celebration	Apx
"	30		"	Apx
"	31		"	Apx

G. Alliante Lieut Col
1 Cmdg. 1 Som. L.I.

<u>Secret</u>

War Diary

of

2nd Bn. Lancashire Fusiliers

From 1st Aug 1917
To 21st Aug 1917

Volume 8

Date 1/9/17

H.W. _____ Lt Colonel
Comdg Lancashire Fus

WAR DIARY
INTELLIGENCE SUMMARY

Army Form C. 2118.

August
Ref. Map. 51.B. N.W. 1/20,000

Place	Date	Hour	Summary of Events and Information	Remarks and references to Appendices
BAROSSA CAMP G.16.a.4.6	1st	3.30	Bn. celebrated anniversary of MINDEN DAY Bn. Parade "Trooping Colour"	9.u.
HIMALAYA TRENCH H.26.a	2nd		Bn. moved to Bde. Reserve in HIMALAYA TRENCH H.26.a	9.u.
"	3rd		Bn. found working parties by day and night for front system (11 O.R. Reinforcements)	9.u.
"	4th		" " " "	9.u.
"	5th		" " " "	9.u.
"	6th		On night of 6/7th Bn. relieved 1st K.O.R. in R in Res. Sub Sector, Right Sector	9.u.
Front Line Right Sub Sector I.31,5,6 & I.25 central	7th		Quiet day. Our Artillery active. Enemy Snipers somewhat active. (1 O.R. Reinforcement)	9.u.
"	8th		Enemy generally active. Artillery T.Mortars and rifle grenades. Casualties. 6.O.R. Killed 1.O.R. wounded	9.u.
"	9th		Enemy Artillery active (2/Lieut G.N. STANCE evacuated from Hospl.) Casualties. 1.O.R. Killed 2.O.R wounded 2/Lieut C. MELLOR to Hospl.	9.u.
"	10th		General Activity Casualties. 3 O.R. Wounded	9.u.
"	11th		Moderately quiet	9.u.
"	12th		" Casualties 1 O.R. killed	9.u.
"	13th		General Activity during day. Quiet at night Bn. relieved in trenches by 1st Bn/R/R Bde. (9.O.R. Reinforcements)	9.u.
"	14th		Bn. moved to BAROSSA CAMP Casualties 1.O.R. Killed 2.O.R Wounded 2/Lieut C. DUNKERY to Hospl	9.u.

Army Form C. 2118.

WAR DIARY
or
INTELLIGENCE SUMMARY.
(Erase heading not required.)

Place	Date	Hour	Summary of Events and Information	Remarks and references to Appendices
BATTROSS CAMP C.18.a.4.6	15th		Bn in Camp. Bn found night working Parties for front System	
	16th		" dayand "	
	17th		Ditto	
	18th		Ditto	
	19th		Ditto	(2nd Lieut E. DAGLIGH and 2.O.R. to Hospl.)	
	20		Ditto	
	21		Ditto	2nd Lieut C. DUNLEVY Rejoined from Hospl.	
	22		Ditto	2nd Lieut G.T. COOPER to Hospl. (4.O.R. Reinforcements)	
	23		Ditto	Capt S.W. HOWARTH from Hospl.	
	24		Ditto		
	25		Ditto		
	26		Ditto	(1 O.R. Reinforcements)	
	27		Ditto		
	28		Ditto		
	29		Ditto		
	30		Bn. relieved 1st/7th Bn HAMPS.R in Bde. Rgt Reserve in Camp H.25.c.5.3	
CAMP H.25.c.M.3	31st		Co. relieved 1st/7th Bn HAMPS.R in LANCER LANE H.29.6.	

H.M.Elwin Lieut Col.
Comdg 1 Hamps Hn.

SECRET

War Diary
of
2 Lancashire Fusiliers
from
September 1st 1917 to
September 30th 1917

Volume No 9

J.W.Watkins.
Major
Commanding Lancashire Fus

Army Form C. 2118.

WAR DIARY
or
INTELLIGENCE SUMMARY.

(Erase heading not required.)

Instructions regarding War Diaries and Intelligence Summaries are contained in F.S. Regs., Part II. and the Staff Manual respectively. Title pages will be prepared in manuscript.

SIGNAL [?] maps

Hour, Date, Place		Summary of Events and Information	Remarks and references to Appendices
September 1st	H.25.c.5.3	Bn in Camp at H.25.c.5.3. in Support to 1st K.O.R. Lanc. R. (75 O.R. Reinforcements)	qu.
2nd		Bn. Relieved 1st K.O.R. Lanc R. in trenches Essex on Right. Seaforths on Left. (2nd Lieut. E.G. Dalglish re-joined from Hosp.)	qu.
3rd		Do Very quiet	qu.
4th	TRENCHES	Do	qu.
5th		Do	qu.
6th		Bn: Relieved in trenches by 10th/11th H.L.I. 1.O.R. Killed	qu.
7th		On relief Bn. moved to No.4 Camp Hendecourt.	qu.
8th	No.4 Camp Hedecourt	In camp. C and R. hanny	qu.
9th		do	qu.
10th		do	qu. (1.O.R. Rejoined)
11th		do	qu.
12th		do	qu.
13th		do	qu.
14th		do	qu.
15th		do	qu. (1.O.R. Rejoined)
16th		do	qu. 1.O.R. Rejoined
17th		do	qu.
18th		Bn. moved to Beaumetz. Entrained for Pesennoer	qu. 2 O.R. sick (A. Hammond to Hospital R. Nairn)
19th		Bn arrived Pesennoer wounded to Sutton Camp arrived 9.45 A.M.	qu.
20th			qu.

Army Form C. 2118.

WAR DIARY
or
INTELLIGENCE SUMMARY

(Erase heading not required.)

Instructions regarding War Diaries and Intelligence Summaries are contained in F. S. Regs, Part II. and the Staff Manual respectively. Title Pages will be prepared in manuscript.

Place	Date	Hour	Summary of Events and Information	Remarks and references to Appendices
SUTTON CAMP	Sept. 21st		Co. & Pn. Training	9am
	22nd		"	9am
	23rd		"	9am
	24th		"	9am
	25th		"	9am
	26th		"	9am
	27th		Bn. entrained at INTERNATIONAL (A.9.a.1.4) CORNER STATION (9ᵒ Lieut N.D. Evans joined Bn.) (153 O.R. Reinforcements) Lieut L.G.C. Chapman to Hospl. Detrained at B.14.a.9.9	9am
To WOLFE CAMP			Marched to WOLFE CAMP B.28.c.b.8	9am
CANAL BANK C.13.c.	28th		Elder Dincke Pde Reserve on Canal Bank.	9am
	29		moved into Canal Bank.	9am
	30		On Canal Bank.	9am

J. McRae Major.
Comdg. 2 Manchester Fuslrs.

Secret

War Diary
of
2nd Lancashire Fusiliers
From 1st October 1917
To 31st October 1917

Volume 10

4/11/17

H.W.E. Ben. Lt Colonel
Comdg Lancashire Fus.

Army Form C. 2118.

WAR DIARY
or
INTELLIGENCE SUMMARY.
(Erase heading not required.)

Instructions regarding War Diaries and Intelligence Summaries are contained in F.S. Regs., Part II. and the Staff Manual respectively. Title pages will be prepared in manuscript.

Place	Date	Hour	Summary of Events and Information	Remarks and references to Appendices
Dunoon Reninie (canal bank)	1/10/17		Bn. relieved in Reninie by Hampshire Regt. Moved back to ROUSSELL Camp. Casualties 1 OR killed 2 OR wounded. Reinforcements 6 OR	
Roussel Camp	2/10/17		Bn. rested at Roussel camp. Casualties 1 OR wounded on working party.	
Roussel Camp	3/10/17		Reinforcements 11 OR.	
Roussel Camp	4/10/17			
Roussel Camp	5/10/17		Bn. moved from ROUSSELL Camp to WOLFF Camp. 1 OR wounded.	
Wolff Camp	6/10/17			
Wolff Camp	7/10/17		Bn. relieved 2 Coy. Hampshire Regt & 2 Coy. Rifle Brigade in the front line in left of POEL CAPPELLE. Casualties 1 OR wounded.	
Front line	8/10/17		Bn. in front line	

Place	Date	Hour	Summary of Events and Information	Remarks and references to Appendices
FRONT LINE	9.10.17		Bn attacked on a frontage of 200 yards with its centre on IMBROS HOUSE A Co Right front C Co Left front B Support D Reserve. Zero hour 5.20 am. The Bn advanced about 400x (yds) (apps) in advance of the own front line. There were three objectives but owing to the resistance on the right by rifle fire the Bn consolidated between the 1st & 2nd objectives. Casualties:- Major T.W. WATKINS Capt G.C. MARTIN M.C. " G.L. ELKINGTON 2Lt M.S. ELLIOT " H.M. DODSON " L. SHIPMAN " E.G. DALGLIESH " W.H. RILEY (Reader Day) } WOUNDED 2Lt A. WARRELL " R.S. THICKNESSE } KILLED Capt R.A. LOWE (Seven) 2Lt E.S. FARGHER missing Estimated Casualties OR 33 Killed 126 Wounded 41 Missing	
FRONT LINE	10.10.17		Bn held consolidated position on left of POELCAPPELLE	

Army Form C. 2118.

WAR DIARY
or
INTELLIGENCE SUMMARY.

(Erase heading not required.)

Place	Date	Hour	Summary of Events and Information	Remarks and references to Appendices
Front Line	10.10.17		Bn relieved in front line by Royal Warwickshire Regt. Proceeded back to REDAN Camp. Arrived at REDAN early morning of 11.10.17	
Redan Camp	11.10.17		Reinforcements 10 OR.	
Redan Camp	12.10.17		Bn moved from REDAN Camp to PENTON Camp near PROVEN by train	
Penton Camp	13.10.17			
Penton Camp	14.10.17		Bn moved from PENTON Camp to PURBROOK Camp near HARINGE	
Purbrook Camp	15.10.17		5 Officer Reinforcements 2Lt C.E. JONES 2Lt R.E.T. WALDEN 2Lt H.W. EVERETT 2Lt A.M. RUSTON 2Lt KEIGHTLEY	
Purbrook Camp	16.10.17		Bn moved from PURBROOK Camp and arrived in ROAD Camp, ST TAN TEN BIEZEN. Reinforcements 1 OR.	
Road Camp	17.10.17			
Road Camp	18.10.17		Bn moved from ROAD Camp at 5:30am & entrained at PEBEL HOEK at 12 noon for HABARCQ. Reinforcements 2 OR.	
Road Camp	19.10.17			
Habarcq	20.10.17		Arrived at HABARCQ at 2:30 am.	

Army Form C. 2118.

WAR DIARY
or
INTELLIGENCE SUMMARY.
(Erase heading not required.)

Instructions regarding War Diaries and Intelligence Summaries are contained in F.S. Regs., Part II. and the Staff Manual respectively. Title pages will be prepared in manuscript.

Place	Date	Hour	Summary of Events and Information	Remarks and references to Appendices
HABARCQ	21.10.17		Reinforcement 2.LT G.T. WATSON 2.LT A.CHILTARN	
HABARCQ	22.10.17		Reinforcement 2.O.R.	
HABARCQ	23.10.17		Bn. moved from HABARCQ to SCHRAMM BARRACKS ARRAS.	
HABARCQ	24.10.17		Bn moved from HABARCQ to ARRAS	
ARRAS	25.10.17		Bn moved from ARRAS to BOIS des BOEUFS	
Bois du BOEUFS	26.10.17			
Bois des Boeufs	29/10/17		Bn. moved from BOIS des BOEUFS & relieved 4th Seaforth Highlanders in ARTOIS Sub-Sector. Reinforcements Lt T. ROBINSON.	
			Casualties 1 O.R. wounded	
Front Line	29/10/17		Casualties 1 O.R. wounded 2.LT R.W. ARMSTRONG 2.LT J.W. KEIGHTLEY to Hospital	
Front Line	30.10.17		Reinforcements 1 O.R. Casualties 1 O.R. wounded	
Front Line	31.10.17		Casualties 2.LT E.G. JONES wounded (Raid or Duty) 1 O.R. wounded	

A.W.Clem Lieut Colonel
Commanding Lancashire Division

Operation Orders
by
Lancashire Fusiliers
Ref Map Belgium 20 S.W. 1/20000   9th Oct 1917
        Belgium 20 S.E. 1/20000

1. The 5th Army in conjunction with the Second Army and the French Army is continuing the attack on Z day.

2. (a) The 4th Div. is attacking with 12th Inf Bde in the Front Line. 10th Inf. Bde in support and 11th Inf. Bde in Reserve.

(b) 6th Yorks Regt. 32nd Inf Bde 11th Div. will be on the Right of 12th Inf Bde, and 1st Lan Fus of 86th Inf Bde 29th Div. on Left.

The Brigade will attack on a front of two Bns and disposition will be as follows:-

Right Assault Battalion   2nd Essex Regt
Left   "   "   2nd Lan Fus
Bde Support   2nd W. Rid. Regt
Bde Reserve   1st K.O.R. Lanc Regt

Brigade Objectives
FIRST - V.14.c.1.5 - STRING HOUSE - V.13.a.2.2
SECOND - V.14.c.85.98 - V.13.b.8.4 - V.13.b.1.8
THIRD - V.14 Central - V.14.a.45.80 - V.7.d.8.5

There will be a halt of 45 minutes on each of the FIRST and SECOND Objectives, during which reorganisation will be carried out and touch regained if lost.

The 2nd Lan Fus will attack on a front of Two Companies and dispositions will be as follows:-

RIGHT Front   A &
LEFT Front   C
Support.   B
Reserve   D

The Brigade, Battalion and Company Boundaries are as follows

BRIGADE.
RIGHT. U.24.c.5.2 - V.14.c.0.4 to V.14.a.98.05
LEFT. U.24.a.7.9 - V.7.d.87.53   P.T.O.

Bn.
    RIGHT. V.B.C.00 — V.H.a.4.9
    LEFT. Brigade Left

Company
  A.Co RIGHT. Bn. RIGHT
  A.Co Left
  C.Co RIGHT. A Co. Left
  C.Co LEFT Bn. Left

7. To ensure that all Ranks know the general direction of the advance, Co. Commdrs. will select guiding points, and have them pointed out to all Ranks. The true bearing of the line of advance is approximately 55°.

Patrols will move on the outer flanks of all Cos. They will be responsible for keeping touch & direction. C.Co. will arrange to get in communication with 1st Lan.Fus at MILLERS HOUSES, WATER HOUSE and V.7.d.8.5

This is to ensure touch and must be done.

8. Throughout advance Cos. must be prepared to form a defensive flank. The remainder must push on and try and turn the obstacle.

Co. Commdrs. are reminded that in this form of Warfare the most effective form of Support is in most cases given by outflanking the enemy, rather than by merely giving more weight to an attack as one does in Trench Warfare.

9. MOPPERS UP B. Co. will detail 1 Pl. Lao Lewis Gun to MOP UP behind A.Co.

D.Co. will detail 1 Pl. behind C.Co.

Definite parties from mopping up Pls will be detailed to mop up special points. e.g. COMPROMIS Farm, WATER HOUSE etc. As soon as they have completed their task they will rejoin their Pls.

10. M.G's One Section (less 1 Gun) of the 2nd M.G.Co will be allotted to the Bn.

P.T.O.

M.G.
These Guns will move with Bn. HQrs. until Final objective is taken. They will then move as follows: One Gun to B.Co. One Gun to C.Co. and One will remain with Bn. H.Q.

11. T.M.B. The 12th T.M.B will move with 2ND W. Rid Regt.
If Companies find they require a Gun they will at once notify Bn H.Q.

12. Contact Aeroplanes.
Probably at each Objective a Contact Aeroplane will fly over.
It will fly over and either drop a white light or call up with a succession of A's (·—) on its Klaxon Horn.
The Co it is calling up will light its Aeroplane Flares in bunches of threes if possible.
These flares must not be wasted and care must be taken only to light them when called for

13. Final Objective
On reaching Final Objective (a) Cos will at once consolidate, covered by posts of Lewis Guns and Riflemen.
D. Co. will consolidate on a line about 200 yds behind front. Cos.
(b). The "Support" Ps of A & C Cos if not absorbed in Front Line, will make Strong Points behind their Front System.
B. Co will make a strong point in BESACE Fm. The Vickers Gun will be used for defence of this post in addition to a garrison from B. Co
(c) Strong Patrols will be sent out from A and C. Cos. as far as barrage will permit.
As soon as protective barrage lifts, these patrols will push on and get in touch with enemy.

P.T.O.

A.C. will send Patrol to MEMLING FARM.
(b). Reorganise.
(c). On reaching Final Objective it is possible that a further Objective may be assigned to the Brigade. In this event the 2nd W.Rid.R will continue attack on the Right and 1st K.O.R. Lanc.R on Left.

Counter Attack Coy

D. Coy is detailed as Counter Attack Coy and will Counter attack immediately O.C. D.Coy thinks it necessary without any orders from Bn HQrs. He will send a Report to Bn H.Q. directly the occasion arises.

14. Barrage.
(a) The Creeping Barrage will take 10 minutes to move over the first 100 yds to allow troops on left to come up.
(b) The Protective Barrage will halt 300 yds in front of the Final Objective
(c) Further orders re Barrages will be notified later.

15. Bn H.Qrs. will move from LOUIS Fm to a Shell hole about U.18.d.6.3 (exact position to be notified later.) at Z – 1 hours.
After Z hour Bn HQ. will move by bounds along Coy dividing line approximately.
The first move will be after Coys have reached first objective. The Second after Second Objective. The third Bound will be to neighbourhood of WATER HOUSE after the final objective has been taken.

17. Reports. Coys will report if possible by runners as they reach each objective, or more often if necessary. Reports should include estimated casualties as well as other headings on the forms issued.

P.T.O.

Within at the most, 2 hours after reaching Final Objective Coos must notify Hd.Qrs. their disposition on maps issued.

18. Communication will be done entirely by
(1.) Runners.
(2.) VISUAL.
The Bn Signalling Officer will arrange to keep in touch by VISUAL with Cos and also with Bde throughout the attack

19. Dress. Dress will be as laid down in S.S. 135 Section XXXI. In addition each man will carry a shovel or a pick in the proportion of 80 shovels to 20 picks

20. ZERO hour will be notified later.

Sgd G. C. Martin Capt Maj
Lan Fus.

Copy No 11

Mr Swan

Secret.

War Diary

of

2nd Bn Lancashire Fusiliers REGT.

From 1st November 1917
To 30th November 1917

Volume II

30-11-17

M.J. [Dunn] Lt Colonel
Commanding
2 Bn Lancashire Fusiliers Regt

Army Form C. 2118.

WAR DIARY
or
INTELLIGENCE SUMMARY.
(Erase heading not required.)

Instructions regarding War Diaries and Intelligence Summaries are contained in F. S. Regs., Part II. and the Staff Manual respectively. Title pages will be prepared in manuscript.

Place	Date	Hour	Summary of Events and Information	Remarks and references to Appendices
LOJEUL SECTOR (GUÉMAPPE)	1/11/17		Bn relieved in Cujeul sector in front of Guémappe by 22nd N.F. & proceeded to Mercatel & bras. Thence by train to Schramm Barracks Arras.	
SCHRAMM BARRACKS	2/11/17			
"	3/11/17			
"	4/11/17			
"	5/11/17		Reinforcements joined 4 OR. 2Lt Thompson & Lt Simpson Lt H.W. Huxley	
"	6/11/17			
"	7/11/17			
"	8/11/17		Reinforcements joined 3 officers. 2Lt N.G. Myers, 2Lt L.S. Adnans Lt H.W. Huxley Bn relieved 1st Bn East Lancashire Regt in the Monchy Defences.	
MONCHY DEFENCES	9/11/17		3 OR reinforcements. 2Lt Dunlevy to hospital.	
"	10/11/17		Casualties 2 OR wounded.	
"	11/11/17		3 OR reinforcements	
"	12/11/17		Bn relieved 1st Bn King's Own in left Sub-sector Monchy defences.	
LEFT SUB SECTOR	13/11/17		5 OR reinforcements 2 OR wounded (gassed).	
"	14/11/17		Bn made a raid in Sunken trench opposite Monchy zero hour 2 am 2Lt Walden + 20 OR	
"	15/11/17		Company raiding party. Casualties 2Lt Walden R.E.T. killed	
"	16/11/17		Bn relieved in afternoon by 1st Kings Own & proceeded down to Brown Line. (Bde Reserve)	
BROWN LINE	16/11/17		Bn in working parties	
"	17/11/17		"	
"	18/11/17		"	
"	19/11/17		"	

Army Form C. 2118.

WAR DIARY
or
INTELLIGENCE SUMMARY.

(Erase heading not required.)

Place	Date	Hour	Summary of Events and Information	Remarks and references to Appendices
BROWN LINE	20/11/17		Reinforcements 2LT FALLOWFIELD-COOPER H.W. 2LT DAVIES H.B. 4 O.R.	
" "	21/11/17		Bn. relieved 1st Bn. Kings Own in Left Sub-Sector	
LEFT SUB SECTOR	22/11/17		Reinforcements 2 O.R.	
" "	23/11/17		1 OR wounded	
" "	24/11/17		Bn. relieved in Left Sub sector by 1st S.O.M.L.I. & marched to SCHRAMM BARRACKS ARRAS, arriving about 10 p.m.	
SCHRAMM BARRACKS	25/11/17		Reinforcements 2LT W.F.HALL Cranston (attd Bde) 2 OR wounded (gassed)	
" "	26/11/17			
" "	27/11/17			
" "	28/11/17		1 OR killed by shell in vicinity of BILLETS 1 OR wounded by shell in vicinity of BILLETS	
" "	29/11/17			
" "	30/11/17			

2/12/17

A.W.Keen Colonel
Commanding 2nd Kings Own Yorkshire

SECRET.

WAR DIARY

of

2nd. Bn. LANCASHIRE FUSILIERS Regt.

From : 1st. December 1917

To: 31st. December 1917.

VOLUME 12.

Date:
31/12/17.

Lt. Colonel,
Commanding
2nd Bn. Lancashire Fusiliers.

Army Form C. 2118.

WAR DIARY
or
INTELLIGENCE SUMMARY.
(Erase heading not required.)

Ref. FRANCE Sheet 51 1/10,000

Place	Date	Hour	Summary of Events and Information	Remarks and references to Appendices
ARRAS	1st DEC	9.15 am	Inspection by C.O.	GRA
		9.30 am	Brigade parade for Medal Presentation by Corps Commander.	GRA
		2 pm	Football Match with Machine Gunners.	GRA
Neuville Vitasse N8 & 57	2nd	6 am	Battery connected for the line at 11.30. Battery HQ changed to Neuville N8 & 57	GRA
		1 pm	12" Trench Mortar Battery relieved 10" Trench Mortar Battery. M.G. Section manned 48 Forward manned into the line. 3" Stokes Mortar fired 50 rounds on to enemy front line in O.21 d 4.0 & 5. Enemy Rifles fire on our communication trench.	GRA
	3rd	6 am	3" Stokes fired 10 rounds during the period in enemy lines at O.21 c 7.0 So. + O.21 d 7.95. Enemy mortars Enemy M.G. active from Bois de Vert on our front systems.	GRA
	4th	6 am	3" Stokes Mortar fired throughout the period on the following targets Junction of Stamp + Pintade. O.21 d 4.0.50 Chapperton. 4 Bombs. Bottle + Ernie. O.6c 8.0.10. SS rounds in all being fired. Enemy activity Artillery shelled during the night with gas shell + high explosive, paying most attention to Spade Reserve + the front line Hostile M.G's active during the night harassing our advanced communication from the direction of the Bois du Vert.	GRA
	5th	6 am	3" Stokes Mortars fired during the period on enemy front line + support between O.21 c 10.30 + O.21 d 8.0.50 95 rounds being fired. Enemy artillery shelled Spade Reserve between 1 am + 11.30 am high barrage. M.G. active enemy harassing trench M.G. on our front Jupiter. O.D. 9.0 Red.	GRA
	6th	6 pm	3" Stokes fired on the following targets. 4 in N.G. Support fired on front line + support between O.9 b 10.50 O.14 b 8.0.50. Gun in Vine Avenue fired on Spoon Boot Trs 3 rounds. 193 rounds in all were fired. Enemy artillery active shelling on communication trenches & reserve Pick Ave + Spade Support in retaliation to our guns. F.A. harassing on trench Gas shells were fired. Enemy light T M.S shelled H.6 Support about N.21.b at 5.30 P.M. & dropped 8 bombs about N.21.b.	GRA

Army Form C. 2118.

WAR DIARY
or
INTELLIGENCE SUMMARY.
(Erase heading not required.)

Instructions regarding War Diaries and Intelligence Summaries are contained in F. S. Regs., Part II. and the Staff Manual respectively. Title pages will be prepared in manuscript.

Place	Date	Hour	Summary of Events and Information	Remarks and references to Appendices
Hebuterne Nrd Sec-	Dec 7th	6 A.M.	3" Stokes fired 147 rounds during the period on the following targets. O.8.d.60.50. O.8.4.t.60.50. & Bucrie Trench. Spoon Trench at O.8.d.75.70 enemy also shelled. Enemy artillery active on tracks behind Monty J.S. O.M.S. 10.0 P.M. MG's active during night on own front system.	GMJ
	8th	6 A.M.	3" Stokes fired 20 rounds during the period on the following targets. Gun fired from Vine Avenue on emplacements on Green detected on aerial photograph at O.2.d.80.0. Scorned. Lewis fired on the target. Junction of Bunny Bucrie Beetle Tri were shelled also enemy front line between O.8.t.40.50 & O.4.b.60.50. Enemy artillery active Spade Res & East Res. Pick Vine Ave'y an supports being shelled during the period. MG's active during the night. Enemy TM's co-operated in the shelling & retaliated to 3" Stokes bombs.	GMJ
	9th	6 A.M.	3" Stokes fired 22 rounds on the following targets Enemy front line between O.8.d.60.50 & O.4.b.80.50. and enemy support line Bucrie Tr & Beetle Tr. Emplacements in Green Lane were again shelled. Enemy artillery active on Pick Avenue & Spade Res. Enemy MG & field active fired on in Crater Subway during the night. O.O.91 and.	GMJ
	10th	6 A.M.	3" Stokes fired 30 rounds during the period on enemy positions at junction of Street Pm across O.8.d.15.10. Junctions of Support & communication trench at O.8.d.80.15. Enemy artillery active on our support & communs. Network nr. 9.30-6.30 Sunniside Corner machine heavily shelled during the day N9c - N9d. Enemy light TM's fired spasmodic on Spade Res, Gordon Avenue & Hue Support 2/Lt Worlick relieved 2/Lt Howarth in N9 sector at about N9 & Sector O.O.92 and.	GMJ
	11th	6 A.M.	3" Stokes fired 10 rounds during the period on enemy emplacement at O.8.d.60's Enemy wire junction of Strong Pm around O.8.d.15.10 junction of O.O.93 and Cas't. Known again from C.R.S. Support & communication trenches at O.8.d.60's & Enemy mortars O.O.93 and Cas't known again from C.R.S. 2/Lt Col Lumor reported from reinforcement.	GMJ

2353   Wt. W2544/1454   700,000   5/15   D. D. & L.   A.D.S.S./Forms/C. 2118.

WAR DIARY or INTELLIGENCE SUMMARY

Army Form C. 2118.

(Erase heading not required.)

Instructions regarding War Diaries and Intelligence Summaries are contained in F. S. Regs., Part II. and the Staff Manual respectively. Title pages will be prepared in manuscript.

Place	Date Dec.	Hour	Summary of Events and Information	Remarks and references to Appendices
Hooge W. N & L. S. ?	12th	6 pm	3" Stokes fired 130 rounds during the period on the following targets. Form Stokes gunners H95 Sp at fired on enemy lines between O.8d.60.50 & O.14.6.60.10. Gun on Vine Avenue open shelled Garrenlan at O.14.b.10. Shots fell into front attack (subsidiary attack) Enemy artillery shelled Gordon Ave & White Tr & Spade Ave intermittently. Enemy TMs fired about 30 rounds on front line.	JPR
	13th	8.30 am / 6 pm	3" Stokes fired 100 rounds on the following targets. Enemy lire between O.8d.60.50 & O.14.6.60.10. Spoon Tr N20. The shelled Enemy artillery active on our communication trenches throughout the day. Enemy TMs fired on front line about 20 rounds.	JPR
	14th	6 am	3" Stokes fired 120 rounds on enemy front line between O.8d.60.60 & O.14.6.60.50 Spoon Tr shelter enemy lit shelters Enemy artillery shelled Gordon Ave intermittently. Slight barrage on Spade Rd at 7 pm & 11 pm. Enemy TMs fired about 30 rounds on & in front supports line.	JPR
		7 pm & 11 pm		
	15th	6 am	Sec 3" Stokes Mortars co-operated in raid by 3rd Essex Regt on enemy front & support lines. (Morning & evening) special attention to the following targets junctions of trenches at Buckle with Long - Bolt with Spoon Pun & Strap Tr — Buckle Tr who junction & Buckle & Bodge & Beetle. Sap in Lanyard at O.14.b.6.95. 41 rounds were fired in all during raid. Gun fired 9th fired during the night on Spoon Tr N War junction. Was opened with expected during the period. Hostile attack artillery shelled Gordon Avenue. Saddle & Hill Support White Tr Dale Tr barrage continually between 7 pm & 10 pm. Enemy MGs retaliated on front system during raid & at night. Usual bursts of traversing fire were 7 pm. 0045 med	JPR
	16th	6 am	3" Stokes fired 127 rounds during the period on the following targets. Enemy Sap T. Tr in Spoon Tr at O.8.d.60.60. Enemy front line system between O.8.d.60.80 & O.14.b.60.80. Hostile artillery shelled Gordon Ave & Saddle Sup & Saddle Res intermittently during the period.	JPR
	17th	6 pm	3" Stokes Mortars fired 100 rounds during period on enemy positions as follows: junction of Pun & Strap Tr. Buckle Beetle & Barge. Enemy front line new trenches between O.8.d.60.50 & O.14.b.60.80. Enemy artillery shelled Gordon Ave & Spade Res intermittently.	JPR

A.5834 Wt. W4973/M687 750,000 8/16 D.D. & L. Ltd. Forms/C.2118/13.

WAR DIARY
or INTELLIGENCE SUMMARY
(Erase heading not required.)

Army Form C. 2118.

Place	Date	Hour	Summary of Events and Information	Remarks and references to Appendices
[Illegible] N8 A57	Dec 18th	6 AM 5 PM	Relieved by the 11th [Bn]. Relief complete by 5 P.M.	J.M.
ARRAS Rue Frederick de George	19	9 AM 11 AM 2 PM	Cleaning equipment. Khaki and Boots inspected by O.C. Battery Billet Inspection	J.M.
"	20	9 AM 11.30 AM 2 PM	Route march in clean fatigue, gas helmets on Sectional football match at cycle track Arras	J.M.
"	21	9.30 AM 9 AM 10.20 11 AM	Parade at 9 AM in fighting order. Inspection + kit (ammunition) turnout &c. Gun drill Arms drill and musketry Stand to	J.M. J.M.
"	22	6.30 AM 9 AM 11 AM 2 PM 6.30	Stand to Parade fighting order. Inspection by O.C. Gun drill Football match between sections Stand to	J.M. J.M.
"	23	9.45 10 AM 11-12	W.O's Classes Parades Room cutter church parade Church of England Service	J.M.
"	24	9 AM	No 2 Section parade fighting order under 2nd Lt Gerrith will take gun contest to gun I exhibition store for O.C. W.O. Seel [illegible] under W.J. [Gannon] for route march. Stand to 6.30 am	J.M.

WAR DIARY
or
INTELLIGENCE SUMMARY

Army Form C. 2118.

Place	Date	Hour	Summary of Events and Information	Remarks and references to Appendices
Arras	24	2 PM	Sectional football match.	
"	25	9.30	Church parade for Church of England in ARRAS theatre	
		9.45	Roman Catholic parade	
		2 P.M.	Battery Christmas Dinner	
		6 PM	Concert given by Battery in billets at Arras.	
"	26	11 AM	No 1 Section present in fighting order for the line under 2nd Lt Kykkwith	
		1 PM	No 1 Section present under 2nd Lt Wrench	
			The 12th Trench Mortar Battery relieved the 10th French Mortar Battery. 50 rounds were fired by 3" Stokes. Relief completed by 5 P.M.	
			Section in line fired 200 rounds on DEVIL TR, MONK TR.	
NS20-8.21	27	6 AM	BOLT TR & GREEN LANE. Guns fired in bursts of ten round at intervals during the night. Enemy TM retaliation is on front	
"	28	6 AM	30 Rounds were fired on POODLE TR (map ref D2 b 6-6) in bursts 5 rounds from 9 PM to 11 PM. 80 rounds were fired on DEVIL TR, HARNESS LANE and junction of two (I 31 c 08-88). Enemy TMs shelled our guns in DALE TR. Enemy TMs retaliation died on fire by silencing CURLU TR where we located her gun.	

Army Form C.2118.

Army Form C. 2118.

WAR DIARY
or
INTELLIGENCE SUMMARY.
(Erase heading not required.)

Instructions regarding War Diaries and Intelligence Summaries are contained in F. S. Regs., Part II. and the Staff Manual respectively. Title pages will be prepared in manuscript.

Place	Date	Hour	Summary of Events and Information	Remarks and references to Appendices
N5a 0-3	29	6Am to 6Pm	All guns in line (5) were registered on MacKen gun emplacement and T.M. emplacements. 180 Rounds were fired at unknown during the night at targets on which they had registered during the day.	
		6Am	Work done. Gun emplacements were improved.	
	30	6Am to 6Pm	40 Rounds were fired in night retreator on SPOON Tr several direct hits were obtained on enemy Trenches. 130 Rounds were fired on DEVILS Tr and HARNESS LANE also Craters in HARNESS LANE (I.31.c.8-75) Tea were fired in bursts of fire from 11.30 PM to 4 AM. Enemy T.Ms silenced a short til a our gun in LINK ALLEY rendering it inoperative. Enemy snipers were active. Also machine guns (Gun M. returned)	
	31	6Am to 6	3" Stokes registered on known enemy loo at O2d 9-05 firing 12 Rounds good observation for clusts. 50 Lewis were fired at clear targets at strength will find enemy revealing at rifle fire enemy/or results. 110 Rounds were fired on BIT LANE CRATER and DEVILS Tr N coll and land of BIT LANE. Enemy T.Ms fairly active.	

4th Division
12th Infantry Bde
2nd Lancs Fus.

January - December
1918

SECRET

WAR DIARY

of

2nd Battalion LANCASHIRE FUSILIERS Regiment

From : 1st January 1918

To: 31st. January 1918

VOLUME 2

Date. 31/1/18.

J W Watkins Major
Commanding:
2 Bn. Lancashire Fusiliers Regt.

WAR DIARY
or
INTELLIGENCE SUMMARY.
(Erase heading not required.)

Army Form C. 2118.

Place	Date	Hour	Summary of Events and Information	Remarks and references to Appendices
JANUARY				
Right Sub Sect. D.2.a.9.	1st		Bn in front line. Right Sub Sector. Moncorn Sector	gen
	2nd		"	gen
Bde. Reserve N.3.F.	3rd	12 noon	Bn relieved by 1st K.O.R Lanc R. On relief moved into Bde. Support	gen
		9pm	Bn relieved by 2nd Duke of Wellington R. On relief Bn moved into Bde. Reserve. 2 O.R. Reinforcements.	gen
	4th		Bn in Bde. Reserve. Day and night working parties found on fire area.	gen
	5th		"	2 OR Reinforcements gen
	6th		"	gen
Right Subsector	7th		Bn relieved 1st K.O.R Lanc R. in Right Subsector	gen
	8th		Bn in Right Sub Sector. 3 O.R. wounded.	gen
	9th		"	gen
	10th		" 1 O.R. wounded	gen
	11th		Bn relieved in line by 1st Bn K.I. On relief Bn moved to Arras. 1 O.R. wounded. Bn to Bn Reserve.	gen
ARRAS	12th		Bn in Arras. B. Co, 1 Bn Training. 2/Lieut. B.T.B. Butler Bowden joins Bn.	gen
	13th		" 2 O.R. Reinforcements	gen
	14th		"	gen
	15th		" 2 O.R. Reinforcements	gen
WILDERNESS CAMP. H.31.a	16th		Bn relieved 1st K.O.R Lanc R. in Wilderness Camp.	gen
	17th		Bn in Wilderness Camp. Night working party found. Day working party found. Shortened trail in Reserve	gen
	18th		" Bn training	gen
	19th		Bn relieved 3/4 Middlesex R in Reserve. Bde. Support. Right Sector	gen

Army Form C. 2118.

WAR DIARY
or
INTELLIGENCE SUMMARY.
(Erase heading not required.)

Instructions regarding War Diaries and Intelligence Summaries are contained in F. S. Regs., Part II. and the Staff Manual respectively. Title pages will be prepared in manuscript.

Place	Date	Hour	Summary of Events and Information	Remarks and references to Appendices
Fosse Farm N11C.95.40.	19th		Bn. Hd. Qrs. in Fosse Fm. 2.O.R. Wounded	qua
	20		Bn in Bde Support. Day & night working parties	qua
	21		" "	2"Lieut W.D. James 2.O.R. Wounded	qua
	22		" "	2 Lieut J.J. Elsworth) Injured	qua
	23		" "		qua
Right Sub Sect D.58a & 0.8c.	23		Bn relieved 1st K.O.R. Lanc R. in front line Right Sub Sect.	qua
	24		Bn in front line	qua
			Lieut Butler-Bowden to Hospl. Sick	qua
	25		" "	1 O.R. Wounded	qua
	26		" "	1 O.R. Wounded	qua
Brown Line	27		Bn relieved in front line by 1st K.O.R. Lanc R. On relief Bn moved to	qua
			Bde Reserve in Brown Line. Capt K.H. Douglas Hamilton to Hospl. Sick	qua
N4.	28		Bn in Brown Line. Night working Parties. 1 O.R. Wounded	qua
	29		" "	qua
	30		" "	qua
	31		" "	qua

J. Whatmough
2 Lieut. tms.

S E C R E T.
xxxxxxxxxxxxxxxxxxxxxxxxx

W A R   D I A R Y

of

2nd. Bn. The LANCASHIRE FUSILIERS Regt.

From:- 1st February 1918

To:- 28th FEbruary 1918.

V O L U M E 2

3/3/18.

J W Watkins Major
Commanding
2nd. Bn. The LANCASHIRE FUSILIERS Regt.

2 L F
Vol 41

40-1.
3 sheets

Army Form C. 2118.

WAR DIARY
or
INTELLIGENCE SUMMARY.
(Erase heading not required.)

Instructions regarding War Diaries and Intelligence Summaries are contained in F. S. Regs., Part II. and the Staff Manual respectively. Title pages will be prepared in manuscript.

Place	Date	Hour	Summary of Events and Information	Remarks and references to Appendices
	1/2/18		Battalion went from Brown Line	Casualties nil
Line	1/2/17		Battalion relieved 1st Bn. the King's Own Regt. in front line	CAMBRAI SA
Line	2/2/18		Held front line	casualties nil ROAD SA
Line	3/2/18		Held front line. 2/Lt G.J.Watson to Hospital. Shelled 6 O.R. wounded. SECTOR SA
Line	4/2/18		Held front line. No casualties.	SA
Line	5/2/18		Battalion relieved by 8th Seaforth Highlanders. and went to ARRAS by busses.	SA
			No casualties.	SA
ARRAS	6/2/18		Battalion moved to BERNEVILLE. 55 O.R. reinforcements arrived.	SA
BERNEVILLE	7/2/18		Reinforcements. 117 O.R. joined.	SA
"	8/2/18		Training	SA
"	9/2/18		Training	SA
"	10/2/18		Training	SA
"	11/2/18		2/Lt E. de B. Cantrill Hatherly joined. aud 13 O.R.	SA
"	12/2/18		Training	SA
"	13/2/18		Training	SA
"	14/2/18		Company marched to WAILLY to the A.R.A. Composition No. 9 Platoon 2/Lt H.C.Chilton training. Reinforcements 1 O.R.	SA
"	15/2/18		Training. WARNING ORDER No I ISSUED.	SA
"	16/2/18		Reinforcement 63 O.R.	SA
"	17/2/18		Training	SA
"	18/2/18		Lt E. Hartley Re-joined. 2 O.R. reinforcements.	SA
"	19/2/18		Training	SA

Army Form C. 2118.

WAR DIARY
or
INTELLIGENCE SUMMARY.
(Erase heading not required.)

Instructions regarding War Diaries and Intelligence Summaries are contained in F.S. Regs., Part II. and the Staff Manual respectively. Title pages will be prepared in manuscript.

Place	Date	Hour	Summary of Events and Information	Remarks and references to Appendices
BERNVILLE	20/2/18		Reinforcements 32 O.R. Brigade Field Day	S.H
"	21/2/18		Company Training.	S.H
"	22/2/18		Range.	S.H
"	23/2/18		C.O.'s Parade. Company in attack. Platoon rounding up Copse filled with M.G.S.	S.H
"	24/2/18		Brigade Church Parade.	S.H
"	25/2/18		Lt E. Hartermann & 2/Lt W.H. Riley. Reconnaissance of 3rd System NEUVILLE ST VITASSE	S.H
"	26/2/18		Captain G.C. Gerrardin R.A.M.C. evacuated from Hospital. Day & Night Patrols. Coy H.Qrs a.d.n. - field kits and wiring. Night work out	S.H
"	27/2/18		No. 9 Platoon 21st H.C. Childrens War 12th Bn A.P.A. Completion (cost) Brigade Field Day.	S.H
"	28/2/18		Range.	

JWSARNS Major.
Commanding 2nd Lancashire Fusiliers.
2/3/1918.

12th Inf.Bde.
4th Div.

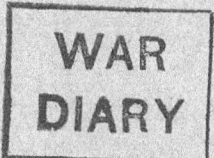

2nd BATTN. THE LANCASHIRE FUSILIERS.

M A R C H

1 9 1 8

SECRET.
xxxxxxxxxxxxxxxxxxxxxxxx

WAR DIARY 12/4

of

2nd Bn. The LANCASHIRE FUSILIERS Regt.

From:- 1st March 1918.
To:- 31st March 1918.

VOLUME 3

3/4/18

Capt
for Lt.Colonel,
Commanding
2nd Bn. The Lancashire Fusiliers Regt.

Army Form C. 2118.

WAR DIARY
or
INTELLIGENCE SUMMARY.
(Erase heading not required.)

Place	Date	Hour	Summary of Events and Information	Remarks and references to Appendices
Field. BERNAVILLE	March 1918. 1.		Coy Training.	Nil
"	2.		Training.	Nil
"	3.		Training. Final of Bn Boxing Competition. L/Cpl Wigram D.C.O	Nil
"	4.		Training	Nil
"	5.		as won by the Featherweight.	Nil
"	6.		Training	Nil
"	7.		Training	Nil
"	8.		Training	Nil
"	9.		Training. *Capt. J. Little. U.S.A. M.O.R.C. joined the Bn. on attached	Nil
"	10.		Officers Training.	Nil
"	11.		Bn moved from Billets in BERNAVILLE to BAUDIMONT Barracks ARRAS	Nil
ARRAS	12.		In Billets in ARRAS. 31 O. Ranks joined as reinforcements	Nil
"	13.		In Billets in ARRAS	Nil
"	18.		Bn moved from BAUDIMONT BARRACKS ARRAS to where 2"A	Nil
LINE	19.		& SCOTS GUARDS in STIRLING CAMP LEMON TR Bn. to R. BLANCY St LAURENT.	Nil

Army Form C. 2118.

WAR DIARY
or
INTELLIGENCE SUMMARY.
(Erase heading not required.)

Instructions regarding War Diaries and Intelligence Summaries are contained in F. S. Regs., Part II. and the Staff Manual respectively. Title pages will be prepared in manuscript.

Place	Date March	Hour	Summary of Events and Information	Remarks and references to Appendices
LINE	19.		Lt. & QM J. Gore joined the Bn. 10. O.R. reinforcement.	MA
	20.		Bn. in Bn. Reserve in STIRLING CAMP.	MA
	21.		Bn. in Bn. Reserve & officers attached to the Bn. from the 1st R. WARWICK REGT. 2/Lts L.H. Hope – A.W.B. Potter – W.G. Wilding. K.F. Lilley.	MA
	22.		2.O.R. Wounded Bn. moved from STIRLING CAMP to BRASS DUGOUTS Reg. to Bn. Support Bn. HQ LEMON TR.	MA
	22.		Bn. in Bn. Support 2/Lt a/Major J. Watkins M.C. to be a/Lt. Col. C.S.M. Sheldon joined Bn. to relieve C.S.M. Granger to England at 6 noon turn of duty.	MA
	23.		Moved Bn. into Bn. SUPPORT. from STIRLING CAMP to relieve 2 ESSEX Reg't Battn. Bn. in FAMPOUX section to LEMON TR.	MA
	24.		Bn. in Bn. Support.	MA
	25.		Bn. in Bn. Support. M of own SCARPE.	MA
26.27			Bn. in Bn. Support. Map Ref. Trench Map. S16 N.W. 1/10000	MA

Army Form C. 2118.

WAR DIARY
or
INTELLIGENCE SUMMARY.
(Erase heading not required.)

Instructions regarding War Diaries and Intelligence Summaries are contained in F. S. Regs., Part II. and the Staff Manual respectively. Title pages will be prepared in manuscript.

Place	Date March	Hour	Summary of Events and Information	Remarks and references to Appendices
LIME. LEMON TR. POE SUPPORT	26.	3.0 a	Enemy bombardment commenced very heavy. Three separate barrages on Front Support and Reserve lines and on the open between. Continued till 7.0 a.m. when enemy launched a big attack from their hola out till practically wiped out. A.Co. in close support to front line Bn. was completely wiped out after a tremendous fight. Bn. stopped the enemy from advancing beyond the front and close support trenches. D.Co suffered fairly heavily. B.C & lightly. Battn. continued to hold remnants of the day. Enemy stopped in our support line after suffering heavy casualties. Our casualties were — Killed. Officers. O. Ranks. 2Lt. R. McCarroly. 16. 2Lt. J. Heron. Wded. 2Lt. G.R. Williams. 87. 2Lt. J.A. Kingsley. Missing. 2Lt. R.J.S. Buther Bowdon 120.	WM

Army Form C. 2118.

WAR DIARY
or
INTELLIGENCE SUMMARY

(Erase heading not required.)

Instructions regarding War Diaries and Intelligence Summaries are contained in F. S. Regs., Part II. and the Staff Manual respectively. Title Pages will be prepared in manuscript.

Place	Date	Hour	Summary of Events and Information	Remarks and references to Appendices
B. LINE. LEMON TR.	29		Bn. absorbed the remains of the ESSEX Regt. into the Strength and became front line Bn. Small isolated fights going on. Bombing up and down communication trenches. Intermittent bombardment throughout the day. Posns in LEMON TR. Casualties inchdn. a/c. 28"	Nil.
" "	30		Bn. in front line, joined by 10th Ch Vds. Lilahm. unchanged. Small bombing fights in communication trenches throughout the day. Casualties inchdn. 29"	Nil.
" "	31		Bn. relieved in the line by 1st K.R.R. K.O. Regt. Situation unchanged. Casualties unchdn. 30"	Nil.
			Posns in LEMON TR still.	

Signed for Lt. Col.
2 Lancs Fus.

APPENDIX 1.

The following congratulatory messages were received and are forwarded in conjunction with the war diary.

From General HORNE, Commanding 1st Army begins:-

Please accept and convey to units which have fought to-day, my admiration of the skill and determination displayed by Commanders, Staffs and all ranks. A very heavy attack pushed home by vastly superior numbers has been repulsed with heavy loss to the Germans. The troops have shown a splebndid spirit and may well feel proud of their achievement.

Following from the Military Secretary begins:-

The Commander in Chief sends his congratulations to Major-General MATHESON and all ranks of the 4th Division on the successful operations carried out by them on the 14/15 and 17th inst, and on the way in which they have succeded in aadvancing their line.

EXTRACT FROM THE TIMES Dated 25th April 1918!

"ESPECIALLY GALLANT 4TH"

The Commander in Chief has requested the Army Commander to convey his congratulations to all ranks of the 4th Division.

(The 4th Divn was mentioned in the official tribute by Sir Douglas Haig which appered in the TIMES yesterday, for "Especially Gallant" service on March 28th, and the operations of April 14th, 15th and 18th were also referred to. "I doubt if any Division" wrote our special correspondent on the 23rd inst" has killed more Germans than the 4th).

12th Brigade.

4th Division.

2nd BATTALION

LANCASHIRE FUSILIERS

APRIL 1918.

SECRET

War Diary

of

2nd Bn Lancashire Fusiliers

From: April 1st 1918
To: April 30th 1918

Volume 4

A. Martin Inger
Lieut. Colonel
Comdg 2 Lancashire Fusiliers

Army Form C. 2118.

WAR DIARY
or
INTELLIGENCE SUMMARY

(Erase heading not required.)

Instructions regarding War Diaries and Intelligence Summaries are contained in F. S. Regs., Part II. and the Staff Manual respectively. Title Pages will be prepared in manuscript.

Place	Date	Hour	Summary of Events and Information	Remarks and references to Appendices
LINE FAMPOUX SECTOR. ARRAS.	April 1918.		Map Sheet 51 M 10:	
	1.		Bn in Support to "C" the Kings Own Regt.	
	2.		Bn relieves A" the Kings Own Regt. in front line.	
	3.		Front line. Situation unchanged.	
	4.		Front line. Situation unchanged.	
	5.		Front line. Situation unchanged.	
	6.		Front line. Situation unchanged. Relief of the Bn. by the Y. & B".	
	7.	9 p.m.	CANADIAN Bn. commenced	
	8.	5 a.m.	Complete relief of the Bn. by the CANADIANS. Bn. proceeded by Light Railway to SIMENCOURT. 2Lt. C.K. KEATES, 2Lt. T.R. WARNE & 113 O.Ranks joined the Bn.	
SIMENCOURT	9.		Bn in Billets cleaning up and reorganising Co. Major H A KIRKBY DSO. joined the Bn. 57 O.Ranks Reinforcements.	
"	10.		Bn in Billets.	
"	11.		Bn in Billets. Major H KIRKBY DSO. attached to Royal Warwickshire Rgt. Bn prepared to move at 4 hour notice.	

WAR DIARY
or
INTELLIGENCE SUMMARY

Army Form C. 2118.

Place	Date	Hour	Summary of Events and Information	Remarks and references to Appendices
SIMENCOURT	12.		Bn under orders to be ready to Entrain at 12 noon. Entraining point is on the ARRAS - DOULLENS Rd 1000 yds S. of BEAMETZ. Proceed to entraining point by Route March. Arrive 12 noon. Bn Entrains 3.45 p.m. Arrive BUSNES NE of LILLERS about 8 p.m. Bivouac for the night in fields and barns on the outside of the Rd.	
BUSNES - L'ECLEME.	13.		Bn moved to L'ECLEME. 10% reinforcements dealt back to Transport. Arrive L'ECLEME 4 p.m.	
Map Sheet 36A'/40000			Bn in billets in L'ECLEME	
36A S.E./20000 15.			Bn in L'ECLEME. Co training.	
LINE.	16	9 p.m.	Bn relieved 15 Bn The HAMPSHIRE Regt. in left subsector 2/4 Brigade Q19 - Q26 Bn HQ. in House at P30 c 5.1. A.C.D Co in trunts. A Co in support.	
RIEZ DU VINAGE.	17.	7 a.m.	Relief completed. Quiet day. Later open warfare then in pits in the open. Enemy artillery began bombarding back area and roads through ROBECQ and RIEZ DU VINAGE.	
	18.	1 a.m.	Enemy bombardment very heavy.	
		3 a.m.	Enemy bombardment intense. S.O.S. sent up by the 7th The KINGS OWN on our right. Bn HQ in telephonic communication with our left Co. Bn HQ. sent up S.O.S in response to call from Co. Artillery put down Barrage on S.O.S. line. Report later on prisoner that they were caught by this Barrage and attack stopped on our front. Co. reported O.K. 4.0 a.m.	

Army Form C. 2118.

WAR DIARY
or
INTELLIGENCE SUMMARY
(Erase heading not required.)

Instructions regarding War Diaries and Intelligence Summaries are contained in F.S. Regs., Part II. and the Staff Manual respectively. Title Pages will be prepared in manuscript.

Place	Date	Hour	Summary of Events and Information	Remarks and references to Appendices
RIEZ DU VINAGE.		4.35am	Enemy shelling slackened and 5.0 a.m Enemy shelling ceased. 7.0 a.m R.B. report that enemy attack their right hand gun post and were driven off leaving about 20 dead. In touch with 1st the King's Own. Relieved A. obtained movement in front of their line and sent a party out who retired with prisoner.	N/A
		7.30am	Situation unchanged and quiet. Remainder of daylight was quiet.	N/A
		2.15pm	Small enemy attack on the front and the King's Own complicated and repulsed. RIEZ DU VINAGE where they had been in the morning. Casualties. 4 O.Ranks wounded. 6 Prisoners of war.	
RIEZ DU VINAGE.	19		Quiet day all day. Some shelling of support (A) Co. 4.0 O.Ranks Killed. 4 O.Ranks wounded.	N/A
	20.		Quiet day. Situation unchanged.	N/A
		9.15pm	S.O.S sent up by A Co on our right. No infantry action. 2/Lt HEMBRYK with 3 men went out against Machine gun and captured it. men and a Machine gun. Situation unchanged. R.C. Co. Relieving ESSEX Reg. in front of RIEZ DU VINAGE. Relief delayed by S.O.S. calls from ESSEX. 9.15pm and again at 10pm. Relief finally carried out by 1.15am. D Co. comes under command C.O. ESSEX Regt. ESSEX Regt. B. between RIEZ & CANAL comes under Cavalli. 2.O.R. killed. 2 O.R wounded.	N/A
RIEZ DU VINAGE.	22.		In line. Quiet day. Situation unchanged. A.G shelled heavily in morning. Casualties. Capt. E.L. van POMEREN. 2Lt. J. ELSWORTH. 2Lt. G.I. WATSON wounded. 2 O.R wounded.	N/A

WAR DIARY or INTELLIGENCE SUMMARY

Army Form C. 2118.

Place	Date	Hour	Summary of Events and Information	Remarks and references to Appendices
RIEZ DU VINAGE	23	3 a.m.	D. Coy & 1 Pl. A. Coy. under 2/Lt N.S. Burns assaulted to attack. Vide Appendix 1.	
		4.30 a.m.	Zero hour. Artillery barrage opened. Offensive in vast Q.2.b.8.7.0 - Q.27.a.0.9. Machine gun fire reached front line in that direction and	
		7.30 a.m.	Objective infantry reached. Reorganising. Their not attacking troops and left a gap between to PIERRE - AU - AISRE and RIEZ DU VINAGE. Owing to the gap artillery fire could not be brought down. Enemy Artillery barrages had already and enemy sniping very active. Pns withdrawn after dark to Q30.d.4.5. - Q.26.b.7.6. Post includes home at Q27.a.0.5	
			CASUALTIES 2/Lt E.I. HSMEL-RYK. H.C.HILTON-HARRISON killed 2/Lt N.S. BURNS W/S GILBERT, T. R. WARNE wounded. 2/Lt W.F. LILLEY missing presumed 4. OR killed 170. OR W/d SE. OR missing	
	24	4 a.m.	Poss of HQ and Slight MG. bns slackened out. Heavy sniping all day. Relieved by 2 Bn SEAFORTH HIGHs.	
GONNEHEM	25.		Rule complete Bn moved BLR to GONNEHEM. B.n in BILLETS.	
	26.	2.30 a.m.	2/Lt E.C. DAGLIESH. 2/Lt W. D. HENSHALL. Reinforcement joined. 2/Lt L.G.C. CHAPMAN	
	27		2/Lt BELL, GONNEHEM shelled. Casualties 2.O.R. wounded. Chevalier. 2.O.R wounded (G.S.G.)	
	28		In GONNEHEM & CALONNE. Shelled. Casualties 1. O.R. wounded.	
	29		2/Lt E.I. HOWL rejoined. 2.O.R. Killed 4. O.R. wounded.	
	30		In BILLETS. Shelled during night 29/5/29 and about 8 p.m. 1.O.R. wounded.	
	31		GONNEHEM shelled 11.30 a.m. & 1.30 p.m. Bn moved up to fill support in HINGES - L'ECLEME line. Pts HQ at Q.5.a.05.00.	

2449 Wt. W.14957/M90 750,000 1/16 J.B.C. & A. Forms/C.2118/12.

OPERATION ORDERS No. 2.
by
Lieut Colonel J.W. Watkins, D.S.O., M.C.
Commanding - Lancashire Fusiliers.

Field. Ref.Map. Sheet 36A. S.E. 1/20,000   22/4/18.

---

1. On the morning of 23rd instant "D" Co. and 1 Platoon of "A" Co. Lan.Fus. under Lt.N.D.Evans will attack and consolidate a line from Q.20.b.7.0. (road junction exclusive) along road to Houses at Q.26.b.9.6.
   At the same time the - Gloucester Regiment will attack and consolidate a line from Farm at Q.14.c.5.6. along road to road junction Q.20.b.7.0. inclusive.
   The dividing line between Battalions will be Q.20.b.7.0. - house at Q.20.d.3.7. (inclusive to Gloucesters) to bend in road at Q.25.b.2.3. Direction of attack 75° Magnetic.

2. BARRAGE. Artillery will open at Zero Hour. It will take the form of a creeping barrage moving as follows:- Start on a line Q.19.b.7.5. - Q.20. c.0.5. - Q.20.c.3.0. - Q.26.b.0.3. for 5 minutes.
   (1) From start till reaching houses. 100 yds in 2 minutes.
   (2) From houses to River 100 yds. in 3 minutes.
   (3) Waits 5 minutes on the River.
   (4) River to finish 100 yds in 3 minutes.
   Finish on line Q.14.d.0.6. - Q.14.d.2.6. - Q.14.d.7.0. - Q.21.a.0.6. - in front and on LA PIERRE AU BEURRE to Houses Q.27.a.5.7.
   Standing till ZERO plus 40 minutes.

3. MACHINE GUNS. Barrage will open at ZERO.hour and continue till 7am unless asked to cease earlier. It will be ready to open up again at any time in case of need until consolidation is completed.
   The 4 M.G's at Q.26.b.9.5. will withdraw with "C" Co. and O.C."C" Co. will see that they re-occupy their positions at ZERO plus 40 minutes.

4. 6" NEWTONS AND TRENCH MORTARS will co-operate on allotted targets Stokes Mortars are at Q.26.b.8.4. and are under command of O.B."B" CO.

5. Aeroplane co-operation has been arranged. Flares will be exhibited to planes calling for them by first line Cos. at about 5am, 7am, noon and just before dark.

5. Attacking troops will form up for the attack ZERO - 30 minutes on a line Q.26.a.1.7. to Q.26.a.6.1.
   The Gloucesters will be formed up on the left and close touch must be maintained throughout the operation.

7. "C" Co. will withdraw to behind the hedges at Q.26.b.9.5. so that troops will be clear of the houses by ZERO - 15 minutes.
   At ZERO plus 40 minutes "C" Co. will re-occupy the houses and get in touch with "D" Co. who will be on their final objective.
   At dusk "C" Co. will move the troops at present in the line from Q.26.b.9.7. to consolidate a support line from Q.26.b.9.7. to Q.20.d.0.4.
   "C" Co. will be ready to assist "D" Co. during any phase of the operation.

8. "B" Co. will assist by firing burts of fire from his Lewis Guns, paying special attention to the houses at Q.27.a.5.7. and the N.W. corner of PACAUT WOOD.

9. Battalion Headquarters will be at P.30.c.6.1.

10. On reaching objectives messages will be sent back by visual station to be arranged by Signals. Telephone wire will be run forward as soon as possible from old "B" Co. H.Q. at Q.25.c.9.0.

11. The platoon of "A" Co. to be attached to "D" Co. will report to Lt. N.D.Evans at 2am. The other platoon of "A" Co. and "A" Co.H.Q. will move at 3am.

No.......2.

move at 3am into area that will be evacuated by "D" Co. and become support.

12. Prisoners will be sent to A Co. H.Q. at Q.25.c.9.0.
"A" Co. will send them straight on to Bn.H.Q.

13. PATROLS. On objective being reached "D" Co. will ensure that the buildings on E.side LA PIERRE AU BEURRE are cleared and also ascertain if LA PIERRE AU BEURRE is held.
"C" Co. will send out a patrol to clear the Houses at Q.27.a.5.7.

14. BRIDGES will be carried by first line attacking troops for crossing the COURANTI.

15. WATCHES Watches will be synchronised at 2-30am by runner from Bn.H.Q.

16. ZERO hour will be notified later.

17. In case of Enemy attack these orders will be destroyed.

18. ACKNOWLEDGE.

(Signed) V.F.S.Hawkins, Capt & Adjt.
- Lan. Fus.

SECRET.

War Diary

of

2ⁿᵈ Lancashire Fusiliers.

From:- May 1ˢᵗ 1918

To:- May 31ˢᵗ 1918.

Volume
5

Wm. Kirkby Major
Comdg 2 Lan Fus

WAR DIARY
or
INTELLIGENCE SUMMARY.

Army Form C 2118.

Place	Date	Hour	Summary of Events and Information	Remarks and references to Appendices
	May			
PACAUT WOOD	1		2h Bn relieved the 2nd ESSEX REGT in the right sub-sector of the Regt's Brigade.	A/M
LA THUILERIE			Relief W.R. 4 H. Appendix A/M/1	A/M/1
Map Sheet 51A			2Lt R.E. Elliott - 2Lt J.S.S. MALPAS - 2Lt J. EDWICH and 2 O.R. joined the Bn.	A/M
1/20,000	2		In the line. Situation unchanged. 3 O.R. wounded.	A/M
Les HARISOIRS	3		In the line. Situation unchanged.	
	4		2Lt A. PICKERING - 2Lt C. NICHOL - 2Lt J. CHALMER - 2Lt L. MORGAN joined. 2 O.R. killed, 6 O.R. wounded.	A/M
			In the line. Situation unchanged. Raid by Bn on our right, casualties to heavy shelling in vicinity of Bn H.Q. Readjustment of the B.C. relieved C.H. of PACAUT WOOD by Essex Regt and moved to the right. C Co closed into the right. A.A. supp. Co moved up to the right. 2 O.R. killed, 5 O.R. wounded.	
	5		B.H.Q. moved to WSBT6.	
	5		In the line. Situation unchanged. 2Lt J. BENNEY born joined Bn from Regt.	A/M
	6		Bn relieved in the line by 1st Bn the Royal WARWICKSHIRES REGT and moved back to billets in LECELEME. Relief completed about 4 am. Thick Appendix B/M	A/M
			2Lt C.R. REDD - A. MITCHELL - D. THOMAS - J. McDONALD joined the Bn.	
LECELEME	7		Bn in billets cleaning up.	A/M

Army Form C. 2118.

WAR DIARY
or
INTELLIGENCE SUMMARY
(Erase heading not required.)

Instructions regarding War Diaries and Intelligence Summaries are contained in F. S. Regs., Part II. and the Staff Manual respectively. Title pages will be prepared in manuscript.

Place	Date	Hour	Summary of Events and Information	Remarks and references to Appendices
L'ECLEME	8		Bn in Billets A.D Co move up to CANAL BANK on account of expected German attack	N/A
	9		1 O.R killed 7 O.R wounded whilst moving to working party. B.C Co. B.H.Q. B.M.O.	N/A
			B.C Co. move up to CANAL BANK	N/A
	10	4 am	B.H.Q. A.D. Co return to L'ECLEME	N/A
		9 pm	B.M.O. A.D Co return to CANAL BANK	N/A
	11	am	Rifle B.C Co. return to L'ECLEME	N/A
RIEZ DU VINAGE		9 pm	Bn relieved 2 Bn. Hampshire Regt in right subsects of the Left Brigade front B.H.Q. P36A6.6	N/A
	12		2 O.R wounded. 21 O.R joined Bn	N/A
	13		Bn in the line. Situation unchanged. 30 O.R wounded	N/A
	14		Bn in the line. Situation unchanged. 2Lt Greenwood wounded. 10 O.R killed 10 O.R wounded	N/A
	15		Bn in the line. Situation unchanged. Capt Stevens joined Bn.	N/A
	16		Bn in the line. A Co relieved D Co front line and D Co went back to support.	N/A
			Bn in the line. Situation unchanged. 30 O.R killed 20 O.R joined	N/A
	17		Bn in the line. Situation unchanged. 4 O.R wounded	N/A

Army Form C. 2118.

WAR DIARY
or
INTELLIGENCE SUMMARY.
(Erase heading not required.)

Place	Date	Hour	Summary of Events and Information	Remarks and references to Appendices
RIEZ DU VINAGE	18.		Bn in the line. Khakis unchanged. Lt. P. HARTLEY killed on patrol. Party 6 O.R. wounded. 30 O.R. neufou events. During night 16-17-18. B. D. Coys. relieved 2 Inch'Killeurs in fort	Nil
	19.		1 RGT DU VINAGE left by C Coy 5½" +1" during the southwest between April 9" - 12". Bn relieved by 1 Bn the Royal INNISKILLING Regt and on completion of relief moved to L'ECLEME. Appendix C. Lt Col. J. B. WATKINS D.S.O M.C. wounded. 2 O.R. killed 20 O.R wounded	Nil
L'ECLEME	20.	3 am	Bn arrived in L'ECLEME. 6/14th cleaning up. Major HARRISON D.S.O assumed command of the Bn.	Nil
	21.		Bn in Billets. Baths at BUSNETTES. 84 O.R. joined.	Nil
	22.		Bn in Billets. Lt. Montgomery joined the Bn. Running parties to Rifle Bn.	Nil
PACAUT WD.	23.	9 pm	Bn relieved 1st T. RIFLE BDE in Right Subsect of Rifle Bde Sec. below	Nil
LA FOURNERE			complete 12 in night. Bn HQ W 8 d 1.6	Nil
LE CAIROY	24.		Bn in the line. Khakis unchanged. 2 O.R. wounded.	Nil
	25.		Bn in the line. Khakis unchanged. 4 O.R. wounded	Nil

WAR DIARY or INTELLIGENCE SUMMARY

Army Form C. 2118.

(Erase heading not required.)

Place	Date	Hour	Summary of Events and Information	Remarks and references to Appendices
PRENTOIS	26		On the line Situation unchanged. Ian to 3.30 am O.C.Coy hill yellow line killed	
LA PANNERIE			Took over by evening in line in rear Butts 2 O.R. wounded	
LE CAUROY	27		An in line. Situation unchanged. 8 O.R. wounded	
	28		An in line. Situation unchanged. 1 O.R. killed. 3 O.R. wounded	
	29		An in line. B Co. relieved C Co. in the front line. C Co. moved back	
			to support. Situation unchanged. 6 O.R. killed	
	30		An in line. Situation unchanged. 1 O.R. wounded.	
	31		An in line. Situation unchanged. 1 O.R. killed. 3 O.R. wounded	
	June		During the time A.D. Co. in reserve found nightly carrying and	
			working parties for front line Co. Quiet tour except nightly gas shelling	
			of all the area for Fort to track back to H.Q. all through gas shell	

J.A. Kirkby Major
O/C 2 Lancashire Fusiliers

SECRET

War Diary
of
2nd Lancashire Fusiliers

From June 1st 1918
To June 30th 1918

Volume

A.H. Kirkby Lt Colonel.
Comdg 2 Lan Fus

WAR DIARY
INTELLIGENCE SUMMARY

Army Form C. 2118.

(Erase heading not required.)

Place	Date	Hour	Summary of Events and Information	Remarks and references to Appendices
Sheet 36A 1/20000. LINE PEAUTWD	May 31st		Bn in the Line. Enemy exchanged Gas Shelling in area W3 and 8.	
to LATANNERIE	June 1918		during night. Casualties 1 O.R. Killed 2 O.R. Wded.	NIL
	1		Bn in the Line. Enemy exchanged Gas Shelling in areas W3 and 8 during night.	NIL
			2 Lt. C.C. CHAPMAN Wded. Gas. 5 O.Rs wounded	
	2.		Bn in the Line. Situation unchanged. Bn relieved by 5/Bn. 9h Royal WARWICKSHIRE Regt. in Right Subsects of the Right Bn front.	NIL
			Bn on relief moved back to billets in L'ECLEME. Casualties 7 O.R. wded	NIL
L'ECLEME.	3	2.40AM	Relief complete. 3 Am Bn in billets	NIL
	4		Bn in Billets. Cleaning up 79. O.R. reinforcements.	NIL
	5		Bn in Billets. Training.	NIL
	6		Bn in Billets. Training. 2 O.R. reinforcement.	NIL
	7		Bn in Billets. Training.	NIL
	8		Bn relieved 1st Bn the 4th HAMPSHIRE Regt. in Right Sub Sector of the Regt. Bn Front. RIEZ DU VINAGE. In position. "A" "D" support. "A" reserve. "B" - Canal Bank. C.	NIL

WAR DIARY
or
INTELLIGENCE SUMMARY.

Army Form C. 2118.

Place	Date	Hour	Summary of Events and Information	Remarks and references to Appendices
Riaz Du Vicage	8th Oct		Enemy activity during the day. 2/Lt C.C. Read noted 2/Lt C.H. Ffoulkes owed to O.R. wounded	
	9.		Bn HQ Rose House 136 O.R. Reliefs complete 2.30 A.M. O.R.	
			Bn in the line. Situation unchanged	
	10		Bn in the line. Situation unchanged. Casualties to O.R. noted	
			2/Lts L.J. Kemp - A. Sewell - D. McIntosh - at A.H. Barker-Jones	
			joined Bn for duty.	
	11		Bn in the line. Situation unchanged Casualties 3. O.Rs killed	
	12.		Bn in the line. Situation unchanged. Casualties 1 Off. killed	
	13.		Bn in the line. Situation unchanged D Co moved up	
			1/c Canal Bank to Kent Reserve. Major W.B. Small	
			joined for duty from England	
	14		Bn in the line. Situation unchanged A/b Whereas D Co in	
			the Bart line. D Co moved back Knypok	
			2/Lt R. Gimour att. 12 Inf Bde HQ noted to O.R.	
	15.		Bn in the line. Situation unchanged 1 O.R wounded	

Army Form C. 2118.

WAR DIARY
or
INTELLIGENCE SUMMARY.
(Erase heading not required.)

Instructions regarding War Diaries and Intelligence
Summaries are contained in F. S. Regs., Part II.
and the Staff Manual respectively. Title pages
will be prepared in manuscript.

Place	Date	Hour	Summary of Events and Information	Remarks and references to Appendices
RIEZ DU VINAGE	16.		Bn in the line. Situation unchanged. Enemy artillery active during the night. 2 OR killed, 2 OR wounded.	M.M.
	17.		Lt. C.V. Longstaff joined for duty. Bn in the line. Situation unchanged. Enemy artillery active during the night. 1 OR killed 5 OR wounded	M.M.
	18.		Bn in the line. Situation unchanged. 2 OR wounded.	M.M.
	19.		Bn relieved by the right Sub-Sector of the left Bde. Front by 1st Bn the Royal WARWICKSHIRE Regt. Relief Active 11 P.M.	M.M.
L'ECLEME.	20.	2.30 A.M.	Relief complete. Bn moved back to L'ECLEME.	M.M.
			Co cleaning up.	M.M.
L'ECLEME	21		Bn in Billets. Co organising and training	M.M.
	22		Bn in Billets. Co training on the range and assault course. 87 OR went for amts.	M.M.
	23.		Bn in Billets. Co training.	
		10.30 P.M.	4 officers & 16 groups working under RS on essential attack assembly trenches in 930 B.D. 1 OR killed 2 OR wounded.	M.M.

Army Form C. 2118.

WAR DIARY
or
INTELLIGENCE SUMMARY.
(Erase heading not required.)

Place	Date	Hour	Summary of Events and Information	Remarks and references to Appendices
L'ECLEME	24		Bn in Billets training on assault course and Range. Competition shooting every evening. Pat Bours and application.	
			2Lt W.C. WILDING - N. COTEER & 120th reinforcements	MH
Line	25		Bn relieved 5th Bn The Rifle Bde in Right subsector of	
PACAUT WD 16			In right Bn post. Relief 12:45pm Complete 12:45am	MH
LA POTTERIE			Bn HQ STURN INN W8 D 1.6 cavalier C.Co Comm Boon A.Co Reserve D.Co	MH
	26		Bn in the line Situation unchanged. 1.O.R. Killed	MH
	27		Bn in the line Situation unchanged. 1. O.R. killed	MH
	28		Bn in the line Situation unchanged. 1 O.R. killed	MH
	29		Bn in the line Situation unchanged D Co relieved Co in support line. C Co moved up and relieved B Co in front line. A Co moved back to Reserve.	MH
	30		Bn in the line Situation unchanged.	MH

H.W. Tylor Lt Col
Cdg 2 hour Bn

SECRET.

WAR DIARY

of

2nd Battalion The LANCASHIRE FUSILIERS

FROM:- 1st JULY, 1918
TO:- 31st JULY, 1918.

VOLUME 7.

[signature] Lieut. Colonel,
Commanding
2nd Bn. The Lancashire Fusiliers.

2/8/18.

Army Form C. 2118.

WAR DIARY
or
INTELLIGENCE SUMMARY.
(Erase heading not required.)

July 1918.

Place	Date	Hour	Summary of Events and Information	Remarks and references to Appendices
PACAUT	1		Bn in the line. Shaton unchanged. Casualties 3 O.R. wounded	
SECTOR	2		Bn in the line. Shaton unchanged	
LINE	3		Bn in the line. Shaton unchanged	
	4		Bn in the line. Shaton unchanged	
	5		Bn in the line. Shaton unchanged	
	6	9.30 AM	Bn carried out a raid on enemy post in the Wood about Q34c 60.7 & Q34c 70.1s. The raiding party consisted of L/H.H.BARKER-JONES - B.Co and 26 O.R. B.Co. The artillery and machine gun Bn operated Punk 3 Prisoners 1 Sh/gll Casualty Gunner to 10 pers L 38 R.I.R. Awards L/H.H.BARKER-JONES - M.C. 2493 Sgt. E.W.WIGGIN - D.C.M. 36584 Pte POOLE A. - M.M.	
			Remaining this night the front supports and supports remain shaton unchanged.	

Army Form C. 2118.

WAR DIARY
or
INTELLIGENCE SUMMARY.
(Erase heading not required.)

Instructions regarding War Diaries and Intelligence Summaries are contained in F. S. Regs., Part II. and the Staff Manual respectively. Title pages will be prepared in manuscript.

Place	Date	Hour	Summary of Events and Information	Remarks and references to Appendices
LIRE	7		Situation unchanged. The Bn. was relieved by the 1st Bn. the Royal WARWICKSHIRE Regt. and on relief moved as follows :- B.C. Co. to CANAL BANK (36 A.0.9 - O.32.c.S.9) A. D Co. to Billets in L'ECLEME	
	8.	10 p.m.	Relieve started	
		2.30am	Relieve finished	
L'ECLEME	8		Casu[altie]s Nil. 1 O.R. killed. 1 O.R. wounded	
	9		B. C. Co. on CANAL BANK. A. D. Co. in Billets cleaning up	
			B. C. Co. on CANAL BANK. A. D. Co. in Billets at 2.30. O.R. rejoined	
	10		B. C. Co. on CANAL BANK. A. D. Co. in Billets	
		6 p.m.	A. D. Co. relieved B.C. Co. on CANAL BANK	
			B. Co. returned to L'ECLEME Relief complete 12 midnight	
	11		A. D. Co. on CANAL BANK. B. C. Co. in Billets cleaning up	
	12		A. D. Co. on CANAL BANK. B. C. Co. in Billets	
	13.		Co. on the CANAL BANK supplying working party to R.E. Bn. relieved by Hampshire Regt. in the night. Returned to left Bn. Front Line. D. Co. Supp. Bn. A. Co. Reserve. B. Co. Res Henon	

Army Form C. 2118.

WAR DIARY
or
INTELLIGENCE SUMMARY.
(Erase heading not required.)

Instructions regarding War Diaries and Intelligence Summaries are contained in F. S. Regs., Part II. and the Staff Manual respectively. Title pages will be prepared in manuscript.

Place	Date	Hour	Summary of Events and Information	Remarks and references to Appendices
LINE.	14		Bn in the line. Enemy artillery fairly active on Reserve	MLA
VILLAGE			Lieut. J.H.H.BORRER loses M.C. and 1 O.R. wounded	MLA
SECTOR.	15.		Bn in the line. Wharton unchanged. Enemy artillery active	MLA
	16		at night. 2 week 2nd Lt. C. DOYLEY joined. Bn in the line. Wharton unchanged. Enemy artillery active in Recloi and vicinity of Ponta Q.2 O.R. wounded	MLA
	17		Bn in the line. Wharton unchanged	MLA
	18		Bn in the line. Wharton unchanged. 1 O.R. killed	MLA
			Lieuts. BLOOR, DESMOND. BRACKWELL join. 10 P. and	
	19		Bn in the line. Wharton unchanged. 1 O.R. killed	MLA
				1 O.R. wounded
	20		Bn in the line. Wharton unchanged. 1 O.R. wounded	MLA
	21		Bn in the line. Wharton unchanged. A Co. relieved	MLA
			D Co in the front line. D Co now held by S.Bn.	
			1. O.R. wounded. Major. W. B. Carrell to Hospital	
	22		Bn in the line. Wharton unchanged. 6 O.R. wounded	MLA

Army Form C. 2118.

WAR DIARY
or
INTELLIGENCE SUMMARY.
(Erase heading not required.)

Instructions regarding War Diaries and Intelligence Summaries are contained in F. S. Regs., Part II. and the Staff Manual respectively. Title pages will be prepared in manuscript.

Place	Date	Hour	Summary of Events and Information	Remarks and references to Appendices
LINE	23		Bn in the line. Situation unchanged. Capt E.E.C. MARTIN M.C. proceeded to England on 6 months Non Effective afc	N/A
			3 years 2 months service with the BEF in FRANCE	N/A
	24		Bn in the line. Situation unchanged. Enemy artillery active. 1 OR killed. 1 OR wounded.	N/A
			Bn in the line. Situation unchanged.	N/A
	25		Bn in the line. Situation unchanged. 1 OR wounded	N/A
	26		Bn in the line. Situation unchanged. D Company being Eg'Onnehoyre that 3.O.R. of A Co. rushed in a daylight Raid 2 snipers from an enemy post. 1 OR killed - 1 OR wounded	N/A
	27		Bn relieved by 1 Bn R.R. Regt WARWICK'S in Pt Piet and moved back to Billets in L'ECLEME Rd BERQUETTE	N/A
			Bn in Billets 3 p.m Bn parade for Bath's to MINDEX	
	28		L'ECLEME Slaughter 11 am - 2 pm Bn sand	N/A
			Bn in Billets. Evening. 35 O.R joined	
	29		5.30pm. Battalion scheme Batt move in Bus Reneehen L'ECLEME Batt man via Bus Reneehen L'ECLEME shelled	N/A

Army Form C. 2118.

WAR DIARY
or
INTELLIGENCE SUMMARY.
(Erase heading not required.)

Instructions regarding War Diaries and Intelligence Summaries are contained in F. S. Regs., Part II. and the Staff Manual respectively. Title pages will be prepared in manuscript.

Place	Date	Hour	Summary of Events and Information	Remarks and references to Appendices
L'ECLEME	30		Bn in Billets. Brigades 11 A.M. - 2.30 P.M. L'ECLEME Stilled during night.	MM
	31		Bn in Billets. Baths etc. elsewhere Bn won the Championship in that turned out Fieldgun. L'ECLEME Shelled during night.	MM

J.W. Nelson Lt Col
Comm'g 2 " New Fus

Secret

War Diary

of

2 Lancashire Fusiliers

From:- August 1st 1918
To:- August 31st 1918

Volume 8

H. Kirkby Lt Colonel
Comdg 2 Lancashire Fus

Army Form C. 2118.

WAR DIARY
or
INTELLIGENCE SUMMARY.
(Erase heading not required.)

Instructions regarding War Diaries and Intelligence Summaries are contained in F.S. Regs., Part II. and the Staff Manual respectively. Title pages will be prepared in manuscript.

Place	Date	Hour	Summary of Events and Information	Remarks and references to Appendices
LECLEME			Map 36a S.E. 1/20000	
	August 1918.		MINDEN DAY 159th ANNIVERSARY.	
	1.	6.30.A.M.	Reveille played by K. Drums	
		11.A.M.	Ceremonial parade. Trooping the Colour. Made Commanded by Lt Col. H.A. Kirkby. D.S.O. Salute taken by Brig Gen. T.H. Wade. D.S.O. xx Lancashire Fusiliers Cdg 11th Inf Bde.	
		P.M.	Gen Wade. C.O. 2nd in Command and Adjt. O.M. visit Co. during Dinners.	
		2.30 P.M.	Sports	
		6.P.M.	Concert by A Div. Follies	
	2.	2.A.M.	LECLEME shelled heavily. Still struck in billets occupied by A Co. Killing 10 O.R wounding 9 2. O.R	
				Mu
		7.30.A.M	Parade for firing on the range at ALCOCQUE. On arrival	
			on range and parade dismissed owing to rain	
		3.P.M	Bn. moved out of LECLEME into to Shilling B.C.Co. A. D Co. & to CANTRAINES and Trench in vicinity. Bn H.Q. to CANTRAINE.	
			Move to BUSDETTES	

Army Form C. 2118.

WAR DIARY
or
INTELLIGENCE SUMMARY.

(Erase heading not required.)

Instructions regarding War Diaries and Intelligence Summaries are contained in F. S. Regs., Part II, and the Staff Manual respectively. Title pages will be prepared in manuscript.

Place	Date	Hour	Summary of Events and Information	Remarks and references to Appendices
CAD TRAINING	3.		Bn in billets	
		9.0.a.m	Bn moves up to Recant Sector to relieve 13th Bn The Rifle Brigade	MM
			Bn HQ STAR INN. Relief Complete 11am. B & D Cy in front line	
LINE	4.		Bn in Line B Co front line. C Co in Support D Co in Canal Bank. A Co in Reserve. Enemy shelling rather unsettled photo during night 4-5th. Situation rather unsettled photo report no enemy seen in front. Expected to Reinwerck & enemy line	MM
LINE	5.		Situation unaltered fighting patrols sent out report no enemy in enemy front line. Enemy shelling heavy early morning 1 OR wounded	MM
LINE	6.		Situation not changed. C Co pushed forward reoccupied enemy trenches on Jan & to LANKHOF WHITE CHATEAU about wood Q6. Established N edge LANKHOF barriers. 2 OR killed	MM
LINE	7.	1am 2 prisoners	2 prisoners captured report enemy withdrawn up Yser	
		4.30am	Orders for the pursuit return issued by to Bdy	

Army Form C. 2118.

WAR DIARY
or
INTELLIGENCE SUMMARY. /MM/
(Erase heading not required.)

Instructions regarding War Diaries and Intelligence Summaries are contained in F. S. Regs., Part II. and the Staff Manual respectively. Title pages will be prepared in manuscript.

Place	Date	Hour	Summary of Events and Information	Remarks and references to Appendices
Line	7.		enemy C Co front, B Co support. A Co move up to Relieve A Co B Co. D Co unknown on CROOK Street.	
		8 a.m.	Co moves forward and occupies line VET-BOIS Fm —	
			N.E. edge of FAGOT WOOD about 100' in advance of Donk line. Heavy Artillery M.A.	/M/1
			fire active. A Co and B Co established	
		10.	HALF WAY HOUSE. A2B to 4.	
			BURKE 9m	
		11.m.	Heavy enemy Shelling BURKE 9m N.E. and 9m	
			Central. 2nd Lt Foulsham wounded. 6. O.R. killed	
Line	8.		Advance continued. C Co occupy BRAN[?] On	
			enemy Artillery fire down promenade barrage	/M/1
			Throughout the day. 9 to 10 a.m. in all. 6 O.R. wounded	
			2nd Lt Longland wounded. - 1. O.R. killed 10. O.R. both	
			1. O.R. died of wounds. + outpost line. C Co relieved B	
		9 p.m.	A Co relieved C Co in outpost line. New BnHq moved from BURKE 9m	
			original support line to support line	

Army Form C. 2118.

WAR DIARY
or
INTELLIGENCE SUMMARY.
(Erase heading not required.)

Place	Date	Hour	Summary of Events and Information	Remarks and references to Appendices
LINE	9.		Clayton Trenches all withdrawing except by fighting rear guards. On reaching the line TURBEAUTE - JONCK'SR - KINGS CROSSROAD - 19th Bn. Right. Advance to take 1700 yds Bn.H.Q shelled 3 30pm - 5 30pm 1 OR wded	A/A
		9pm	1st The Kings Own took over Rt. support Co. Bn. retiring to Front Line A Co. - Support Co. Canal Bank D Co. - Reserve B Co. 2/Lt Dickson & 43 details employed carrying when on duty, 2 L ORs killed - 8 ORs wded	A/A
			Bn in Support	
LINE	10.		" " Support	A/A
	11.	9pm	Bn relieved Kings own in support line Right Front Co A Co - Left Front D Co Right Support B Co - Left Support C Co Bn.H.Q. TRACENT WOOD D.33.B.8.5. 1 OR wded	A/A

WAR DIARY
or
INTELLIGENCE SUMMARY.

Army Form C. 2118.

Place	Date	Hour	Summary of Events and Information	Remarks and references to Appendices
LINE	12		Bn in outpost line. No change. Capt A.H. Shimmin joined Bn.	N/A
LINE	13		Bn in outpost line.	
		9am	Bn relieved by 2 Gordon Regt in outpost line.	
			Bn into bath & grd Sen clo Hopkey Wd to Copse Wd.	N/A
			CREPOT WOOD — 2nd Bn clo - support line D.Co to HEPBURN	
			COPSE A B Co Pon Res.	N/A
			HOOSE L O.P. wood	
	14		Bn in support	N/A
	15		Bn in support	
		8pm	Bn relieved by 2 M. Sea forth H.Q.R. & two Coys back to KICHEME Bn H.Q. in CHATEAU DE QUESNOY remainder with 7pm 10th Bath have moved to BURBURE	N/A
ECLEME	16		Bn in Billets. Remainder to attend Dvl. O.K.	N/A
	17		Bn in Billets at ECLEME. Pm relieving front by outgoing ALLOUAGNE 7am - 8pm. Punctured by Train killed Pte [?]	N/A

Army Form C. 2118.

WAR DIARY
or
INTELLIGENCE SUMMARY.

(Erase heading not required.)

Instructions regarding War Diaries and Intelligence Summaries are contained in F. S. Regs., Part II. and the Staff Manual respectively. Title pages will be prepared in manuscript.

Place	Date	Hour	Summary of Events and Information	Remarks and references to Appendices
LECLUSE	18	pm	Bath. Church Parade 10.15 a.m.	MM
	19	pm	Bn. in Billets. Pm bathing & games for teams	MM
		5 pm	Bn. in Billets. Main Rising Bar Lines for teams	MM
	20	pm	Bn. in Billets.	MM
	21	pm	Bn. in Billets. Pm started when R.B. in pieces	MM
			SECTOR Relief. Another to S.W. Wilkenham from the	
Mr P. Sheet 51 B.S. 11			Line	
LARRY	22	10 am	pm. moved by Monti Rote & Leguy to Are-	MM
LES		1.30 pm	Bn. arrived Leguy & Ares	
ARRES	23		Bn. billeted in Leguy, les Ares	MM
	24		Bn. in Billets	MM
	25	7.15 am	Bn. marched to BURQUETTE – entrained and arrived BAVRANS 4.0 pm – marched to CROISETTES	MM
CROISETTES				
	26	6 pm	Bn. billeted in CROISETTES	MM
	27	pm	Bn. marched to BURLES	MM

WAR DIARY
or
INTELLIGENCE SUMMARY.

Army Form C. 2118.

Place	Date	Hour	Summary of Events and Information	Remarks and references to Appendices
BURLES	27		Bn. to billets in BURLES-MONCHAUPT.	WM
	28		Bn. marched to HAUTE-AVESNES at 11 a.m. and moved by motor Bus to BETHUNE area arriving at SCOTTS WATCH at 8.15 pm. Bn. moved forward	
	29		taking over trenches in O.7k.	[9.1]
	30		The Bn. remained in trenches in O.7k.	[9.1]
	31		During the evening companies were shifted into trenches in O.8.c. Bn. H.Q remaining at O.7 a 2.5	[9.1]
			The Bn. was awaiting orders all day. It eventually moved up to relieve the Rifle Brigade (11th Bde.) in support in trenches in O.17 c + O.12.c at 11.30 pm.	[9.1]

W.R.Kelly Lt. Col
Cmdg. 2nd Lancashire Fusiliers.

War Diary

of

2nd Lancashire Fusiliers

From Sept 1st 1918

To Sept 30th 1918

Volume 9.

H. A. Kirkby Lt Colonel
Comdg 2 Lancashire Fus

WAR DIARY
INTELLIGENCE SUMMARY.

(Erase heading not required.)

Army Form C. 2118.

Place	Date	Hour	Summary of Events and Information	Remarks and references to Appendices
REMY Sector ARRAS Map sheet 51 B SE 1/20,000	Sept 1		All preparations being made for the attack on the DROCOURT-QUEANT line. The following arrangements Coy Comdrs conferences as to how the attack was to be carried out. Lieut Abrahams, 2/Lieut Dunkley M.C. were passed & Lt Stange M.C. joined Coy in the afternoon. Two carrying parties from A & D Coys in the evening to carry up ammunition to forward dumps.	S.9.d
	"2nd"	2 am	Bn assembled in P.7.6 & d & P.13.6. in support. 2nd ESSEX Right Front, 13' KINGS OWN Left front.	
		5 am	Zero 5 A.M. All objectives taken with the exception of ETAING on the left. Coy consolidated in DROCOURT - QUEANT line in P.15.b & P.16.a. A Co attacked	
		NOON	2 platoons to block trenches in P.8'b. Heavy enemy shelling of ETERRIGNY in afternoon very quiet in the evening & throughout the night.	S.9.d

WAR DIARY
or
INTELLIGENCE SUMMARY.
(Erase heading not required.)

Army Form C. 2118.

Place	Date	Hour	Summary of Events and Information	Remarks and references to Appendices
	3rd		During the night A/Bn had to move & form up on a line from P8.d central — P9.c central with 2nd ESSEX on the left & 1st KINGS OWN on the right. Our Bn to attack ETAING in support.	
		Zero 5 a.m.	ETAING taken early with only 11 prisoners. The enemy having evacuated it overnight. Total prisoners during operation 440 excluding 7 officers. Casualties. Capt P.G. Bowen M.C. killed. 2nd Lt Stanger Dundas, Morgan, Montgomery, Sewell, Lund wounded + 1 B.O.R. being killed. 22 killed.	
	4th		Reconnoitred position from 2nd Bde. (10thDiv) also were relieved two that night, came up to that 10th Relief Royal Sussex Regt. Taken over from ero — Relief completed by 12.30 a.m.	57 D

WAR DIARY
or
INTELLIGENCE SUMMARY.

Army Form C. 2118.

Place	Date	Hour	Summary of Events and Information	Remarks and references to Appendices
	4th	2.30 am	The Bn arrived in new area near O.13. entrn	
		5.30 pm	the QM Stores had moved to & from ARRAS. 10/ inch. Major Ayrel joined the Bn.	
	5th	12.30 pm	The Bn moved to ACHICOURT where section Brigade entrained. Station shelled on train	
map sheet 44 1/40,000		10.30 pm	was moving out. Detraining at TINQUES adv. we entrained for MAGNICOURT-en-COMTÉ. Arrived 12 midnight	5.9D.
MAGNICOURT.	6.		Bn in billets in MAGNICOURT. Day spent cleaning up and looking aft. H.H. Banks, joined M.C. rejoined fr England	MM
"	7.		Bn in billets in MAGNICOURT. Co training. fr Channel	MM
"	8.		up and temporary Bn in billets. Co training. Churchparade	MM
"	9.		Bn in billets. Co training	MM
"	10.		Bn in billets. Co training. General Conference by Colm	MM
"	11.		Bn in billets. Co training. B.C.C. 2 B.f. Bn. inspected a platoon	MM

Army Form C. 2118.

WAR DIARY
or
INTELLIGENCE SUMMARY.
(Erase heading not required.)

Instructions regarding War Diaries and Intelligence Summaries are contained in F. S. Regs., Part II. and the Staff Manual respectively. Title pages will be prepared in manuscript.

Place	Date	Hour	Summary of Events and Information	Remarks and references to Appendices
			a fighting army. No 18 Platoon of A. Co. also all M.G. Sect. under 2/Lt Ribey. M.C.	
MAGNICOURT	12		Bn in Billets. Co. Training. Brigade N.C.Os on weather	
			Course to front was very wet and having some somewhat	
			held up. S.O.R. new Placements.	
	13		Bn in Billets. Co. Training. T.C.M. STANGE. M.S.L. Wounded	
	14		Bn in Billets. Bn scheme. Route march CHEERS and Beehive	
			attack back to MAGNICOURT.	
	15		Bn in Billets. Bn Church Parade cancelled. O.O.R. Issued	
	16		Bn in billets. Bn Scheme. Pursuit of and attack on enemy	
			withdraws to a considerable portion	
	17		Bn in Billets. Bn On the ROCOURT Ranges attacky field firing	
			and application. Lewis gun under L.G Officer	
	18		Bn in Billets. Brigade Scheme cancelled. Bn outpost scheme	
	19		Bn in Billets. Inspect K. worn only morning by Co. on training ground	
			Marching order kit inspection by Co. on training ground	
			H. R. J. G. Park 1(M30) W. W. 20826/1992 50,000 8/17 S&M B&L 18/M31C/2128/17	C.S. Jones rejoins from England

Army Form C. 2118.

WAR DIARY
or
INTELLIGENCE SUMMARY.
(Erase heading not required.)

Place	Date	Hour	Summary of Events and Information	Remarks and references to Appendices
MAGNICOURT			Brig-Gen. R.A. YAGAR. C.M.G. D.S.O. took leave of the Bn. on being invalided to India. The period from the 6th – 19th inclusive being spent in training – was an opportunity to a certain amount of educational training to the platoons. Platoon football matches were played and an inter Co. run under country was organised and won by B. Co. Bdier played a good match against the Brigade at cricket after a good match against the front of the training were spoilt by very dull weather. The Twad lost 1 to 5 days Bullring on the service Riffle, but to do work to bring up the men steadily. Bullets with detail. B/O. i/c SS-15 details been spread to another Pm ready to move every 19.14.	
Put Sheet hut 9 Billion Sh	20th	4.45 am	Bn marched to MURPHY-A COTON in Kirbein – arriving at entraining point at 5.15 am	
BATTERY-VALLEY.		7 am	Bn entrained	
		10 am	Bn detrained and arrived in new area i.e. BATTERY-VALLEY.	

Army Form C. 2118.

WAR DIARY
or
INTELLIGENCE SUMMARY.
(Erase heading not required.)

Place	Date	Hour	Summary of Events and Information	Remarks and references to Appendices
	20th	C.O.	Bn. was in Quval Cump X and shelld. Moved through of reserve in Valley on 1st stage only. FEUCHY - ARRAS Road about 100 x from Sun.Q. Transport on the Hill near FEUCHY CHAPEL X Roads.	
BATTERY VALLEY	21st		Bn. in BATTERY VALLEY	
	22	11 AM	Church parade	
		3 PM	Bn. moved to HAPPY VALLEY. Remainder of HAPPY VALLEY soon in the system of trenches - dugouts and accommodation was vary crowded. Orders to improve shelter and van paul heavy drawn to purpose. Penning west abbey Coy went up about 10 pm. to reconnoitre line.	
	23		Bn. in HAPPY VALLEY Training by Platoons, C.O.R. accidentally wounded.	
	24		C.O. who was accompanied him was also slightly wounded.	
half Sheets		7pm	Bn Rd'ed relieves 1st Rn Bn Rifle Bde in the left sector of the Left Bn Frt. Disposition: Right front Coy C Co - Centre A Co. - Reserve Co B Co. Pushq 03a89.	
51B N.W. 51B S.W.		11.30pm	Relief Complete.	

Army Form C. 2118.

WAR DIARY
or
INTELLIGENCE SUMMARY.
(Erase heading not required.)

Place	Date	Hour	Summary of Events and Information	Remarks and references to Appendices
LINE.	25.		On the line Skaton very quiet. Certain amount of gun shelling to JIGSAW wood BOIS DES SARTS.	M.M
	26.		On the Skaton very quiet. During the morning to ready to "prevent" trouble on our right. Nothing to report by Scouts etc. Enemy by himself pretends to be prepare everywhere. Scouts who talk the Germans - bomb snatchup	M.M
		8.30pm	A.C. in conjunction with 9th & 10th R.B. offering a opening by enfilading village in Rue griv & His emerging and established point in enemy lid without casualties. B.G. erected diversion to simulate attack at dawn 27. Casualties Nil	M.M
	27.		From the line the situation in sectors with 9 RNT. 1 Otto Rankinmura 3d. H.Q brought up much up to Ap. the line. No alliance with the situation.	M.M
	28.	7pm	Relieved by 9th R.B. in front line and proceeded by Rue Baux O.O. Col Ruth to O.S.O. it. Relief complete 11 Pm 10 R. between	M.M M.M
Reserve.	29.		Arm Reserve. Cleaning up and salvaging.	M.M
	30.		Arm Reserve. Cleaning D.B to practice platoon organising up M.G. etc.	M.M

Maj. A.K. Roth M. Col
Cmdg 13th Middlesex Reg Bn.

Secret

War Diary

of

2 Lancashire Fusiliers

from Oct 1st 1918
to Oct 31st 1918

Volume 10

H W Kirkby Colonel
Comdg 2 Lancashire Fus

Army Form C. 2118.

WAR DIARY
or
INTELLIGENCE SUMMARY.
(Erase heading not required.)

Instructions regarding War Diaries and Intelligence Summaries are contained in F. S. Regs., Part II, and the Staff Manual respectively. Title pages will be prepared in manuscript.

Place	Date	Hour	Summary of Events and Information	Remarks and references to Appendices
Map Sheet 51B N.W. 1/20000	October 1918			
Line	1.		Bn in Reserve Bn in old front line however relieves 11th Bn and Twin Copse. Arty Order 1/4. Reconnaissance of Bn Right Sector. Carried out by 2 Bn Officers. Patrols arranged in the line night 1/2 in rear to examine the night pats.	AAA
	2.		Bn in Reserve.	
		1830pm.	Relief of 1st Bn Kings Own Regt. started by the Bn. Guides met Coys at Railway crossing just west of B.O.I.47.	AAA
		2345	Relief complete. B Co - Right front. C Co - Left front. D Co - Centre front. A Co in Reserve B.H.Q. O.50.8.0 Headquarters of a minor character in contemplate. It is very important that a cunning stands be made over R. TRINQUIS Brook and bridge heads established. Co Cdr told to remark took a view to attempt crossing night 3/4th.	
SAILLY-EN-OSTREVANT 16 HAMBLAIN Sheet 51B. 1/10000	3			
51B. 1/20000		Noon.	D Co. effect a crossing at J.26.c.6.3. Enemy found little opposition and took enemy posts only established at J26.C.55 - 76 - 9.5	

WAR DIARY or INTELLIGENCE SUMMARY

Army Form C. 2118.

Place	Date	Hour	Summary of Events and Information	Remarks and references to Appendices
LINE	3.	2100	Situation fairly quiet. Enemy ones what demoralised by our evening strafe and running short a great deal of ammunition. Enemy snipers active all night. A carrying party of 2 officers 50 O.R. and A.C. arrived material to the R.E. to make a bridge.	
	4	0100 to 0300	but the enemy put down a heavy barrage and bridge was not finished. Enemy artillery very active all night. C Co 3 O.R. died - D Co 2 O.R. wd. to B Co 1 O.R. wd.	
LINE		0700	Barrage established at J.26.c.6.3.	
		0930	2Lt. Orchard D Co. crawled out to enemy post at J.26.c.4.8. which was unoccupied. One dead german in it with no identifications.	
		1900.	Enemy put down a barrage. Enemy artillery put up a burst then Yangel signal RED - RED - RED which is the same as an S.O.S. Our gunners turned on for 10 minutes, enemy trench and bridge heads, pk but up finished.	

Army Form C. 2118.

WAR DIARY
or
INTELLIGENCE SUMMARY.
(Erase heading not required.)

Instructions regarding War Diaries and Intelligence Summaries are contained in F. S. Regs., Part II. and the Staff Manual respectively. Title pages will be prepared in manuscript.

Place	Date	Hour	Summary of Events and Information	Remarks and references to Appendices
	4.		Casualties. 6 O.R wounded. 2/Lt S. MUTCH was wounded at duty.	
LINE	5	0300	Enemy again attacked Bridgehead post but was driven off	
		0545	Enemy again attacked and repulsed	
			Enemy right L/5" Shrapnel cracks near the dam in J26c.	
		0800	Enemy artillery obtain heavy bombardment which was kept up all day on the post, and followed by another attack which was again repulsed Casualties 2 O.R killed 4 O.R. wounded 2/Lt D BLORE wounded.	
		1930	Platoon 7 A Co under 2/Lt ASHLEY sent up to support one of our 6. Co. when 2 Co. to 38. our 6 Co. put out 2 posts at J26a a 44 and J26c Post was unsuccessful in their attempt to bridge the Sluice. R.E. unsuccessful in their attempt to mend the post but was stopped.	
		2100	Enemy again attempted to mend the post but was stopped.	
		2130.	Another enemy attempt beaten off.	

Army Form C. 2118.

WAR DIARY
or
INTELLIGENCE SUMMARY.

(Erase heading not required.)

Place	Date	Hour	Summary of Events and Information	Remarks and references to Appendices
LINE	6.	0500	Pat on enemy side of TRIPTWIS held by D Co. Later relief by 2 pltn A Co. Fairly quiet day. All Coy to Fampoux	
		1915	Relief of Bn by Canadian BLACK WATCH started	
		2200	Relief complete. Bn moved back by march route to BATTERY VALLEY arriving 0100.7th.	
BATTERY VALLEY	7.	0115	Bn marched via ARRAS - DUISANS - to MAGARR arriving	
		1800hrs	Good billets.	
	8.		Men billets cleaning up. Details rejoined Bn from Louez.	
			Maj Gen LIPSETT, Coy in Div lectured Kott Officers 1000 hrs. Bn in Billets Platoon & Co. training.	
	9.		Brig Gen McNaughton tooks over command 12 Inf Bde	
MAGARR			Bde O.R. reinforcement truned	
	10.		Bn in billets. Bn Scheme set reamed out by the Bn	
			L.A.B Kinnear joined the Bn.	

WAR DIARY
or
INTELLIGENCE SUMMARY.
(Erase heading not required.)

Army Form C. 2118.

Place	Date	Hour	Summary of Events and Information	Remarks and references to Appendices
MAROEUIL	11	1200	Bn entrained near MAROEUIL and moved by BAARAIN - HENINEL-SUR-COJEUL - CROISELLES - QUEANT - INCHY to area E. of BOURLON. Map sheet 57C. 1/40000. Transport moved by road taking 2 days and staging night 11·12th at WANCOURT. 11 O.R. reinforcements joined	
BOURLON	12		Bn having ready to move at 2 hours notice. Transport rejoined Bn at 1700 hours. 1 O.R. reinforcement.	
BOURLON	13	0845	Bn moved by route march to FAUBOURG ST. ROCH - CAMBRAI.	
CAMBRAI		1400	Bn arrived in billets 9. St Roch, map 57B. A 11.4.9.	
	14		Training in billets. A.B Co. Coy reconnoitred front.	
	15		Maj Gen. LIPSETT C.M.G. D.S.O. Coy to Bn killed. Bn in billets. Platoon training Co. C.D Coy Co. Coy reconnoitred front area	
	16		Bn in billets. Platoon & Co training. 1 O.R. reinforcement.	
	17		Bn in billets. Bn training. Orders received to move to new area near IWUY. T.D. map 51A 1/40000	
	18	1100	Bn moved across country to area near IWUY. arriving in new area 1430 hours. Route in open hours T12.A.9.2. Men bivouaced in bivouac sheets in the open.	
IWUY				

Army Form C. 2118.

WAR DIARY
or
INTELLIGENCE SUMMARY.
(Erase heading not required.)

Instructions regarding War Diaries and Intelligence Summaries are contained in F.S. Regs., Part II, and the Staff Manual respectively. Title pages will be prepared in manuscript.

Place	Date	Hour	Summary of Events and Information	Remarks and references to Appendices
Area near IWUY	19.		Training. C.O. to Can. sent up to reconnoitre Autrwad area pending an attack by 10.11 Inf Bde.	
		15.00	Enemy reported to have withdrawn and operation altered accordingly	
	20.		Small attack by 10.11 Bde captured HOSPRES & SPOLZOIR. 12 Inf Bn ready to move at 30 mins notice. 2.0.R Bn forward	
	21.		Bn ready to move. A number of drafts horses etc arrived. Games etc	
VILLERS-EN-22.	22.	09.00	Bn moved by platoon at 100 x distance across country to VILLERS-EN-CAUCHIE.	
CAUCHIE hopSTA'/pows		11.00	Bn arrived in billets. 6 Rounds H.E. H.V. fell in the village about 13.00 hours	
	23.	05.00	6 Rounds H.E. H.V. in village. CO. & Co Cdn reconnoitred front train received for move forward. 11.00 - orders altered - 16.00 hours	
		10.00	orders altered again and again at 23.00 hours Bn to be ready to move by 11.30 24th inst	

WAR DIARY
or
INTELLIGENCE SUMMARY.

(Erase heading not required.)

Army Form C. 2118.

Instructions regarding War Diaries and Intelligence Summaries are contained in F. S. Regs., Part II. and the Staff Manual respectively. Title pages will be prepared in manuscript.

Place	Date	Hour	Summary of Events and Information	Remarks and references to Appendices
VILLERS - EN - CAUCHIE.	Oct. 24.		Bn. ready to move to area p.i. map 51A S.W. 1/20,000. at 1130 hours	
		1200	Bn moved by platoons at 100x distance across country to area P.31 near SAULZOIR	
P.31 Central		1400	Bn arrived P.31.	
VERCHAIN.		1830.	A Co. attached to 1st Bn. The King's Own Regt. Bn. HqrsA Co. moved up and relieved 2Bn. The Seaforth Hdrs. in VERCHAIN. Bn arrived in billets. All good cellars in VERCHAIN An occasional round of H.E. Put into VERCHAIN during night. 24th - 25th.	MM
		2300	Bn. operation order received to to be ready to move in support to ESSEX & King's own about 9am Zero hour for attack in morning is 0700 hour.	
VERCHAIN.	25.	0700	Zero hour.	
map 51A S.E. 1/20,000.		0900	Co. moved on Johnson B Co. to K31a - C Co to K31A - D Co K16 - T36.	MM
SIA N.E. 1/20,000		1300	Orders received and moved to Co. B Co to relieve King's Own on Railway line K28 c + 0. to K27 D O 8.	

WAR DIARY or INTELLIGENCE SUMMARY

Army Form C. 2118.

Place	Date	Hour	Summary of Events and Information	Remarks and references to Appendices
Map 51 N.E.	25"	1/5000	C Co. to relieve ESSEX Regt. on railway line K27 D.c.8. to K20 D9.9.	
			A Co retired to Bn and moved in support to B Co	
			Sunken road K33 B.	
		1500	D Co moved in support to C about DEFFERRIERE Fm. K26A.	
			move in two's. A Co moved to craters in QUESNAINE	
			K32 D 4.6. which was being heavily shelled at time. 9hr	
			village had been captured the morning by KINGS own	
		1600	B Co relieved Kings own. 51st Div on our left counterattacked	
			and driven back slightly. Relayed eleq of ESSEX by C Co.	
		1800	ESSEX relieved by C Co.	
			B Co was unable to get touch with 61st Div on right and	
			C Co was unable to get touch with 51st Div on left. Two	
			defensive flanks formed. B.C. Co Hdq punch out	
			patrols. If practicable occupy ARTERS and get in	
			touch with the enemy	
		2300	Then received to establish a line of outpost on sunkenroad	

Army Form C. 2118.

WAR DIARY
or
INTELLIGENCE SUMMARY.
(Erase heading not required.)

Place	Date	Hour	Summary of Events and Information	Remarks and references to Appendices
QUERRIEUC	25th	22.00	Map Sheet 51A N.E. 1/20000 K28 B.8.7 to K15 C.5.5. Orders issued to Coy.	
		22.40	B.C. rang up and asked if we would rather establish ourselves as above, with advance guards' answer 'Yes'. Orders given to the right and left ack [?] worked to E S E to come up and spread with no on our left.	
		22.30	Orders issued to Coys to form up as follows — B Co. Right Ack on Railway from K28 D.4.0 to Railway bridge K27 D.8.4. C Co left Ack from K27 D.8.4 to K27 D.0.8. A Co Right Support in Sunken Road K33 B.8.7. D Co. Left Support in Sunken Road K33 A.0.8. to K27 C.0.1. Pte H8 wounded at K32 D.4.0.	
	26	04.00	Bn formed up ready for the attack as above	
		05.00	Orders for Bns is received from Bde	
		05.30	Orders as Bn was issued to Coys. Objectives of the attack. Sunken Road K28 B.8.7 – K22 A.5.6. including the village of ARTRES. A Co to form a defensive flank along Road from K28 B.8.7 – K28 C.4.0.	

WAR DIARY or INTELLIGENCE SUMMARY.

Army Form C. 2118.

Place	Date	Hour	Summary of Events and Information	Remarks and references to Appendices
	26.10		Boundaries of the attack. Between Bn & 6⅟₂" Div. on the right. Road N.33.B.8.7.	
			Through ARTRES along ARTRES - RESEAU Road.	
			Between the Bn & the ESSEX REGT on the left. K27 D.0.8 to K12 A.5.3.	
			Between Cos. K27 D.8.4 - K28 A.3.1 - K22 D.0.3.	
		0900	B.C.C. issued orders over the Telephone to the effect that a Special Platoon under an Officer was to be detailed to establish a bridgehead across the La PITONELLE RIVER as soon as the objectives were captured, whilst the protective barrage was on the moving ground. R.23.A. B.Co. was ordered to detail a platoon under 2/Lt. HEMSHALL.	
		1000	Zero hour. A Co. of the Kings Own attached to the Bn. and went forward at 1030 to establish Liaison Posts between B.Co. & the 6⅟₂" Div.	
		1009	Attacking Cos. close up on the barrage and attack.	
		1030	Support Co. move off 500⁰ in rear of attacking Co. Telephone wire run out by Signal Officer to keep communication between Bn H.Q. and Support Co.	

WAR DIARY or INTELLIGENCE SUMMARY

Army Form C. 2118.

Place	Date	Hour	Summary of Events and Information	Remarks and references to Appendices
	26"	1200	All objectives reported captured. A Co in position on flank & four platoons pushing on to river. In touch with 61st Div at K29c0.0 and Essex Regt. D Co in junction road K28 A & C. Bn Battle HQ. consisting of Major Cured, Signal officer, Intelligence Officer & runner. 4 cmgs established with Bn HQ in CHATEAU at K28 A32.	
		1300	Bridgehead posts established on every side of the LA RONELLE River covered by a Coy. Bn. Tuck passable bridge at K29a2.9. Post established by Kings Own Coy at K29c1.9 - K29 A11 - K29A1.4 and K29a8.7. A Co rendered unnecessary.	
		1330	A Co under Capt S. CLARKE M.C. pushed across the river and a line of posts established K29A8.4 - through M of JERNE in K29a and across the junction road to trench at K23c.24 4D. This gave in possession of both bridge and in K29a. The special platoon of B Co to attack B Co in the junction road K288 and established posts K29A1.9 - K23c.0.0.	

WAR DIARY or INTELLIGENCE SUMMARY

Army Form C. 2118.

Place	Date	Hour	Summary of Events and Information	Remarks and references to Appendices
	26	1200	Communication by telephone established from C.O. at Battle HQ K18 A.3.2. to Regt. at Bn HQ K32 D.4.6. b-By at LA TARAVISE Fm. This line was maintained through almost continual shelling until relief night 28th/29th.	
		1530	Heavy Enemy shoot on K10.11.12.23.24 from Bullet M.G. This developed into a counterattack against Essex & 5th Div. at 1600. Artillery warned and many casualties caused amongst the enemy. The counterattack was preceded by heavy enemy artillery bombardment lasting 1600 to 1700. with M.G. & Gas. ASTRES and valley K29 - K22 - 1216 Shell & gas all night.	
		1700	Rations arrived and taken up under very difficult conditions by L. JOPLING, M.C. & 2L. ORCHARD in Limbers to Chateau K18 A.3.2.	
		1800	Inspection of Bn as under. A Co - Sunken Ridge head K29.4.6. - M in FERTIS K29.0 - K23.c.4.40. B Co. - K29.0.9. - K23.0.0. - K29.0.3. - K22.c.5.3. C Co. K22.D.0.3. - K22.D.0.3. A.Co. Bn Bullet HQ K28 A.3.2. Bn HQ K32 D.4.6. D.Co. Sunken Road K28 A.C.	

WAR DIARY or INTELLIGENCE SUMMARY

Army Form C. 2118.

Place	Date	Hour	Summary of Events and Information	Remarks and references to Appendices
	26	0600 / 2400	Fairly quiet except for enemy Spasmodic Artillery shots. Estimated casualties for 26th 2/Lt W.D HERSHALL wounded. 6 O.R. Killed 43. O.R. Wounded 7.O.R. missing L/Cpl LLOYD reported Captured. 68 Proven including 3 Officers. Situation unchanged.	
ARRAS & QUERENANG	27	0400	2/Lt C.V. LLOYD & 12 O.R. patrolled ARRAS-PRCBEAU Road upto 500 enemy seen moving from K23 to K16. Except for enemy artillery activity on ARRAS and QUERENANG many was uneventful.	
		1600	Capt. G.M SATTG. F. M.C. Eng. C. Co. moving between Killed whilst on forward reconnaissance.	
		1300 / 1800	Very heavy bombardment by enemy of CHATEAU K28 A 3.2 Co of Kings own withdrawn and it is unknown wh'ich wh Gi. on at Skakon unchanged enemy artillery active on K29 A 8 4. ARRAS and QUERENANG with gun K2.	
	28	1800	Relief of Bn by 1st RIFLE B.D.E. ordered.	

Army Form C. 2118.

WAR DIARY
or
INTELLIGENCE SUMMARY.
(Erase heading not required.)

Place	Date	Hour	Summary of Events and Information	Remarks and references to Appendices
	26	2030	Relief completed. Bn. move by march route to YPRES where all men are in billets.	A/A
			Casualties 26th - 28th are.	
			Capt. C.N. STANGE M.C. missing believed killed. 6 O.R. Killed	
			2/Lt. W.D. HENSTOCK 2nd Bn. of Wellington Reg: att/d 10000 46 O.R. wounded	
			2 O.R. missing	
YPRES	29	0100	Bn. arrived billets. Day spent cleaning up and reorganising	A/A
	30		Bn. in billets. Coy training. Capt. J. TODD M.C. - 2/Lt. COCKER -	A/A
			FINCH - HILL - KEELY. - KEATES joined the Bn.	A/A
	31		Bn. in billets. Coy training	A/A

H.P. Kirkby Lt. Col.
ag 2 Bn. The Lancashire Fusiliers

SECRET.

WAR DIARY.

OF

2 Bn. Lancashire Fusiliers Regt.

From. 1st. November. 1918.

To. 31st. November. 1918.

VOLUME. II

Date.   [signature]   Lieut.Col.
                         Commanding.
                       2nd Lancashire Fusiliers.

Army Form C. 2118.

WAR DIARY
or
INTELLIGENCE SUMMARY.

(Erase heading not required.)

Instructions regarding War Diaries and Intelligence Summaries are contained in F.S. Regs., Part II. and the Staff Manual respectively. Title pages will be prepared in manuscript.

Map Sheet 51A 1/40000. VALENCIENNES, 12.

Place	Date	Hour	Summary of Events and Information	Remarks and references to Appendices
HASPRES	Nov. 1918 1.		Am in billets. Cleaning up and reorganizing.	NIL
	2.	9.00	Battn. had to move to make room for 4th Div. HQ.	
		14.00	Am moved by march route to billets in VILLERS-EN-CAUCHIE.	NIL
		14.30	Pm arrived in VILLERS-EN-CAUCHIE. 2.O.R. Rein/cement. 2 Lt. Capt. A. HOWARTH M.C. & Ireland on 6 months leave of duty.	
	3.		Pm in billets. Churning up Capt. CONSTANCE M.C. killed in action 27.10.19. buried in civil cemetery.	NIL
VILLERS-EN-CAUCHIE			1. O.R. reinforcement.	
	4.		Platoon training. Pm mounted at Bn. HQ. guard.	NIL
	5.		1.O.R. reinforcement. Platoon training. Billets under Capt. A.D. Howarth M.C. lifted from CAMBRAI. Orders received to move to QUÉRÉNAING.	NIL
	6.	11.30	Am moved by march route to QUÉRÉNAING. Very wet weather giving march movement somewhat impracticable. No billets available in QUÉRÉNAING. Bn marched on to ARTRES. captured by the Bn 24.10.18	NIL

Army Form C. 2118.

WAR DIARY
or
INTELLIGENCE SUMMARY.
(Erase heading not required.)

Instructions regarding War Diaries and Intelligence Summaries are contained in F. S. Regs., Part II, and the Staff Manual respectively. Title pages will be prepared in manuscript.

Place	Date	Hour	Summary of Events and Information	Remarks and references to Appendices
ARRES	6.	1600	On arrival in ARRES which was full of troops and no available billets. Men billeted in town and broken down houses. M.H.Q. in a Factory with 2 Essex Reg't.	M.H.A
	7.		On in ARRES. Men to billets throughout the day and M.H.Q billetted in N.E. end of village. On parade settled by 1600 hours.	M.H.A
	8.		On in billets. Wet weather prevented training. A/Co moved in to factory on old ARRES-PRESEAU Road. One naval crossed RIVER NELLE. 3. O.R. reinforcements. Platoon training carried out. 1. O.R. in M arrived.	M.H.A
	9.		Church parade in the afternoon. An hrs kit things Over by 4 — 5. in Bn Football League.	M.H.A
	10.		ARMISTICE SIGNED by German delegate. News of this received on Bn Ceremonial Parade at 1000 hours.	M.H.A
	11.		News taken very quietly. Hostilities ceased at 1100 hours. 4. O.R. reinforcement.	M.H.A

Army Form C. 2118.

WAR DIARY
or
INTELLIGENCE SUMMARY.
(Erase heading not required.)

Instructions regarding War Diaries and Intelligence Summaries are contained in F. S. Regs., Part II. and the Staff Manual respectively. Title pages will be prepared in manuscript.

Place	Date	Hour	Summary of Events and Information	Remarks and references to Appendices
ARTRES	12		Co. Training. In the evening Brig. Gen. CARTON de WIART V.C. - C.M.G. - D.S.O. late B.E.C. 12 Inf. Bde. came over to see the Bn.	AAA
	13		Co. Training. Many civilians returning to the village and men with knowledge of building stores of building duty to help civilians repair their houses. Soup kitchen started in the village by the Bn. to help the refugee civilians. Order to cameras suspended and part of Censorship regulations modified. Bn. training 2 Essex Regt. 2-0 in Bde football Cup. Brig Gen McNAGHTON C.M.G. - D.S.O. Marea cup to be called the RHONELLE Cup to the Bn in the Brigade that proves the most small armed efficient between now and return to England on demobilization.	AAA AAA AAA

WAR DIARY
or
INTELLIGENCE SUMMARY.
(Erase heading not required.)

Army Form C. 2118.

Place	Date	Hour	Summary of Events and Information	Remarks and references to Appendices
ARRAS	14	—	Co. Training. 1.O.R. reinforcement	MMM
	15		Co. Training. Bn played and beat Banks in football. League by 4-1	MMM
	16	1000	Bn Ceremonial Parade. The Mayor of ARRAS came up to present the C.O. and K.R. to reacting village and looking after the civilians. 1.O.R. reinforcement	MMM
			1.O.R. reinforcement. V.1.O.R. wounded accidentally	
	17	1030	Bn Church Parade and Thanksgiving Service. Bn played and beat 12th 2o Zouaves 4-1. 40 R. reinforcement	MMM / MMM
	18		Co. Training	MMM
	19	1300	Bn moved by march route to ST SAUVE in Suburb of VALENCIENNES on V.-MONS Road.	MMM
		1300	Bn arrived at ST SAUVE. 1.O.R. reinforcement	
ST SAUVE	20	0930	Bn Ceremonial Parade. Inspection and review by G.O.C. 40 D.	MMM
	21		Co Training. Lt. Long M.M. Junior Bm. to O.R. reinforcement	MMM
	22		Co. Training. 1.R.E. Glow reinforcement forming 2nd A.W. Scrounger (arrival). 40 R. reinforcement	MMM

Army Form C. 2118.

WAR DIARY
or
INTELLIGENCE SUMMARY. AFW

(Erase heading not required.)

Instructions regarding War Diaries and Intelligence Summaries are contained in F. S. Regs., Part II, and the Staff Manual respectively. Title pages will be prepared in manuscript.

Place	Date	Hour	Summary of Events and Information	Remarks and references to Appendices
ST. ANNE'S	23	—	Co. Training. Lt. A.C. Mitchell leaves for England. 2 O.R. reinforcement	AFW
	24	10.15	Church Parade Service.	AFW
			Ployed 9th Co R.E. in Base Football League & drew 1-1.	AFW
			2 Lt. Osborne and 08 O.R. NCO joined Bn.	
	25		Bn Training in morning. 1.S.to I.work reinforcement	AFW
			England. Pte R. ana Battle changed Khaki. Brushes	
			started. 4 O.R. reinforcement.	
	26		Bn Training. 2 O.R. reinforcement.	AFW
	27		Bn Training. 2 O.R. reinforcement.	AFW
	28	10.30	Bn Ceremonial Parade. Inspected by Gen. Hume Gen O'Kerry.	AFW
			1 O R reinforcement.	
	29	9.00-9.30	Bn Ceremonial Parade. 5 O.R. reinforcement.	AFW
	30		Co. Parade in morning. Bn. and held Marching van inspection	AFW
			Bn. played Battle in Football League and won 1-0.	

3-12-18

Secret.

War Diary

of

2nd Bn Lancashire Fusiliers Regt

From 1st Dec. 1918.

To 31st Dec. 1918.

Volume 12.

H.M. Kirkley [?] Lieut Colonel
Comdg 2" Lancashire Fusiliers.

Army Form C. 2118.

WAR DIARY
or
INTELLIGENCE SUMMARY

(Erase heading not required.)

Instructions regarding War Diaries and Intelligence Summaries are contained in F.S. Regs., Part II. and the Staff Manual respectively. Title Pages will be prepared in manuscript.

Place	Date	Hour	Summary of Events and Information	Remarks and references to Appendices
St. SAUVE	1st	11am	Church Parade -	E.P.D.
		2p-	Games -	E.P.D.
"	2nd	9a-	Training	M.H.
		11.30	Education classes -	M.H.
"	3rd	0800	Range	M.H.
		14.30	Education	
		11.30 - 14.30	Boy Training	
"	4th	9am	Education	M.H.
		11.30	Games	
		2pm	Platoon Training	
"	5th	9am	Education	M.H.
		11.30am		
		11.30		
"	6th	0900h.	Platoon Training	M.H.
		11.30h	Education	
		14.00	Recreation	
"	7th	0930hrs	Bn. Parade	M.H.
		11.30hrs	Education	

Army Form C. 2118.

WAR DIARY
or
INTELLIGENCE SUMMARY

(Erase heading not required.)

Instructions regarding War Diaries and Intelligence Summaries are contained in F. S. Regs., Part II. and the Staff Manual respectively. Title Pages will be prepared in manuscript.

Place	Date	Hour	Summary of Events and Information	Remarks and references to Appendices
St Sambre	8th	0930 hrs	Parade Services	M.H.
"	9th	0900	Coy Training	M.H.
		1130 hrs	Education	
"	10th	0900	Route march by Coys	M.H.
		1130	Education	
		1400	Recreation	
"	11th	1030	Medal Ribbon Presentation Parade by the Corps Commander held owing to inclement weather in the theatre S. Sambre.	M.H.
"	12th	0900	Bn. route march & practice of deploying to Artillery fire from line of march.	M.H.
		1130	Education	
		1400	Recreation	
"	13th	0800 to 13.30	Range	M.H.
		1130 to 1230	Education A & C Coys.	
"	14th	0800	Baths	M.H.
		1700		

Army Form C. 2118.

WAR DIARY
or
INTELLIGENCE SUMMARY
(Erase heading not required.)

Instructions regarding War Diaries and Intelligence Summaries are contained in F. S. Regs., Part II. and the Staff Manual respectively. Title Pages will be prepared in manuscript.

Place	Date	Hour	Summary of Events and Information	Remarks and references to Appendices
St Andre	15th	10:15	Parade Services	N.A.
"	16th	0900	Platoon Training	N.A.
		11:30	Education	
"	17th	0900	Coy Training	N.A.
		11:30	Education	N.A.
"	18th	0900	Range - 'A' Coy	N.A.
			Otherwise Coy Training	
"	19th	0930	Bn. Parade & Tactical Training	N.A.
"	20th	0800	Range	N.A.
		1300hrs		
"	21st	0930hrs	Bn. Route march & Ceremonial	N.A.
		11:30	Education	
"	22nd	10:15	Parade Services	N.A.
"	23rd	0900	Baths and Coy training	N.A.
		16:00	Coy S.A. range	
"	24th	0900	Coy. Training	N.A.
		11:30	Education	

Army Form C. 2118.

WAR DIARY
or
INTELLIGENCE SUMMARY
(Erase heading not required.)

Place	Date	Hour	Summary of Events and Information	Remarks and references to Appendices
St Saulve	25th	1030	Parade Services	N/A
		1245	Commanding Officer visited men at their dinners at the same time inspecting the character of dining halls - finally awarding the prize to D'coy	
"	26th	0900 to 1200	Physical Training	N/A
"	27th	1200	Inspection of billets by Commanding Officer	N/A
"	28th	0900 & 1130	Coy Training. Education	N/A
"	29th	1030	Parade Services	N/A
"	30th	0900 1130	Coy Training. Education	N/A
"	31st	0800 to 1600	Baths - B'coy 50 x range -	N/A

J.W. White Lt Col.
Cmdg. 2⁄⁰ Lancashire Fusiliers

2nd Lancs. Fus.
Jan – Feb. 1919

26F Army Form C. 2118.

Vol 5.2

WAR DIARY
or
INTELLIGENCE SUMMARY.
(Erase heading not required.)

Place	Date	Hour	Summary of Events and Information	Remarks and references to Appendices
ST SAULVE	1st	9am	16 Bn went out for the whole morning in relation to a Batt. pontoon drive — 1 O.R. reinforcements	
" "	2nd	10am	Bn parade — 16 Bn. Getting ready left for the new area East of Mons. 10 O.R. reinforcement — 2 O.R. demobbed	
ST SAULVE to LAHESTRE	3rd		16 Bn moved from St SAULVE to LAHESTRE by lorries arriving at the latter place about 3.15 p.m. 26 O.R. reinforcements sent in the previous night.	
LAHESTRE	4th		Day given up to settling down in the billets. 7th Bn. The Leinsters offer on a pistol billet.	
"	5th	9.30am	Bn parade for about 2 hrs mostly visual training — rather stationary — Rode up to games in the evening 5 O.R. Reinforcement.	
"	6th		Parade until Company arrangements	

51.V
5 wheels

Army Form C. 2118.

WAR DIARY
or
INTELLIGENCE SUMMARY.
(Erase heading not required.)

Instructions regarding War Diaries and Intelligence Summaries are contained in F. S. Regs., Part II, and the Staff Manual respectively. Title pages will be prepared in manuscript.

Place	Date	Hour	Summary of Events and Information	Remarks and references to Appendices
AHLESTRE	7	9am	Parade under Company Commanders. Chest coverets.	
			Route march	
	8	9am	2 O.R. reinforcements to Regiment	F.R.
		9am	Physical culture	
		10a	Bn. Commander Inspecting the colour	
		11.30	Lecture at MORIANWELZ	
	9	9a	2 O.R. reinforcement	F.R.
		9a	Physical Training	
		10	Bn. Ceremonial Trooping the colour	
		10.30	Tactical scheme	
			1 O.R. casualty at—	F.R.
	10	9.30	C.O.'s Church parade	
			To be fired and no nearer about 2am	
			The morning	
	11	9a	Company training	F.R.
		9.45	N.C.O. detailed out to LA BRUYÈRE to watch enemy	

Army Form C. 2118.

Army Form C. 2118.

WAR DIARY
or
INTELLIGENCE SUMMARY.
(Erase heading not required.)

Place	Date	Hour	Summary of Events and Information	Remarks and references to Appendices
LAHESTRE	12th	9am	of A.L. Div. Association Competition between 2nd ESSEX + 2nd DUKE OF WELLINGTON'S - 2nd ESSEX won - 2 O.R. Reinforcements - 9 O.R. dispatched -	FFO
"	13th	11.30	Company Training - Educational Classes - 12 O.R. + 1 Officer dispatched -	FFQ
"	14th	9am	Bn. Tactical exercise Coy concentration gave in points - 1 O.R. reinforcement 11 O.R. dispatched -	FFQ
		9am	Physical Training -	
		10am	Bn. Ceremonial - Trooping the Colour.	FFQ
	15th	11.30		
		9.30	Bn. Tactical scheme - Coy concentration at a given point	
		1pm	The Bn. marched out to EM LOUVIERE to watch final of the Div. association Competition - 2nd ESSEX won - 1 O.R. reinforcement -	FFQ
	16th	9.30	Training at Coron -	FFQ
		11.30	Education -	

Army Form C. 2118.

WAR DIARY
or
INTELLIGENCE SUMMARY.
(Erase heading not required.)

Instructions regarding War Diaries and Intelligence Summaries are contained in F.S. Regs., Part II. and the Staff Manual respectively. Title pages will be prepared in manuscript.

Place	Date	Hour	Summary of Events and Information	Remarks and references to Appendices
LA HESTRE	17th	9 a.m.	Physical training	
		10	The C.O. inspected Bn billets -	
		11.30	Education -	
"	18th	11.30	C of E Church parade -	
		2 p.m.	The Bn Rugby team played 4th Bn. M.G.C. in the Div cup tie and won -	
"	19th	9 a.m.	Physical training + Platoon tactics -	
		10.45	Bn marched down to MORLAN WELZ for lecture -	
			15 O.R. demobilised -	
"	20th	9 a.m.	Company training.	
		11.30	Education. 1 officer + 12 O.R. demobilised -	
"	21st	9 -	Physical Training -	
		10 a.m.	Trooping the colour -	
		11.30	Education - 11 O.R. demobilised -	
	22	9.	Coy Tactical Training - Outposts.	
			16 O.R. reinforcements	

Army Form C. 2118.

WAR DIARY
or
INTELLIGENCE SUMMARY.
(Erase heading not required.)

Instructions regarding War Diaries and Intelligence Summaries are contained in F.S. Regs., Part II. and the Staff Manual respectively. Title pages will be prepared in manuscript.

Place	Date	Hour	Summary of Events and Information	Remarks and references to Appendices
AHESTRE	23rd	9am	Company training.	
		10.15	The Bn. marched down to MORLANWELZ to a lecture.	I.9.J
			7 O.R. reinforcements.	
"	24th	9am	Bn. tactical scheme - Outposts - Platoon football matches in the afternoon.	I.9.J
			1 Officer + 17 O.R. dimissed.	
"	25th	9am	C.O. Kit inspection on Bn. parade ground.	
			15 O.R. dimissed.	
	26th	9.30	C of E Church Parade. 1 Officer + 16 O.R. dimissed.	I.9.J
	27th	9am	Coy + Platoon training. 14 O.R. dimissed.	I.9.J
	28th	9am	Company training - Physical drill + Ceremonial.	
			1 Officer + 13 O.R. dimissed.	I.9.D
	29th	9am	Companies went for short route marches.	I.9.J
	30th	9am	Company sports meeting + judging distance on the road.	I.9.J
	31st	9am	Short lecture - Coy Bn + Cos marchout for short route march.	I.9.J
			14 O.R. dimissed.	C.9.J

[Signature] Major
Lieut. Col. CoMMᵈ,
2ND LANCASHIRE FUSILIERS.

WAR DIARY or INTELLIGENCE SUMMARY. — FEBRUARY 1919

Army Form C. 2118.

2 L Fus

Place	Date	Hour	Summary of Events and Information	Remarks and references to Appendices
LA HESTRE	1st		No parade during the morning – Football in the afternoon – 7 O.R. Demobilised –	F.9.D
"	2nd	9.30	Church Parade service C of E.	
			3/O/R/Reinforcements. #90 R. Demobilised 1 Officer,	F.9.D
"	3rd	9.	Physical Drill. Platoon drill. Platoon tactical training in Outposts. 3 O.R. Reinforcements. 11 O.R. Demobilised –	F.9.D
"	4th	9.	Physical Training. Bn. ceremonial education – 3 O.R. Reinforcements	F.9.D
"	5th	9.	Physical Training – Co. tactical training in Outposts	F.9.D
		11.30	education –	
"	6th	9 am	Physical Training – Co. short route marche –	
		11.30	C.O Lecture Conditions for the Army of occupation – 1 Officer + 8 O.R. Demobilised –	F.9.D
"	7th	9.	Company Training – education – 12 O.R. Demobilised –	F.9.D
"	8th		No parade during morning – 200 O.R. 10 Officer Chest wound	

52-V
Highest

Army Form C. 2118.

WAR DIARY
or
INTELLIGENCE SUMMARY.
(Erase heading not required.)

Instructions regarding War Diaries and Intelligence Summaries are contained in F. S. Regs., Part II. and the Staff Manual respectively. Title pages will be prepared in manuscript.

Place	Date	Hour	Summary of Events and Information	Remarks and references to Appendices
LA HESTRE	8th		For 10th Bn Von Fus. 11 O.R. demobilised	(I.9.)
"	9th	9.30	Church Parade service – C of E. 12 O.R. demobilised	I.9.
"	10th	9a	Physical Training –	
		9.30	Education A & B Coy. Tactical Training C & D Coy	
		11a	Education C & D Coy. Tactical Training A & B Coy	I.9.
"	11th	9	Physical Training – Coy at disposal of Co Cmdr	I.9.
		10.30	The C.O. inspected the draft	
"	12th	9a	Physical Training – Short route march & education	I.9.
			9 O.R. Demobilised	
"	13th	9a	Physical Training – Co Tactical Training outposts, education	
			10 O.R. demobilised – 12th T.M.B. attached to 4th Bn.	I.9.
"	14th	9a	Physical Training – Bn Tactical scheme. Outposts	
			6 O.R. demobilised – 2 Reg Officers to England (2 months leave)	I.9.
"	15th		No parade during the morning – 7 O.R. demobilised	I.9.
"	16th	11.5	Church parade service C of E. 6 O.R. Demobilised	I.9.
"	17th	9a	Physical Training – Explanation of Turnery scoped N° 13 "De Soft Spot."	

Army Form C. 2118.

WAR DIARY
or
INTELLIGENCE SUMMARY.
(Erase heading not required.)

Instructions regarding War Diaries and Intelligence Summaries are contained in F. S. Regs., Part II. and the Staff Manual respectively. Title pages will be prepared in manuscript.

Place	Date	Hour	Summary of Events and Information	Remarks and references to Appendices
LACHESTRE	17"	11	Education	C.P.S
"	18"	9 a	Physical Training - Platoon Training - Soft Spot	
		2.30	Rugby match v Somerset Lgt Infantry	S.D
"	19"	9 a	Physical Training. Co route march, education	
		11 "	The C.O inspected the draft. 10.O.R Demobilised	C.F.A
"	20"	9 a	Physical Training - Co Tactical Training - Final part of men went to see Cup Boxes at MONS - 10.O.R Demobilised	S.P.A
"	21"	9a	Physical Training - Bn Tactical Training - 9.O.R Demobilised	P.D
"	22"		No parade - 4 O.R Demobilised - Demobilisation of horses commenced. 14 to CALAIS.	S.D
"	23"	10 "	Church Parade Service C of E. Draft of 2 Officers + 100 O.R warned for 15th Lan Fus - 2.O.R demobilised	E.P.D
"	24"	9 a	Physical Training - Platoon tactical exercise	S.P.D
		11	Education	

Army Form C. 2118.

WAR DIARY
or
INTELLIGENCE SUMMARY.

(Erase heading not required.)

Instructions regarding War Diaries and Intelligence
Summaries are contained in F. S. Regs., Part II.
and the Staff Manual respectively. Title pages
will be prepared in manuscript.

Place	Date	Hour	Summary of Events and Information	Remarks and references to Appendices
LA HESTRE	25	9a	Physical Training	
		10a	On parade, march down to MORLANWELZ for lecture	App 1
	26	9a	Physical Training — Company short route march —	
		11	Education — 1 Off + 70 O.R. Demobilised — Cpl Ron Nulin MONS	55 D
	27	9a	Physical Training — Company tactical training	
			Left Shot. Education. 2 O.R. Demobilised.	
	28	4a	Physical Training — Short Route march — a part	
			of 3 Off + 48 O.R. went for dip bath KBR at 2.25.	
			6 O.R. Demobilised.	

M.J.N. Ribby Lieut. Colonel,
2ND LANCASHIRE FUSILIERS.

R. 4th Division

War Diaries

All Formations

1919

1. Bn. Ryl Warwks
2. Seaforth
3. Rudyd Welch
1/4th Pike A-O
1/1st Hampshire
1st Bn Bedf. Rgt - L. 9
1st Bn Som. Rangers
1st Bn. East

2 Line Inf.

www.ingramcontent.com/pod-product-compliance
Lightning Source LLC
Chambersburg PA
CBHW081425300426
44108CB00016BA/2306